# The Seer's Gift

## A LOOK AT THE LANGUAGE OF VISIONS & DREAMS

*Fred Raynaud*

Book 1, Second Edition, The Seer Series
Dreamweaver Publication

Fred Raynaud/The Seer's Gift, second edition
www.kingdomwind.org

Ordering Information:
Quantity sales. Special discounts are available on quantity purchases by corporations, associations, and others. For details, contact the "Special Sales Department" at our website.

The Seer's Gift/Book 1, The Seer Series/Fred Raynaud. —2 ed.
ISBN 978-0-9892811-3-3

# Contents

*To my son*
*Jamisen Liberty Raynaud*
*(12/11/80 - 1/19/05)*

*"Pain and suffering produce a fork in the road. It is not possible to remain unchanged. To let others or circumstances dictate your future is to have chosen. To allow pain to corrode your spirit is to have chosen. And to be transformed into the image of Christ by these difficult and trying circumstances is to have chosen."*

- Tim Hansel

The first day I walked back into the kitchen, I knew it was going to be rough, but I had no idea how rough it would be. I dreaded that walk along the beach that lead to the restaurant where I worked. I had spent many hours on that beach. It ran across the front of the resort and ended at our condo where we live. I spent many a night, often in the middle of the night, walking on that beach and talking to God. At times, I would just sit there at the end of the pier staring out at the stars that lit up the Tampa Bay sky. I was searching for answers. My heart was in pain. I dreaded going back to work. My mind was a million miles away. I was an emotional wreck. In spite of all that, I had to get back, if I was going to remain sane.

My staff was there with their arms wide open with a warm welcome as I entered the kitchen. There were many tears and hugs and words of comfort but even to this day, it all seems like a fog. I had to do this, to bring some normality back into my life. I needed to clear my mind and try to be strong for my family's sake. Boy, this was going to be tough. They say staying busy will heal many wounds. I suppose it does, you definitely do not want to be paralyzed to the point where life just stops.

I went to my office and stared at my monitor. I shuffled through my mail and tried to get caught up on all the work I missed. That night we were busy. I rushed to the line to expedite. I was there a good 20 minutes before I fall apart. As I stared across the line at my cooks, I kept seeing, in my mind's eye, my son Jamisen. He was standing there with his black floppy chef's hat staring back at me with that ear-to-ear smile of his. "What's up Pops?" I heard him say as I tried to push back the tears. No matter what I did, I couldn't get his beautiful face out of my mind. I pushed a few more orders out of the kitchen, then bam that memory flashed across my mind again. There he was, just smiling at me. That's when I lost it. I turned to my Sous chef Bryon, "It's yours I can't do it." I turned and walked out of the kitchen, headed for home. On the way back, I stopped at the park, sat on a bench and cried. I don't know how long I was there time had disappeared.

You see, five days earlier, my wife and I, buried our son, together with my father. Four months earlier, my wife, and I were sitting on the patio, when we heard the front door open. To our surprise, Jamisen had walked through the door. He stood there with an overnight bag strapped across his shoulder. There was that all too handsome ear-to-ear-smile again. With a wink and a smile, he reached over, picked up his mother in a bear-hug embrace, and gave her a kiss.

"Dad, mom, can I stay with you guys for a while?"

I couldn't contain myself. I was so pleased to see him. He was my heartbeat in so many ways. "You bet you can stay," I said with a bigger smile. We rolled a bed out to the living room. "This will work, not too bad, you get a waterfront view."

Jamisen Liberty Raynaud was our first-born, and boy was he a charmer. He was a man of many talents as well... a cook, salesmen, weight-trainer, and all-around entrepreneur.... Sales was his passion, shoot, he could sell you the shirt off your back. It was wonderful having him home. He was twenty-four years old but lived a life of a fifty-year-old. This was October 2004.

Due to my work and the many business decisions, both good and poor, in the last twenty-six years, my family and I have lived virtually everywhere. Culinary had brought us from Michigan, to California, to Canada, and back to California. We lived on the beach, up in the mountains, and in the deserts of Palm Springs. My career had called again and no longer had we settled ... we were off again ... this time up to Wisconsin, then to Florida, off to Virginia, then back to Florida, then Texas, Florida again, Minnesota, Nevada, back to California, then Nevada, and now back in Florida, where we were firmly planted, and God willing, would stay for good. When we moved to Minnesota, my son was turning seventeen. We decided to keep him in Orlando so he could finish out the school year. All our traveling had taken its toll on Jamie. He decided to park it and stay in Orlando once and for all.

That afternoon, when Jamie showed up, was the beginning of the best four months of our lives. It was as if God had given us our son to recapture all the lost years I had given up to career. There was an eight-year gap between Jamisen and his little sister Nicole. They really never had a chance to grow up together. My son had become a young father and his job in

Orlando and his commitment to his community kept him planted where he was. Excluding a month here and there when he knocked on the door with his overnight bag and a smile. We hadn't seen him as much as we wanted or needed.

This time was a time for catch-up. Nicole and Jamisen, in truth, became siblings. He would scope-out her boyfriends and flex his muscles as he explained to them the definition of "respect." They would argue, fight over the lack of hot water in the shower, laughed, go to the mall, and the movies. Life was good for the two of them. As for Jan and I, it was awesome.

The resort I work at is a rock throw from our house. Jan worked in banquets, I worked in culinary, and my son…? He went from working with his mom in banquets, to tending bar, and then to the kitchen to work with me. He was a good line cook and I just loved having him near me. I can't tell you how many times in the last six years he would call me up on his cell phone, from the market. He wanted to cook for his girlfriend Daisy, and he wanted it to be good. I would verbally walk him through each course, and its preparation, as he roamed the isles on the other end of the phone. Then, when he got back to his place, he would call again, just sure up all the details. He really didn't need to brush up – he just wanted to talk, and be loved, and get some affirmation. I, on the other hand, would have talked for hours. Oh, how I miss those phone calls.

We played basketball, worked out in the gym, watched TV, went to the movies, and out to dinner. We spent Thanksgiving, Christmas, and New Years together. In my wildest dreams, I could not have planned a better holiday season.

On January 15, 2005, Jamisen informed us he was moving back to Orlando ... and soon. My heart was breaking at the thought of him leaving. At the time, I couldn't tell you why ... he was 24, and been on his own for the last six years, but inside I had this incredible weight of grief in my soul. In retrospect, I understand now, but at the time, I didn't have a clue. On January 18, I received a phone call at work. It was my son.

"Hey Dad ... I'm on my way to Orlando..."

"So soon..., why don't you stay awhile? You don't have to leave."

"Dad, I got my old job back. I start in the morning."

"You sure you wana..."

Apologetically, Jamie interrupted, "Dad, I have to go.... Please tell mom I love her and give her a hug. I'll call tomorrow when I get home from work. I love you guys. Don't forget... Tell mom I love her."

"I will, I will, Drive safe, please." My heart was breaking, I didn't know why. Orlando is only a couple hours away.

Those were the last words I heard from my son. It was 4:00 AM when the phone rang. Jan jumped out of bed to answer. I was half-asleep, almost in a dream state.... Then I heard her voice begin to raise, "What? Yes, it is... What..." There was a long pause then she cried out to me in a tone I will never forget, "Fred, FRED... Its our baby boy!"

Startled, I jumped out of bed, instantly, that song by John Lennon, "Beautiful Boy," kept running through my mind, every lyric. I hadn't heard that song in years, but there it was, over and over again.

*"Close your eyes,*

*Have no fear,*

*The monsters gone,*

*He's on the run and your daddy's here,*


*Beautiful,*

*Beautiful, beautiful,*

*Beautiful Boy..."*


I stood paralyzed as I listened to Jan talking to the priest on the other end of the phone.

"Our baby's hurt daddy. We GOT to go. Hurry, get Nicole up, we have to go..." Jan stood there in a total panic, shaking, and crying, then trying to pull herself together.

Nicole heard us and knew something was wrong. We threw together some cloths and ran down to the car. We were all floating in and out between prayers and tears. It was all a fog. I was trying to muster up faith to believe it was going to be ok. I was trying to be strong. Jan did the same. Nicole was trying so hard not to fall apart; she put her headphones on and sat numb in the back seat of the car as we sped down the highway towards Orlando.

I don't know how fast I was going. Under normal conditions, it would take two, maybe two and a half hours. In between my prayers, all I could hear were the lyrics of that song….

*"Before you go to sleep,*

*Say a little prayer,*

*Every day in every way,*

*It's getting better and better,*


*Beautiful,*

*Beautiful, beautiful,*

*Beautiful Boy…"*

The drive was a complete daze … every moment fighting the tears and fears with petitions to God for His healing grace. We got to the hospital at about 5:30 AM. When we arrived, there was no place to park. We drove around the block … then pulled the car over onto the grass and ran to the ER entrance.

At the emergency room – a hospital representative and a priest were there waiting for us, "I'm Father Donavan … (Not his real name) I will take you to him." He placed his arm around Jan's shoulder and comforted her as he led us to the elevator; "We're going to the trauma center on the third floor. We're almost there. Hold on." Jan's body was shacking uncontrollably. My wife grabbed hold of the father's arm and almost collapsed, shaking, and crying.

When we got upstairs, we saw Rob, my son's best friend, and his dad standing there. All we could do was hug him. Rob was hurting real bad, and he was scared. "What happened, Rob?" I said.

"It was an accident, I don't know." Rob said, confused and crying.

They took us to the trauma center and placed us in a private room. Father Donavan said, "Stay here and I'll try to get you in to see him now."

"Where is he?" I asked. "Take us to him... Now! PLEASE!" All of us were in a complete state of shock.

Another priest had entered the room, "I'll stay with you ... my name is Jonathan, we'll get you right in there... I promise!" Dazed and confused I sat on the sofa, broke-down and cried. My wife was shacking couldn't even catch her breath. Jonathan put his arm around her and said, "We can see him now."

We walked down the corridor to a door that leads to the trauma wing, hitting the buzzer to gain access and we went through the doors. The wing was lined with glass-enclosed rooms on the left and a long nurse's station on the right. The floor had an unforgettable smell ... a medicinal smell that lingered in the air. The tile walkway went on forever and the paintings on the walls were flashing by, like billboards on a highway moving in slow motion. The world had come to a stop, and I felt as if I couldn't move.

When we got to Jamisen's room, he was lying in bed with a bandage wrapped around his head and machines hocked up on both sides. A nurse was standing at the foot of the bed greeted us. I walked up and grabbed a hold of his hand ... he was motionless... I was afraid I was going to hurt him. I didn't know what to do.

Jan was holding onto his shoulders, trying to hug him, whipping his face with her sleeve, "Jamisen... *baby*... you're going to be fine... we love you so much, baby... Jamie, *sweetie*... you have to be ok."

I started crying as I rested my head on his chest. I could hear the sound of his heart beating... it was moving to the rhythm of the oxygen being forced into his lounges. His body was warm, almost hot... and his breathing loud. His eyes were closed and all I saw was his beauty... Every detail stood out... His long golden lashes and thick eyebrows, the scar on his arm, his chin and check bones. "Jamie..., wakeup, please?" I prayed silently in desperation.

The nurse let us be, and the priest stood by to comfort us. In slow motion, I turned my head and looked up at the nurse, tears rolling down my face, "What happened to him? What is going on?" Anger was starting to rise inside of me. I felt as if the whole world was ending.

"Well... he's been in a terrible accident. A serious trauma has been inflected to his brain. The doctor is on his way down here. Ah, he will give you more information." She was chocked up as she tried to answer my question.

A police officer had entered the room, "Hello... Mr. and Mrs. Raynaud?" he said apologetically, "My name is Detective Stevens, and I will be investigating your son's accident... I am sorry.... I will be down the hall to answer any of your questions when you're ready."

Jan had recognized him. He was one of the tenants at the apartment complex Jan managed when we lived in Orlando. "I know you… Oh my, I know you." Jan was, for a split-second relieved that she knew a familiar face, it was comforting.

I stood up and said, "Investigate… What is going on? What happened to my son?" We were all numb, confused, and angered. "Tell me what happened!" I said, as I squeezed Jamisen's hand in despair.

"Please, sit down." He said, as Father Jonathan pushed a chair back towards Jan.

"Tell me… Please!" Jan said with a broken heart. We were all in a panic – we had to know what happened, we had to know now.

"From what I can gather at this time, your son… he has been shot and… was struck in the head." Detective Stevens, was shaken as he tried to explain what he could, "I am so sorry… I will be right outside."

At that moment the Doctor arrived. "Mr. and Mrs. Raynaud, I am Doctor Nasaki [not his real name], Head of Neurosurgery here at the hospital." He reached out to shake our hands. "Here's what we have: Your son has obtained a serious injury to the lower quadrant of his brain damaging his brain stem and a good portion of his brain. The area of the brain struck governs his thought process as well as his motor functions. We have been running tests since he arrived and have concluded at this time, he is brain dead."

"**Brain dead!** *What does that mean?*" I interrupted.

"There is no activity in the brain, we have run several tests but are unable to find any activity." The Doctor continued, "The State of Florida requires conformation from at least two physicians to determine brain death. We have called in another specialist to confirm our findings and should have more information for you in a couple hours. I assure you Mr. and Mrs. Raynaud; we are doing everything possible. In the meantime, we have your son on a breathing machine and we are monitoring all his vitals."

We stood there paralyzed by the news. All of us were in complete shock, crying uncontrollably. My heart was breaking... "Why God Why?" I cried as I held onto Jamisen not letting him go. I was confused, not knowing what brain dead meant. I thought it meant a comma, which he would come out of it when the doctors were done working on him.

The family started to arrive. Jan's folks and her sister Yvette were the first to get there. Jamie's grandpa had almost fainted, and they had to put him in a wheelchair. Yvette embraced Jan squeezing her and crying together. "What happened honey, is he going... to be all right?" she could barely get the words out. Jan started weeping, "It's going to be ok sweetie... its' all going to be fine, Jamisen is going to be fine." Yvette wanted to comfort her; she had to help hold things together.

Rob's mom Cindy arrived and took control, being a buffer with the doctors, police, and friends, anyone that would cause us to be overwhelmed and distracted. She truly was an incredible help. She called her husband's doctor who had operated on his brain to get a third opinion. Jamisen's friends started arriving. There were at least thirty close friends standing in the hallway, all crying, wanting to see him and say goodbye. One at a time, I escorted each one of them to his bedside. Many of whom I had known since they were all kids, playing soccer and football together.

The minuets turned into hours as we sat by his side. It was all a blur – we didn't understand why this had happened. Father Donavan entered the room and knelt down asking if we wanted something to eat or drink. Jan shook her head in a daze… "I'm fine."

I was resting my head on Jamisen's chest and whispering in his ear, "You're going to be ok…."

Jan was wiping his forehead with a damp cloth. "Jamie… can you hear me? Honey… Wake-up baby… wake-up now… we need you baby."

A hospice representative walked in and asked if we could meet. We walked down to a private meeting room. She sat us down and looked over at us, "I am so sorry… As you know, your son was pronounced dead at 3:03."

"WHAT?" I said.

"You do know he was diagnosed as being brain dead, don't you?"

"Yes, but I didn't know that meant he was dead, I thought it was a comma." We were so confused. She went on and asked us about his wishes on organ donations. We knew he would want to help as many people as possible. A year earlier, he had volunteered to give up a kidney for Cindy. Nothing ever came of it but he was ready to do it to ease her pain. In his death, he had saved the lives of at least ten families that we know of and have received several heartfelt letters from the recipients. We signed the papers and let it be so. She said she would call us when he was out of the operating room. I shook her hand, turned, and walked away.

When we got back to Jamie's room, a priest had come in to give him his last rights. There we stood, all of us around his warm body, praying and asking God to receive him into His presence. For me I knew he was still alive, that though his brain was dead his spirit was still in that tent we call a body. The end of the operation was the moment for that was the moment is spirit would be released into the presence of his Lord. I looked at him and those lyrics filled my mind ounce again.

> *"Close your eyes,*
>
> *Have no fear,*
>
> *The monsters gone,*
>
> *He's on the run and your daddy's here,*
>
>
> *Beautiful,*
>
> *Beautiful, beautiful,*
>
> *Beautiful Boy…"*

I was standing on the patio at our dear friend Marline's house when the phone call came in. The surgery was over – Jamisen was now seated in heaven, and I crumbled.

The weather had kicked up the same as it was when I penned these words. Tropical storm Alberto was making its way across the gulf heading for our coastline. I remember the fear, thinking the storm wasn't going to let up. We thought Captain Kendrick was going to cancel our sea journey. My sister Jean, Greg, my brother Paul, and their kids, were all there supporting us and doing anything and everything they could, to help ease our pain.

The next day, on the morning of January 25th, 2005, it cleared. At the church, my nephew Chase read for me the poem I had written. He knew I was in no state to read anything. After the services - which are still a blur... we headed to the marina in Bradenton Beach and boarded a 50-foot Schooner, called the Frances Crow, with my son, his grandfather Libby, who had passed almost exactly one year early, with family, and friends.

 When everyone was settled, we headed out to sea. We were struck by the awesomeness of the change in the weather. The sun was shining in full strength, the sky was clear above us and the wind... well it had completely stopped... as if it was being held back by the hand of Almighty God. As we cut through the water, making our way out to sea the ocean was silent before us. My mind was going a hundred miles an hour... thinking of my son... thinking of my wife and desperately not wanting to see her hurt anymore - and my daughter - how gentle she is - and so young to feel this kind of pain - then back to my son... and my dad.... I walked around the boat with a blank look and tried to smile or comfort all around - but I was a million miles away. I heard that song continue as the ocean breeze brushed across my face.

*"Out on the ocean sailing away,*

*I can hardly wait, to see you to come of age,*

*But I guess we'll both, Just have to be patient,*

*Yes it's a long way to go, But in the meantime,*


*Before you cross the street, take my hand,*

*Life is just what happens to you,*

*While you're busy making other plans,*


*Beautiful,*

*Beautiful, beautiful,*

*Beautiful Boy..."*

On January 25, 2005, at 12:25 PM, we arrived at Latitude north 27, 25.27 feet and Longitude 82, 42.58 feet. When we got there, we played Beautiful Boy, by John Lennon, Calling All Angels - a song for my wife, and a Wonderful World by Louie Armstrong - for my dad. As the music played, we sprinkled their ashes mingled with the petals of a hundred flowers into the sea. Everyone had a flower.... They were all white roses except two sunflowers - one for Jan the other for me.... As we sailed away, the flowers in the water began to circle our boat. We couldn't believe our eyes; it was as if they were saying good-bye. We stood there hugging and crying together. Part of me was paralyzed - but another part was thanking God for His hand that day - when He blew away the storm. The Lord had stopped the storm and pulled back the winds… in reception of my son and my father. It was a day unlike any other… and a day I will surely never forget.

## In Dedication…

I dedicate this book to my son, a cook, a father, and the heartbeat of my soul. He was a child born to children. We were young parents and Jamisen was our heart's delight and joy. There are so many things I could have told you about Jamie that if I wrote them all it would be a book in and of itself…. I will leave you with this—His life is summed up in five simple passions:

**His Love for his daughter Kayla…** Whom he simply adored, and with every thinking hour, strived to be near her - now he is with her always.

**His love for his family…** Which he cherished so deeply that his passion for us is engraved deeply within our souls.

**His faith in God…** Which echoed within the framework of his very being - and guided his steps as he blazed through this life.

**His love for his friends…** Which marked the footprints of his life.

**His self-determination…** to live life to the fullest and plow into every situation - head-on, with no fear or hesitation.

Jamisen Liberty Raynaud was a melody of our lives, a song written by his creator pointing us to a higher place. He was a tune that played within our hearts in times of trouble or triumph.... His message is that of a life lesson – his proclamation is on the fragility of life and purpose. Please see life in all its fragility and make decisions that respect. Honor life and God's master plan. This is the poem I wrote on the morning of his funeral:

*"How do you describe a shooting star?*
*A life, so bright, so fast, so far...*
*How do you describe a mighty mountain?*
*A heart so big, so wide..., a flowing fountain...*

*How go you describe the ocean blue?*
*A love so deep, so vast, so true...*
*How do you describe this Son of mine?*
*A baby, a child, a man so kind...*

*His hopes, his dreams, his eternal optimism...*
*He loved, he laughed... a glorious prism...*
*A caring soul with depth... and vision...*
*To help the downtrodden... his heart felt*
*mission...*

*Jamisen Liberty was his name...*
*A man of distinction, of laughter, of pain...*
*He took his lumps, and marched on through*
*life...*
*A call to us all in this world of strife...*

*So now, he rides on wings from above...*

*Sheltered in heaven... nurtured in love...*
*His Lord has called him home at last...*
*To watch over us all, his final task...*

*Heavenly peace has entered his heart...*
*This, our example... a place to start...*

*So how do I describe this Son of Mine?*
*An ocean, a mountain, a shooting star...*
*A father, a son, a spirit so far...*
*So far away - have you flown...*
*We will miss you... my son...*
*We love you... we moan...*

*Please God... Please...*
*Heal us... We pray...*
*At the foot of your throne...*
*We will see him some day..."*

- Fred Liberty Raynaud

To my son Jamisen, whom I miss so incredibly much. He taught me what it means to believe in myself and always see my glass half-full. He inspired me to stay the course and run this race with all my heart, I am so grateful to have my son my life for the time we had together, and one day we will see each other face to face.

*"For there is nothing hidden which will not be revealed, nor has anything been kept secret but that it should come to light. If anyone has ears to hear, let him hear. Then He said to them, 'Take heed what you hear. With the same measure you use, it will be measured to you; and to you who hear, more will be given. For whoever has, to him more will be given; but whoever does not have, even what he has will be taken away from him.'"*

- Mark 4:22-25, NKJV

# Acknowledgement

There are several people I would like to acknowledge in the preparation of this book. Foremost I want to thank my wife Jan for putting up with my crazy schedule and supporting me while I got up in wee hours of the morning to take on this task.

Of course, no writing effort would be complete without the diligence of a good Godly copyeditor, and Christy Jones, in spite of her tight schedule raising kids and preparing for various triathlons, heeded that call and helped me to hone my writing and stay focused on the subject at hand; thank you Christy, your work was a true blessing! Then there is my sister Jean, whose fine eye caught what we all missed, simple spelling and phraseology. Her attention to detail is incredible! Love you, Jean. Finely, I would also like to thank my dear friend Leo Griego, for reading my early drafts and giving invaluable feedback and support.

# Preface

*"Now the Lord spoke to Paul in the night by a vision, 'Do not be afraid, but speak, and do not keep silent;"*

- Acts 18:9

*"But when He was alone, those around Him with the twelve asked Him about the parable. And He said to them, 'To you it has been given to know the mystery of the kingdom of God; but to those who are outside, all things come in parables, so that seeing they may see and not perceive, and hearing they may hear and not understand; Lest they should turn, and their sins be forgiven them.' And He said to them, 'Do you not understand this parable? How then will you understand all the parables?'"*

- Mark 4:10-13

This is the first book in a series on the life of a Seer and the gracious gift of God's pictorial language to His bride, the Church. In this revised volume we will not only explore the language of visions and dreams and dive into the depths of the Seer's Gift but will also study this gifting as it relates to the prophetic. In the second book of this series, we will look at the Seer's Gift and how the Holy Spirit uses the language of visions and dreams while ministering healing to those in need. In the third book in this series, we will look the seer's gift and its relationship to prophecy. In the fourth book in this series, we look at the metaphoric language and discuss common symbolism within the body of Christ.

It's a timely work. We live in exciting times! Everywhere you turn God is pouring out the Spirit of prophecy and revelation upon his people, often through the language of dreams and visions. Dreams and visions are one of those mysterious things that always seem to intrigue people. Everyone, at one level or another, is interested in dreams and visions. We all have dreamt.

Nevertheless, for some in the church community, dreams from God are fantasy, something too uncomfortable to consider; and visions... forget about it, you're written off as a loon or one being deceived by the devil. There is a tendency to dismiss visions and dreams as a flight of the imagination. Some people get spooked when you talk about having a dream or seeing a vision. They view these phenomena as emotionalism, extreme fantasy, or even worse occultism. There are segments within the body of Christ that view such happenings through a lens of fear and disbelief. Fear often stems from a lack of understanding which fogs the ability to see God move in this way; lacking the ability to believe it is easy to judge and cast off all who move in revelatory gifting.

The truth is, God always has, does, and will continue to speak to us, whether through that small still voice, a good sermon, a dream, a vision, a prophetic word, a word of knowledge, a word of wisdom, circumstance, or even by nature, Jesus speaks loud and clear. Get this; it's important, He does it all through the consistent truth of His revealed Word – the Bible.

Our God has not changed. His desire to speak to His children is no different today than it was in the garden, or the days of Samuel, or during the time of John the Baptist. The bible speaks of dreams and visions 171 times, 96 of which deal with visions. Virtually every major turning point in scripture was proclaimed, accompanied by, or foretold through the language of visions and dreams. Dreams and visions are one of the tools that God uses to communicate to His children.

James Goll, founder of the Encounter Network (www.jamesgoll.com) and a leading authority on the prophetic, dreams, and visions states:

> *"What God did then, God does today, and God will continue to always do. Dream language is the language of the ages. It is this mysterious way that God comes into our lives, invades our uncomfortable zones, and simply comes to speak to us."*

In a recent article entitled, "The Master Dream Weaver Is Downloading His Dreams Within Us," James Goll, references several historical facts regarding church history and belief in God's ability to speak through dreams.

Great portions of the church father's writings record dreams and visions and have only recently been translated into English. Consider the following:

- Thomas of India, received instruction from his dreams

- Polycarp was given a vision of his martyrdom
- Irenaeus had wise understanding of dreams
- Clement believed that dreams come from the depth of a soul
- Tertullian devoted eight chapters of his writings to dreams
- Gregory of Nyssa spoke of the meaning and the place of the dream.
- John Chrysostom, called "golden mouthed" because he had such oratorical grace upon him, called dreams the source of revelation.
- Constantine was directed in a dream regarding the Heavenly sign that he was to carry into battle.
- Thérèse de Lisieux life was changed through a dream.
- John Newton, an early slave trader, was stopped in his tracks in his lifestyle and his vocation by a dream from God. This became the man, who so turned around his life, he eventually became chaplain to the King of England. He went on to write the hymn that is possibly one of the greatest Protestant hymns of all ages: "Amazing Grace."

By understanding this type of communication, you will be better equipped to fulfill your destiny and walk with God in new and exciting ways.

## The Populist Perspective

The general populace, on the other hand, dives into anything and everything that appears to offer a way to hear from God. Today's interest in spirit guides, eastern mysticism, psychic reading, horoscopes, new age spirituality, and other practices are evident of humanities desire to seek God. It is built into their DNA. What they don't know is, that the "who" they are seeking, is seeking them. Jesus is on the move and His heart is to seek and save that which is lost. That God shaped hole in the heart of humanity is seeking a relationship with the Lord of Glory.

Now here's the rub; if the Church doesn't come to grips with its fear and place revelatory language in its proper perspective they will miss the opportunity to proclaim Jesus to the lost while the world continues to run to anyone that claims to have a connection to deity – even if it is false. We must be like Daniel in Babylon, who was surrounded by astrologers and false revelators, yet he rose to the top like cream in a sea of nonfat milk, proclaiming the truth and exposing the falsehoods of the spirit of antichrist. We must move out in power within the marketplace and take our rightful place as messengers of righteousness for the Kingdom and for our God.

## Why this Book

This series is for the everyday Christian, the average Joe, the layperson, people like you and me. I have written this book to release the folks that are sitting quietly in the back of the church and are not sure of how they fit in or what they can do to contribute to the Kingdom of God. With this series, I want to stir their hearts to go deeper, and dream and understand that, in Christ, they can do all things. I want to ignite their destiny with vision. This series is written as a training manual. It offers insight into practical ways of "how" to listen to God and move out in effective ministry.

The Lord does speak to His people. He speaks to them through His Word. He speaks to them with that small still voice. He speaks to them through circumstance, and He speaks through the language of visions and dreams. This series will help you listen in a new way as you operate to fulfill God's will in your life. You will learn to understand how visions and dreams operate through gifting... wither it's a word of knowledge, prophecy, healing, or discerning of spirits. I pray this series will meet my intended goal.

## The Days in Which We Live

We have been living in the fulfillment of Joel's prophecy for about 2,000 years and as the "*signs of the times*" increase in magnitude and scope, we should anticipate the outpouring of the Holy Spirit would come in the same manner. Many recognize the times we are living. There is not a segment in the church, or in the world for that matter, that questions wither we are living in the last days.

The truth is, we are just a little bit farther down the timeline than the New Testament church was. I am troubled about modern teachings on eschatology is the emphases on an escape plan. Too many evangelicals have hanged-their-hat on a rapture mindset. The high watermark of their theology is to be "caught-up" before the going gets tough, instead of moving out in power to bring in a harvest in this final hour. This series is about being the gospel. It is about doing the gospel.

The hardest thing for me growing up as a Christian in a church community in the midst of change was the lack of information and teaching, on the practical side of dreams and visions. To understand this pictorial communication as a type of language is important. We need to know how dreams and visions function when we are conducting ministry. No matter what the manifestation of God's Spirit is operating within your ministry, dreams and visions often become an active part of the process.

We have many books on the gifts of the Holy Spirit and its operation within the body of Christ. We have seen a flood of books on the prophetic in the church today. Even several study bibles are available that take a charismatic theme. I am not here to take up the cause of defending the place of spiritual gifts in the church today. There are many solid works out there from writers more competent than I that have taken up that cause. My assumption is that the gifts of God are alive and well, and if you're reading this book, chances are you do too. If you are one of those folks, this book is for you.

## Who is this Book For?

This book, for the most part, is for those who are presently moving in the operations of the Holy Spirit and seeing the pictorial language of God operating in their lives. I have written this book to illuminate the realm of visions and dreams. I have written it to show that often times, the Seer (1 Samuel 9:9-19; 2 Samuel 15:27, 24:11), moves in more arenas than that of classic prophecy. This book was written to show the relationship of "*seeing*" and the other revelatory gifts of the Holy Spirit. Frequently, people who "*see*," see while operating in words of knowledge, discerning of spirits, prophecy, revelation, healing, and words of wisdom.

The challenge arises when the Seer, after seeing, has to listen, interpret, and then with Godly wisdom, obey and implement, what God has commanded. It has been my experience that the Seer's ability to listen is twofold: First, the Seer listens with his eyes, or the eyes of his mind, while God speaks to him through visions or dreams. Second, he must listen with his ears and his spirit, sifting that experience through the truth of scripture and prayer to gain understanding on what he has seen, thus, getting a fuller understanding of what God is saying in a given situation.

For the Seer, an understanding of how various gifts function is necessary in applying the Lord's will in a given situation. It is helpful for a Seer to know what gift is operating while ministering so that he may move in the appropriate stance. In this book, I hope to give incisive information on the operation of "seeing" in most applications. However, the main areas that I plan to cover involve healing, inner healing, healing the demonized, and the prophetic, it must be understood that the language of visions and dreams, function alike within all the gifts.

Throughout this series, I will share many personal stories. Stories are important. Remembering what God has done can become seeds for you in your own life. They are invitations for Jesus to do again what He did in the past. Set your hearts to find the seeds of blessing in these stories, for yourself. Sharing stories can ignite a future generation. Stories are testimonies that push and propel us forward. In Joel 1:1-3, it says:

> *"The word of the Lord that came to Joel the son of Pethuel. Hear this, you elders, and give ear, all*

> *you inhabitants of the land! Has anything like this happened in your days, or even in the days of your fathers? Tell your children about it, let your children tell their children, and their children another generation."*

Moses understood the power of remembering and proclaiming when he said in Deuteronomy 4:7-10:

> *"For what great nation is there that has God so near to it, as the Lord our God is to us, for whatever reason we may call upon Him? And what great nation is there that has such statutes and righteous judgments as are in all this law which I set before you this day? Only take heed to yourself, and diligently keep yourself, lest you forget the things your eyes have seen, and lest they depart from your heart all the days of your life. And teach them to your children and your grandchildren,"*

In 2 Timothy1:3-7, Paul says to Timothy:

> *"I thank God, whom I serve with a pure conscience, as my forefathers did, as without ceasing I remember you in my prayers night and day, greatly desiring to see you, being mindful of your tears, that I may be filled with joy, when I call to remembrance the genuine faith that is in you, which dwelt first in your grandmother Lois and your mother Eunice, and I am persuaded is in you also. Therefore, I remind you to stir up the gift of God which is in you through the laying on of my hands.*

*For God has not given us a spirit of fear, but of power and of love and of a sound mind."*

Sharing stories and reminding people of the wonderful things Jesus has done is our testimony. In the book of Revelation, it says that the testimony of Jesus is the Spirit of Prophecy.

Read the words John in Revelation 19:6-10:

> *"And I heard, as it were, the voice of a great multitude, as the sound of many waters and as the sound of mighty thunderings, saying, "Alleluia! For the Lord God Omnipotent reigns! Let us be glad and rejoice and give Him glory, for the marriage of the Lamb has come, and His wife has made herself ready." And to her it was granted to be arrayed in fine linen, clean and bright, for the fine linen is the righteous acts of the saints. Then he said to me, "Write: 'Blessed are those who are called to the marriage supper of the Lamb!'" And he said to me, "These are the true sayings of God." And I fell at his feet to worship him. But he said to me, "See that you do not do that! I am your fellow servant, and of your brethren who have the testimony of Jesus. Worship God! <u>For the testimony of Jesus is the spirit of prophecy.</u>"*

What that means to you – is YOU can hear the word of testimony, and say, "That word is for me ... for my life, for my house, for my generation."

# The Seer Gift is for You

I believe that every Christian can receive the Seer's Gift and see into the heavenly realms.

Paul says in Ephesians 1:15-18:

> *"Therefore I also, after I heard of your faith in the Lord Jesus and your love for all the saints, do not cease to give thanks for you, making mention of you in my prayers: that the God of our Lord Jesus Christ, the Father of glory, may give to you the spirit of wisdom and revelation in the knowledge of Him, the eyes of your understanding being enlightened; that you may know what is the hope of His calling, what are the riches of the glory of His inheritance in the saints,"*

Paul is praying that the eyes of your spirit would be opened. Every believer has two sets of eyes. Obviously, we have our physical eyes to view the world around us. However, we also have our spiritual eyes, or the eyes of our heart, to perceive the spiritual realms around us. We are first spirit beings housed in a body of flesh. When we trust the heart of Jesus and what He did on the cross, we move to that place of hearing God more clearly. As our minds are renewed the clarity of the Hearing Ear and the Seeing Eye becomes sharpened. In essence, the Holy Spirit flips the switch of our imagination giving God another access point for the Him to speak to us. To make this happen it takes childlike faith. Notice the words of Jesus in Mark 10:14-15:

> *"But when Jesus saw it, He was greatly displeased and said to them, "Let the little children come to Me, and do not forbid them; for of such is the kingdom of God. Assuredly, I say to you, whoever does not receive the kingdom of God as a little child will by no means enter it."*

The kingdom of God is here and now. As you read this volume, let your heart be stirred to press into His kingdom as a little child and be transformed!

The Seer Series includes the following books:

- The Seer's Gift - a look at the Language of Visions and Dreams (this volume).
- The Seer and Healing - How visions and dreams operate in the ministry of healing.
- The Seer and Prophecy - The Gift and Office of the Seer Prophet.
- The Seer's Guide to Symbolism: Similitudes, Metaphors, and Symbolism - a reference work on similes, metaphors, and symbolism commonly seen in the life of the believer.

CHAPTER 1

# Seeing Cross-eyed

*"For in Him dwells all the fullness of the
Godhead bodily; and you are complete in Him,
who is the head of all principality and power."*

– Colossians 2:9-10, NKJV

hat an amazing gift we have in Christ Jesus! As
believers in the saving grace of Calvary we have
been given something the world longs to see and
know. We have been grafted into the bosom of Christ Himself,
born again, and seated at the right hand of majesty. This
incredible gift cannot be earned. It is not something that we
strive for as if the works of our hands can somehow bring us to
that place of reconciliation with God. It is a gift of grace for all
that call Him Lord.

The problem is that the same church that understands the
nature of saving-grace struggles when it comes to believing
that they are filled with fullness of the Godhead. That
somehow, after receiving salvation, we have to work at, or
struggle even, to receive all that the Holy Spirit has to offer. We
pray for an open Heaven. We strive to be filled with His

presence. We work with all that we can muster, to try to obtain what we already have. What we fail to understand is that this striving is often based on a works mindset. Now that does not mean that we should not hunger and thirst for more. We should we do for His presence is drawn to the thirst and hunger of His children. Our souls crave for more of Him. However, that kind of hungering is birthed out of relationship and longing, like a bride for her groom.

Works, on the other hand, is performance driven. We call out wanting what Christ has already given us. What we fail to understand is in Christ, all the fullness of the Godhead dwells. The promise of Jesus is that the believer would be filled to the full with Christ, Poppa, and the Holy Spirit, for all the Godhead is in Him. Consider the following Scriptures:

> *"Jesus answered and said to him, "If anyone loves Me, he will keep My word; and My Father will love him, and We will come to him and make Our home with him."*

> – John 14:23

> *"And of His fullness we have all received, and grace for grace."*

> – John 1:16

Paul reinforces this truth when he tells us:

> *"Do you not know that you are the temple of God and that the Spirit of God dwells in you?"*

> - 1 Corinthians 3:16

So, I can think of no better place to start this volume than with a very foundational truth. You have been redeemed and all the fullness of God dwells in you. You are the temple of the Holy Spirit, bought and paid for. It was the Father's good pleasure to fill you even as Christ is full (Colossians 1:19). When you were born again, you were crucified with Christ, raised from the dead with Christ, and are now seated with Him in Heavenly places.

> *"I have been crucified with Christ; it is no longer I who live, but Christ lives in me; and the life which I now live in the flesh I live by faith in the Son of God, who loved me and gave Himself for me."*
>
> – Galatians 2:20

> *"And raised us up together, and made us sit together in the heavenly places in Christ Jesus,"*
>
> – Ephesians 2:6

You have a completely new nature. You have a dual citizenship. You are a child of the King with residency in Heaven, seated at His right hand, and you are an ambassador of Heaven on Earth, created to bring the Kingdom of God to the rest of humanity. You have more of God in you than you can imagine.

> *"But if the Spirit of Him who raised Jesus from the dead dwells in you, He who raised Christ from the dead will also give life to your mortal bodies through His Spirit who dwells in you."*
>
> – Romans 8:11

You did not earn your Poppa's DNA. You do not "press in" for it. It is who you are. There is nothing you can do to gain the Holy Spirit. Christianity is not a lifelong course of moral activities and performance. You are a new creature in Christ. It is not about doing, it about being. You have the same power living in you that raised Christ from the dead. You just have to believe it.

*"Most assuredly, I say to you, he who believes in Me, the works that I do he will do also; and greater works than these he will do, because I go to My Father. And whatever you ask in My name, that I will do, that the Father may be glorified in the Son. If you ask anything in My name, I will do it."*

– John 14:12-14

Belief is the catalyst for all that is in Christ. No longer do you have lack. At that very first moment of faith in Christ, you became a source of Kingdom blessing. Jesus was very clear, *"The Kingdom of God is within you"* (Luke 17:21). You are much larger on the inside than you are on the outside; you just have to believe it. You were meant to be a spring overflowing with living water.

*"On the last day, that great day of the feast, Jesus stood and cried out, saying, "If anyone thirsts, let him come to Me and drink. He who believes in Me, as the Scripture has said, out of his heart will flow rivers of living water."*

– John 7:37-38

You are not alone. He has sent His Spirit to dwell in you in fullness.

> *"And I will pray the Father, and He will give you*
> *another Helper, that He may abide with you forever—*
> *the Spirit of truth, whom the world cannot receive,*
> *because it neither sees Him nor knows Him; but you*
> *know Him, for He dwells with you and will be in you. I*
> *will not leave you orphans; I will come to you."*
>
> – John 14:16-18

Everywhere you go your life should spill over with God's abundance. I don't know why it is easier for us to believe that someday Jesus is going to do a work in us, instead of believing that the work was finished at the cross of Calvary. On the cross, your old sinful nature was abolished and you were given access to a glorious new world. All of your problems were solved on that cross. It may seem hard to believe but it's true. That's why they call it *"good news."*

Jesus died to give you what you could never gain on your own. Religion wants to give you formulas, keys, and tasks to perform, when you already have the ultimate gift in you. The problem for us is that so often we are not outwardly manifesting the fullness of God so we lower our theology to meet the standard of our experience, or lack thereof.

The truth is the perfect sacrifice of Christ was, in truth, good enough to get the job done. If you are not manifesting the fullness of God it is simply because you don't believe. I know that this sounds harsh, but it is the truth. Stop striving and rest in the fact that you have it (Hebrews 4). As you rest and trust in His finished work on Calvary, you will begin to act and live like a completely different person. A person always manifests what he believes.

The word *"believe"* in the Greek literally means *"reality."* Hebrews 11:1 tells us that faith is a tangible substance. True believing always involves demonstration. The Kingdom of God is not a matter of mere talk, but of demonstration of power.

*"For the kingdom of God is not in word but in power."*

- 1 Corinthians 4:20

Really, this is a process of changing the way we think. It is a call to have our minds renewed to believe the truth. I like the way John Crowder puts it.

*"You have become an oasis in the desert. Your inner life bubbles up like pools of fresh water in a thirsty land. On the one side of the cross, you were a beggar, longing for a blessing. But on this side of the cross, you have truly become a source of blessing. You are provision for the hungry. You are drink for the thirsty. You are an endless supply of supernatural oil."*

- John Crowder, Seven Spirits Burning

Remember the primary goal of salvation was not to empty you of evil, but rather to fill you with Himself. The work of the cross gave Him a Holy vessel to fill. Your purpose is "to be" the temple of the Holy Spirit! Calvary is our foundation and our capstone. It is the Spirit Filled life. It is the open door in Heaven. When we seek to move in the fullness of Christ, and understand the mysteries of the Kingdom, it takes faith.

Without faith, it is impossible to please God. It is faith that causes us to access the things of the Spirit. Faith is the magnet and the aroma that attracts the dancing hand of the Spirit (John 3:8).

> *"The wind blows where it wishes, and you hear the sound of it, but cannot tell where it comes from and where it goes. So is everyone who is born of the Spirit."*

Encounter with the Holy Spirit is not a onetime event. We should be receiving the Spirit fresh every day! The cross put us into forever union with the Spirit. By abiding in Christ, we can continually drink from His presence. We already have an open heaven, and it is open because the veil of Christ's flesh was torn.

As you seek to understand how God communicates, please understand the depth of your relationship with Christ and know *"who"* you are in Him. The blood of Jesus is the anchor of our faith, it's the oil of our anointing, it's the fountainhead of our praise, and it is the lens to peer into the mysteries of the Kingdom. It is our stairway to Heaven.

When I speak of seeing cross-eyed, this is exactly what I am talking about, *peering through* the finished work of the **cross** and completely being submerged into this vat of His glorious wine and finished work. Revelation of this truth creates a true sense of peace and freedom to pursue the lover of our souls. It is the place of rest!

## Understanding the Power of Rest

*"Rest,"* boils down to understanding *"who"* you are in Him, but more importantly, who He is in you. Before we were saved, we were trapped in the cycle of performance. After we were saved, we found out that we are accepted in Christ, unconditionally. It is the revelation of *"acceptance"* that solidifies our identity. It is out of the reality of that identity that we move into rest.

Rest is that confidant reassurance of the Father's love-nature towards you. He is good all the time. He does not waver from His goodness or love towards you. When the revelation of your identity merges with the understanding of His incredible love and commitment to you and you receive a fresh understanding of the finished work of Christ on the cross, you have found the secret to the place of rest (Psalm 37:1-7).

*"Do not fret because of evildoers, nor be envious of the workers of iniquity. For they shall soon be cut down like the grass, and wither as the green herb. Trust in the Lord, and do good; Dwell in the land, and feed on His faithfulness. Delight yourself also in the Lord, and He shall give you the desires of your heart. Commit your way to the Lord, trust also in Him, and He shall bring it to pass. He shall bring forth your righteousness as the light, and your justice as the noonday. Rest in the Lord, and wait patiently for Him; Do not fret because of him who prospers in his way, because of the man who brings wicked schemes to pass."*

When you are at rest, you are no longer driven by the pressure to perform. You don't feel or have the need to strive to prove yourself worthy of His grace. You become comfortable in your own skin, in Him. Because He is good and He is for you and not against you, you can inter into His rest.

In Hebrew, the word "*rest*" has two definitions. The first is "*to stand still.*" The second meaning has the notion of "*going for a stroll or walk.*" The latter, I believe captures the essence of rest the best. I am reminded of God walking in the garden in the cool of the day with Adam, or what Jesus said in Mark 6:31 "Come away by yourselves to a secluded place and rest a while." He was asking them to go for a walk, a stroll with Him to a place of rest and solitude. The beauty and power of this is amazing.

Rest is that place in life where we learn to simply walk with Jesus in all circumstances. There is no striving or performance. In all things, we just want to be with Him. It really is that simple.

The process of abiding in Him is the process of adoration, worship, and love ... resting in Him, no matter the circumstances. When you remember that peace is a person and that person is in love with you, rest is at your door. Listen to the words of Jesus in Matthew 11:28-30....

> "*Come to Me, all you who labor and are heavy laden, and I will give you rest. Take My yoke upon you and learn from Me, for I am gentle and lowly in heart, and you will find rest for your*

> *souls. For My yoke is easy and My burden is*
> *light."*

Again, Jesus says

> *"Then He said to His disciples, "Therefore I say to you,*
> *do not worry about your life, what you will eat; nor*
> *about the body, what you will put on. Life is more than*
> *food, and the body is more than clothing. Consider the*
> *ravens, for they neither sow nor reap, which have*
> *neither storehouse nor barn; and God feeds them. Of*
> *how much more value are you than the birds? And*
> *which of you by worrying can add one cubit to his*
> *stature? If you then are not able to do the least, why are*
> *you anxious for the rest? Consider the lilies, how they*
> *grow: they neither toil nor spin; and yet I say to you,*
> *even Solomon in all his glory was not arrayed like one*
> *of these. If then God so clothes the grass, which today is*
> *in the field and tomorrow is thrown into the oven, how*
> *much more will He clothe you, O you of little faith?"*

> - Luke 12:22-28

The closest example I can come up with is something that happened, just a short while ago. I was writing this very topic, when suddenly, my little baby granddaughter Anise (19 months old), came running over to me and grabbed a hold of my leg and began to just hold me. She looked up and lifted her arms with her fingers wiggling, saying in beautiful baby talk, "Hold me." Well, my response was like any grandpa in their right mind. I dropped everything, picked her up, and just held her. She snuggled in all the more, so I rocked her and cuddled her, and whispered to her a soft little song, kissing her on the cheek, as she cuddled, even more. I have to tell you, I could have stayed in that spot for hours.... That is the whole point. If I, a frail human, treasures such a moments, how much more will our Father treasure us in His embrace. That is rest.

Get this - rest attracts rest. I am reminded of the story of Noah. In Genesis 8:8-9 we read:

> *"He also sent out from himself a dove, to see if the waters had receded from the face of the ground. But the dove found no resting place for the sole of her foot, and she returned into the ark to him, for the waters were on the face of the whole earth. So he put out his hand and took her, and drew her into the ark to himself."*

Here we see the symbolism of the Holy Spirit seeking a place to rest. The parallel verse to this is found in the gospels. Jesus is at the Jordan (the same place the people of Israel crossed to enter the Promised Land) getting ready to be baptized by John the Baptist. John records it this way:

> *"The next day John saw Jesus coming toward him, and said, "Behold! The Lamb of God who takes away the sin of the world! This is He of whom I said, 'After me comes a Man who is preferred before me, for He was before me.' I did not know Him; but that He should be revealed to Israel, therefore I came baptizing with water."*
>
> *And John bore witness, saying, "I saw the Spirit descending from heaven like a dove, and He remained upon Him. I did not know Him, but He who sent me to*

*baptize with water said to me, 'Upon whom you see the Spirit descending, and remaining on Him, this is He who baptizes with the Holy Spirit.'"*

- John 1:29-33

Jesus knew who He was. He had no problem understanding His identity. Obviously, Jesus was already full of the Holy Spirit; after all, He is God incarnate. This was the place of public confirmation, the place where the Father and the Holy Spirit display their affirmation and joy for the mission that Jesus was about to fulfill. It is also interesting that the dove remained on Him. Jesus lived a life of true spiritual rest, totally dependent upon the Father. He walked with the Father everywhere He went and in everything, He did.

Jesus promised to give us the same Holy Spirit, as witnessed in Acts chapter two. The thing is, the Holy Spirit is drawn (in fullness) to people that have learned to abide in Christ and find their rest in Him. He, like the dove of Noah, is searching for that place of rest. He wants to live (in power) on a people that know their identity in Heaven and simple want to worship and walk with God in all they do. Through their ability to simply rest in Him, the Holy Spirit is more able to bring the Kingdom of Heaven in demonstration and power. Jesus is that model. My heart's cry for you is that you will seek to be at rest in your identity in Him, that you will know the power of His love towards you, and that your life will be lived in that state of rest.

Pray - Father, show me your love towards me. Teach me your ways. Teach me to walk with you in the comfort of your love. Let my mind be fixed on you and may my heart be as a child and know who I am in you. Let me be comfortable in my own skin, in you! Fill me to overflowing with the dove of your Holy Spirit. Amen!

# CHAPTER 2

# What is a Seer?

*"Now the acts of David the king, first and last,
behold, they are written in the book of Samuel
the seer, and in the book of Nathan the prophet,
and in the book of Gad the seer,"*

- 1 Chronicles 29:29"

## Modalities

A few years ago, I was speaking to our corporate head of training. During the Conversation, she looked over at me and said, *"You're a visual learner, aren't you?"* I asked her what she meant. She went on to explain to me how people process information through both the right and left-brain hemispheres. Most people, however, use one side more than the other, which makes learning some subjects far easier than others. She went on to say that everyone also has a preferred learning style, depending on the side of the brain and learning modality that is most developed. She explained to me that modes or styles of learning include kinesthetic (touching, feeling), audio (hearing) and visual (seeing).

Research has shown that visual, auditory, kinesthetic, gustatory, olfactory, and digital, are the six primary sensory modalities that we use to experience the world around us. These modalities are also known as representational systems. They are the primary ways we represent, code, store and give meaning or language to our experiences. The three main representational systems are visual, auditory, and kinesthetic, although digital, gustatory, and olfactory senses do not play a major role and are often included with kinesthetic.

We use all of our senses and depending on the circumstances may focus on one or more of them - when listening to a favorite piece of music, we may close our eyes to more fully listen and to experience certain feelings. As a chef, I work with aroma and fragrances, and I use and rely on my gustatory and olfactory senses to a large degree in my profession. However, in general, my preferred representational system is visual.

Each of us has preferred representational systems. For example, when learning something new, some of us may prefer to see it or visualize it being performed, others need to hear how to do it, others need to get a feeling for it, and yet others have to make sense of it. One system is not better than any other. However, depending on the context, one or more of the representational systems may be more effective: artists - visual, musicians - auditory, athletes – kinesthetic, and mathematicians - digital. Typically, people at the top of their profession can use all of the representational systems and to choose the one most appropriate for the situation.

Annette Moser-Wellman in her book, "*The Five Faces of Genius*," outlines five modalities that governed the greatest minds of history. The first modality is that of the Seer. She states:

> "*Seers see pictures in their mind's eye, and these pictures become the impetus for ingenious ideas. In the same way that someone can imagine his team's final jump shot at the buzzer or how his living room would look with a new color of paint, highly creative use the skill of the seer to imagine new ideas.*"

Though Mrs. Moser-William is speaking of the natural creative nature and power of the mind to dream and envision, the idea is similar. God has given humanity the ability to create and envision, it is built into that incredible muscle called the brain.

What is powerful to me is the consistency of the world's scientific observations of learning and the creative process of innovation and the way that the Lord chooses to speak to His children. The Lord's method of communication spans the entire spectrum of sensory modalities and beyond. However, that should not be a surprise He created us that way. We were programmed in our very DNA to experience and communicate with God.

The Christian life should not be lived in silence, waiting for that final day in heaven when we can finely speak to Him. We are designed to speak and hear from Him today. We are His temple, and He does live in us after all. We need to interact with Him. Our souls long to have vivid, two-way conversations with Him. We need to see what He is saying. We need to hear the sound of His voice, to feel His heartbeat and passion. We are driven with a desire to taste His goodness and smell the aroma of His presence. We are incomplete in our life with Christ without interaction. Our senses were designed that way.

## The Seer

When I speak about the "*Seer's Gift*," I am talking about folks that operate in God's modality of "*seeing*" what He is saying. These folks operate through the gift of "seeing." Visions and dreams are normal for the Seer. They, often see first and hear second. However, it is my firm convection that the gift of seeing is available to every believer. Like all gifts of the Spirit they are grace endowed, given freely to the hungry. I also believe that they can be given through impartation (more on that later).

The "*Seer Prophet*," on the other hand operates out of all modalities, however he is heavily weighted in the "*seeing*" arena. Bob Jones, a father of this last generation's prophetic movement, said it best.

> "*...A seer is everything. Prophets are the eyes, but seers are the entire head: eyes, ears, smell, taste, and feelings. That is what Isaiah 29:10 says: 'He has shut your eyes, the prophets; and He has covered your heads, the seers.' ... As a seer you move in all five realms, and because of that, you are more discerning. The enemy is never really able to fully shut you down. The prophet can be momentarily blinded, but if the enemy blinds you, you will still be able to hear, smell, taste, and feel.... The*

*prophet can speak the future, but the seer can see what
the people need to let go of in the past, tell them what
the Lord is saying to them today, and declare what the
Lord is offering them tomorrow.... A seer can feel the
strongholds of a town.... You can smell what's
happening. You can discern what's wrong with a
church or a city or even a nation, because you can smell
it."*

In Old Testament Hebrew the word "Seer," is found 34 times, 22 come from the Hebrew word "chozeh," a noun meaning: seer, a prophet who sees visions, a beholder in vision. Gad, Heman, and Iddo are good examples of the word Seer.

*"Now when David arose in the morning, the word of
the LORD came to the prophet Gad, David's seer,
saying,"*

- 2 Samuel 24:11

*"All these were the sons of Heman the king's seer in the
words of God, to lift up the horn. And God gave to
Heman fourteen sons and three daughters"*

- 1 Chronicles 25:5

*"Now the rest of the acts of Solomon, first and last, are
they not written in the book of Nathan the prophet, and
in the prophecy of Ahijah the Shilonite, and in the
visions of Iddo the seer against Jeroboam the son of
Nebat?"*

- 2 Chronicles 9:29

The second Hebrew word for "*Seer*" is "*ra'ah,*" meaning: to see, look at, inspect, perceive, consider; to cause to look intently at, behold, cause to gaze at. Samuel is a good example of this word.

> *"For when David was up in the morning, the word of the Lord came unto the prophet Gad, David's seer, saying"*
>
> - 2 Samuel 24:11

## How the Seer Operates

*Ra'ah* takes the definition of the word seer and expands upon the way a seer operates. Unlike the word "*Nabi,*" meaning "*prophet,*" whose root means to "*bubble up*" as in spontaneous prophecy, the seer receives a word from the Lord as in a vision or dream, but then has to ponder, look at intently, inspect it, and consider it. I call this process "*marination*" or "*stewing.*" So often, when the Lord shows me something, it is only during the process of letting that word "*stew,*" sometimes for days or weeks, and in this process, the Lord expands His thoughts, and speaks to me regarding the depth and width of the vision. He will show me various visions in the same context. He will speak to me regarding the word repeatedly, expanding its meaning. He will drive me into the Scriptures and slather more marination on it.

Only after a season of listening and digging, will I find the richness of what He is saying. Usually, this takes place when he is speaking, what I call "*big words,*" a word that is meant for the global body or group of people. Still, I find this process at work even when the context is personal prophecy, or spontaneous prophecy. I have learned that it is critical for me to stop in those moments, relax, dial down, and listen. I need to hear more from the Lord, to look for its interpretation and application, before sharing it.

This process applies to all folks moving in the prophetic, however, for the Seer, even more so. Every time I have been wrong in the interpretation, it was because I didn't wait for God to confirm the meaning in my spirit. Because I think metaphorically and God usually starts speaking to me metaphorically, I tend to lean on my own experience in this arena.

This needs to be kept in check. If I don't listen, stew, and wait for that peace of God in confirmation with my spirit and rush into the interpretation, I can miss what God is really trying to say. Without the Holy Spirit's guidance, we will find ourselves treading the waters of assumption. Jim Driscoll, author of "*the Modern Seer*," said it well.

> "*If we are overly optimistic in nature, we'll be prone to assume that everything we see is positive, when something might be corrective. If we're overly pessimistic, we'll tend to think everything is negative and therefore may have a hard time accurately revealing the Father's heart to those around us. There is a moment when we're looking for metaphorical understanding and we let go of all our preconceptions. At that moment, it feels like we have no idea what we are doing. We don't have a clue what God is going to tell us about what we're seeing, but based on our*

> *history with Him, we know He's going to tell us something. In that moment of being completely open, we experience great growth, because that is when we experience the spark."*

In the next chapter we will dive into the topic of metaphorical language.

# CHAPTER 3

# Metaphorical Language

*"I have also spoken by the prophets, and I have multiplied visions, and used similitudes, by the ministry of the prophets."*

- Hosea 12:10 (KJV)

Visionary language is a wonderful metaphorical language, but it is critical to be well grounded in the Word. The Word of God paired with your relationship and intimacy with the Lord is the plumb line for your discernment meter. Discernment is very important in sifting out the meaning of metaphorical speech. God loves speaking metaphorically. He can pack so much truth in a simple picture, its mind blowing.

Just a walk through the Scriptures and gleaning from all the ways God spoke to the prophets of old or listening to the words of Jesus as He used simple stories and parables to illustrate powerful truths of the Kingdom, and you will come away with a wealth of insight and a love for "the way" God speaks.

It has been my experience that much of the metaphorical speech that the Lord uses is rooted in scripture; however, He also uses metaphors from our own life experiences. As a Chef by trade, the Lord has used the world of culinary to speak powerful truths to me in metaphorical language. He draws it out of my life like water from a well. The emulsification of a hollandaise sauce becomes a word of salvation, the simmering of a stew on a hot stove, points to something rich and savory the Lord cooking up, breaking down the fleshly sinew, to create tenderness in the life of an individual. Both examples are types of metaphor.

## To Illustrate

Several years ago, I saw a vision of the Lord seated by a river's edge. He was seated next to a flat rock. He had in His hand stalks of wheat. He took the wheat and beat it against the rock. As He beat it, the kernels of wheat were separated. The wind rose up and blew against the chaff, releasing the kernels. He then reached down and began to grind the wheat with His hands on the rock. As He was grinding, He reached into the river and pulled up some water. He drizzled the water into the floury substance, and then He started to work the mass into dough with His hands. As He was kneading the dough, He turned and looked at me and said, "*I knead you.*"

At that moment I was overcome with His Spirit and His love. I not only understood that He wanted me and needed me, but I understood the process of kneading, and the structure it produced in the dough. When water and flour are kneaded together, the proteins in the flour expand and form strands of gluten, which gives bread its texture. The kneading process warms and stretches these gluten strands, eventually creating springy and elastic dough, and thus giving it strength. If bread dough is not kneaded enough, it will not be able to hold the tiny pockets of gas ($CO_2$) created by the leavening agent (such as yeast or baking powder), and will collapse, leaving a heavy and dense loaf. The $CO_2$, like the breath and power of the Holy Spirit, needs a vessel "*kneaded*" to sustain it.

Jesus will take us to that place of kneading. He will massage us into a work of His hands. Like the master potter, He will keep at it until we are at a place to sustain what He pours into our lives. This is a powerful example of the Lord speaking a word that is not only rooted in my life experience, but also established in the Word of God.

Of course, God is not limited in the metaphors He uses. In my world, I see the Lord speaking virtually everywhere, through dreams, visions, aromas, nature, feelings, hearing, the whole gambit, and I wouldn't have it any other way. When I heard the sound of geese honking as they flew by, I also heard the voices of a platoon of angels declaring a season in transition. When I was surrounded by butterflies and a butterfly landed on my shoulder, I heard the Lord say, "*Metamorphoses, it's time to take flight and pollinate – stir up the next generation.*" When I tasted honey in my mouth, I knew there was a sweet prophetic word for someone. When I saw the wind rise up and blow leaves off a tree, I heard the Holy Spirit say, "*I am shacking the trees and releasing my servants into the streets and to the communities they influence.*" When I smelled the flowers of spring and saw flower petals falling from the wind, I knew that the Lord was ready to shower His bride with love and grace. When I heard the sound of dogs barking in the streets, I was caught up into a place of warfare prayer, knowing that the enemy was biting at the heels, of something or someone.

The key in this endeavor is to simple pay attention; always have Jesus on your mind; and listen to what the Holy Spirit is saying. He is speaking all the time.

---

## Similitudes and Symbolism

*"As I walked through a great wilderness I came to a certain place where there was a Den, and I laid myself down in that place to sleep: and as I slept, I dreamed a dream.*

*I dreamed; and I thought that I saw in my dream a man standing with his face turned away from his own house. He was clothed in rags, a book was in his hand, and a great burden was on his back.*

*Then I saw him open the book and read; and as he read, he wept and cried out, 'What shall I do?'."*

- John Bunyan, The Pilgrim's Progress

When I first started thinking about these similitudes and symbolism in the glorious language of God I was drawn to that incredible pilgrim and warrior in the faith, John Bunyan. He is best remembered for his book *"The Pilgrims Progress"* which he says, was *"Delivered under the similitude of a DREAM."* He wrote it from a prison cell almost three hundred fifty years ago (1678). John Bunyan's dream story has become the most famous allegory in English literature. It has been read by more people than any other religious book in history, second only to the Bible, and it has been translated into more languages than any other book in the English tongue.

In the book of Hosea we read:

*"I have also spoken by the prophets, and I have*
*multiplied visions, and used similitudes, by the*
*ministry of the prophets"*

- Hosea 12:10, KJV

The Hebrew word for *"similitude"* in this verse is *"dama"* meaning to liken, to compare, to imagine, think, a symbol, or similitude. To that definition I would include the words, metaphor, allegory, simile, and parable. As you can see from this book the Lord loves to speak through stories. His language is so broad and wide it defies our linear mindset.

Moving in dreams and visions is available to every believer in some degree or another. While everyone is not called to the ministry of the seer-prophet, all can move to some extent in this realm.

In this book I have tried to show the value of metaphor and teach you how God uses the language of visions and dreams to speak to you. I want to encourage you to learn to think metaphorically. Consider the way God speaks. Much of the Old Testament is given to us veiled in allegory, shadows, types, and metaphor. From Genesis to Revelation, we see the fundamental truths of the Gospel and the face of Jesus woven throughout the Scriptures like nuggets of revelation tucked away in the melody of the Word.

The main reason people miss interpretations is by thinking in literal rather than metaphorical terms. God uses symbolism that is familiar to your life. He knows every aspect of your being and will speak through your makeup and the things that have marked your life experience. He knows your life, your makeup, who you are, and what you do. He knows your passions, and interests, He is interested in you. If you are a mechanic, God may speak to you along those lines. If you are a Chef, God may show you an area that you can relate to. Jesus spoke to the people of His day in parables that they could relate to. As an agrarian society that worked the land and fished in the Sea of Galilee they understood when Jesus spoke of tilling the soil and casting out nets for a catch.

God may show you the same type of symbols and their meaning and be very consistent in their use, interpretation, and application. For instance, in the Word of God a lamb is a common symbol that has a consistent thread of meaning throughout Scripture. Whenever certain symbols manifest pictorially to you, it will become fairly obvious what they mean.

On the other hand, God does not want us to turn His creative voice into a formula. His desire is to stretch us and cause us to dig for truth through fellowship with Him. He wants us to be constantly dependent upon Him and His Word. When we think we have it down pat, He will show us a symbol that we thought we knew, and suddenly it made no sense at all. The Lord does this to keep our dependency on Him. Always seek Him and His Word to search out the meaning of His speech. John Paul Jackson put it this way regarding visionary interpretation:

> *"The closer we can maintain our intimacy with the Holy Spirit, the better we can begin to hear*

> *His voice in understanding what He is speaking to us. We can learn all the mechanics and they are immensely helpful, but after that we must depend upon His voice to lead us."*

Follow Daniel's lead. Daniel knew that *"Interpretations belong to God"* and He sought the Lord through prayer and the Lord revealed the meaning of the dream (Daniel 2). In the end, it is hearing His voice that brings the revelation.

Symbolism found in visions and dreams are often similar, however, the interpretation may be quite different. Often visions operate through the gifts of *"the word of knowledge,"* *"discerning of spirits,"* or *"prophecy"* and the interpretation and application may come quickly, as God speaks to your heart regarding the matter. Dreams on the other hand may need more digging and often revolve around your life destiny, mission, life, and God's desire for you personally. I will try to bring this to light as we discuss similitudes.

As you learn the metaphorical language of the Holy Spirit your ability to see will reach new heights.

Proverbs 25:2 says that:

> *"It is the glory of God to conceal a matter, but the glory of kings (or man) is to search out a matter."*

God places great value on our seeking out the things that He conceals. Use this section of the book as a reference tool to spark your mind to think metaphorically. Press in and press on dear saints. The Lord desires to speak to you!

In book four of this series, we will explore the various Similitudes, Metaphors, and Symbolism that are commonly found in the body of Christ.

The following is an example from that volume.

## Ladders, Steps, and Stairs

Often the Lord will use symbols that point to ascension, such as a ladder, a flight of stairs, climbing or taking steps, or ascending up an escalator (modern form of a ladder). I have often seen ladders in visions ascending into Heaven. At the heart of the revelation was God's call to climb higher, to press into His presence and seek that deeper place in Him. He wants us to press into Him, to ascend to new levels of intimacy. This often is the meaning of ascension symbols, but not always.

In Genesis 28 we read where Jacob had a dream, and in his dream, he saw a ladder that stretched from earth to heaven and angels were ascending and descending on it. This is what God had to say about this dream.

> *"Also your descendants shall be as the dust of the earth; you shall spread abroad to the west and the east, to the north and the south; and in you and in your seed all the families of the earth shall be blessed. Behold, I am with you and will keep you wherever you go, and will bring you back to this land; for I will not leave you until I have done what I have spoken to you."*

> - Genesis 28:14-15

God did not mention angels though it is evident they were engaged in fulfilling the declaration of the Lord regarding Jacob and the nation. His dream was about the promise of inheritance and that his decedents would be vast and cover the earth, and that God would be with him and sustain him on his journey. Always look at context, ask yourself what activity is happening. Am I climbing or descending? The answer to that will drive the context. Summary, ladders, steps, and stairs could mean the following:

As you move through this series embrace the beauty of God's pictorial language. Nothing compares to a relationship with God that overflows with communication, adoration, and love.

- A call to you, your church, or others to climb higher and press into the presence of the Lord.
- A word regarding promotion, that God is taking you to a higher place, spiritually or in your occupation.
- A word regarding progression, such as *"step out"* *"take the next step,"* or *"move forward."*

CHAPTER 4

# Types of Seeing

*"In a dream, in a vision of the night, when deep sleep falls upon men, while slumbering on their beds, then He opens the ears of men, and seals their instruction. In order to turn man from his deed, and conceal pride from man, He keeps back his soul from the Pit, and his life from perishing by the sword."*

- Job 33:15-17

## Seeing

**A**"*Seer*" sees three basic ways. The first is internal. A person receives images, pictures, or visions in his mind. This can happen any time but often happens during worship or while the person is in the mode of ministering to someone's need. They can be single frame pictures, but more often than not, they are more like a movie being played out. This type of activity can happen in a vision or a dream.

## Dream Camps

Holy Spirit inspired dreams fall into three camps. In the first camp, you're the object of the dream. You are in the dream and are doing something, or a story is being played out and you're in it. This type of dream can be metaphorical or be direct communication from the Lord to you. When it is not a metaphor, it is very clear, and may even involve an angelic visitation.

The second dream camp is being shown something. You are watching the dream, as an outsider. It's as if a story is unfolding. This type of dream is often metaphorical, but can be more literal.

The third camp of Holy Spirit inspired dreams is the forgotten dream. This is the type of dream is where the Holy Spirit downloads something into your spirit. Your involvement is not necessary; He is simply dropping and sealing instructions into your spirit. Job 33:15-17 says:

> "In a dream, in a vision of the night, when deep sleep falls upon men, while slumbering on their beds, then He opens the ears of men, and seals their instruction. In order to turn man from his deed, and conceal pride from man,"

Have you ever had one of those moments where you walked into a place and felt as if you were there before, like déjà vu? This often is a result of the third dream camp. You were shown something for that moment. When this happens, pay attention, and ask the Lord how you should respond to that situation.

## External Seeing

The second type of seeing is external. The person sees a vision in front of them. It may be translucent or solid. This type of vision can also come as written words over someone. The words can be a sign of a condition in someone's life such as a sin or sickness, example being the word "*adultery.*" They can be declarative or a word of destiny for a person's life, like the word "*Teacher*" or "*Prophet.*"

## Angelic and Visions

This type of vision is also active in the areas of discernment, where you see the spirits behind a situation such as in the demonic. We read in Hebrews 5:14:

> "*But solid food belongs to those who are of full age, that is, those who by reason of use have their senses exercised to discern both good and evil.*"

On the other hand, you may see the angelic in their ministry to the body of Christ. David says in Psalms 34:7:

> "*The angel of the Lord encamps all around those who fear Him, and delivers them.*"

Moreover, in Psalm 91:11-12:

> "*For He shall give His angels charge over you, to keep you in all your ways. In their hands they shall bear you up, lest you dash your foot against a stone.*"

The writer of Hebrews 13:1-2, tells us:

> *"Let brotherly love continue. Do not forget to entertain strangers, for by so doing some have unwittingly entertained angels."*

Angelic activity can be externally seen as translucent (most common), or an actual physical encounter. This type of seeing is not really seeing, as in visions, but peering, as in seeing into the Spirit realm.

An example of this can be seen when Elisha prayed for the eyes of his servant to be opened so he could see the angelic forces around them.

> *"And Elisha prayed, and said, "Lord, I pray, open his eyes that he may see." Then the Lord opened the eyes of the young man, and he saw. And behold, the mountain was full of horses and chariots of fire all around Elisha.*

> - 2 Kings 6:17

Just recently, I had an angel encounter that brought me great comfort. I walked down into my study and felt the presence of the Holy Spirit in the room. As I looked across the room, I saw an angel. He was standing in the corner, wings, and all, about 6 feet tall, big, soft-spoken, strong like confidence wrapped up in love. All I could do was walk over, stand in front, bow my head, and say thank you to the Father. I kept telling the Father, repeatedly, thank you. The angel wrapped his wings around me, caressed me, and said, *"Child, the Father is very pleased with you."* I cried. Then he said, *"I am here to encourage you and help you fulfill your destiny. You are loved; the Father is so very pleased."* I was blown away. Still am. The next day I was driving. I thought I felt his presence. So I spoke up, *"Are you still here?"*

I heard him say, *"Yes child, this is my assignment. The Father is very pleased."* Then the Holy Spirit just flooded my heart. Since that encounter, I have had a new level of acceptance, love, and boldness fill my heart. That encounter was a blend of translucence and physical manifestation. To be honest, in the last thirty years, not counting the sensing of angelic presence during worship, I have had no more than seven encounters with the angelic that I am aware of, two in dreams, one physical encounter, three in visions, and this last event. God has sent his angelic forces to minister to the saints, to assist us in fulfilling our destiny, and to battle on our behalf.

However, like all things, decrement is your lifeblood. Test all things, hold fast to that which is good, for we know that Satan himself can transform into an angel of light, and his only goal is to deceive, lie, steal, and destroy.

## Trances

The third type of *"seeing"* is what the Scriptures refer to as a *"Trance."* A trance is not the vision itself but the mode the Holy Spirit puts you into to receive it. The Greek word for *"trance"* is *"ekstasis."* According to Strong's it means a displacement of the mind, i.e., bewilderment, ecstasy: amazement, astonishment, a trance. It is where the mind and emotion are transported, as it were, out of oneself, and into a raptured state.

One may be awake, but the mind is drawn off from all surrounding objects and wholly fixed on things divine. It is in this state that one sees nothing but the forms and images lying within. The event is so real that it feels as if you have been transported to heaven or wherever the Lord is taking you or showing you. The root word means *"amazement"* a state of wonderment, a state of Holy drunken perception. It is a place where our hunger for the Lord becomes so rich, we have to move into His realm. Peter had such an encounter in Acts 10:9-16. (cf. Acts 11:4-5):

> *"The next day, as they went on their journey and drew near the city, Peter went up on the housetop to pray, about the sixth hour. Then he became very hungry and wanted to eat; but while they made ready, he fell into a trance and saw heaven opened and an object like a great sheet bound at the four corners, descending to him and let down to the earth. In it were all kinds of four-footed animals of the earth, wild beasts, creeping things, and birds of the air. And a voice came to him, "Rise, Peter; kill and eat." But Peter said, "Not so, Lord! For I have never eaten anything common or unclean." And a voice spoke to him again the second time, "What God has cleansed you must not call common." This was done three times. And the object was taken up into heaven again."*

Paul had a similar experience in the book of:

> *"Now it happened, when I returned to Jerusalem and was praying in the temple, that I was in a trance and saw Him saying to me, Make haste and get out of*

*Jerusalem quickly, for they will not receive your testimony concerning Me.'"*

- Acts 22:17-18

John Crowder, in his book, the Ecstasy of Loving God, said it this way:

> *"The word ecstasy refers to an intense, euphoric experience. It can be hard to define, as it refers both to a heightened state of spiritual contentiousness, as well as an intensely pleasant experience. As one's concentration comes into a divinely heightened state of focus, our awareness of exterior senses and intellectual thoughts are often diminished. It is often accompanied by a cessation of voluntary physical mobility. The resulting "spiritual drunkenness" is what the early apostles experienced on Pentecost-what the priests of Solomon's temple experienced as they were unable to stand up under the glory cloud. It is what the Christian mystics encountered in the deep throes of inner prayer, and it is the Charismatic Christian practice which we all call being "slain in the Spirit." It has accompanied the First and Second Great Awakening revivals in the Americas, and was present in the birthing of every significant new move of God or new denomination in church history."*

## Illustrative Example of Visions in a Trance

To illustrate this further I would like to share three other examples of visions I had while in a trancelike state.

### Preparing a Banquet Table

A while back, the Lord gave me the following vision. I was in the midst of worship at church. All of a sudden, I was transported. I was standing in a carpenter's shop like you would see on a farm. It was so real I could smell the wood and feel the dust in the air. Jesus was standing there next to a carpenter's bench. The room was filled with particles of wood dust like a cloud. The sun was shining in the door to the wood shop so you could see the particles floating in the air, almost in slow motion. He was leaning over a large flat piece of wood like a door or a tabletop. He was working with a plane very meticulously; removing layer after layer until the top was perfectly smooth. I asked the Lord what He was making.

He said,

*"Don't you know that when I want to take you higher, to take you to the next level, into that next season, that I need to take you deeper? I take the place where you are, right now, and I plane it, stripping away the last season in order to reveal the next. You see, what worked in the last season will not work in the next. What worked in the wilderness will not work in the Promised Land, the manna has ceased, and the fire and the cloud have disappeared. Go in and possess the Land."*

He went on to say,

> *"I am bringing you from a place of personal protection; Where your shoes never wore out; Where I fed you daily with manna from heaven; Where I caused water to flow and quail to fall from the sky; Where I nourished you and cared for you throughout the last season - to a place of proclamation and position; Where you will become a feeder; Where you become a person – that stills the storm; Where you become the extension of my hands; This is a place where slaves become friends; Where paupers become Kings and Priests; and where the kingdoms of this world will see the Glory of the My Kingdom.... The planning process creates a door into the next season of your life. And when the dust settles, and you allow Me to take you deeper, and you enter in - that door will become a banquet table prepared in the presence of your enemies ... and waves of Mercy and Grace will fill the streets."*

Then I saw the Lord standing at a lathe working a piece of wood. I asked the Lord what He was making, and He said,

> *"I'm creating a scepter out of trees of righteousness. I am creating a people that will walk in My authority and carryout My great commission."*

Then He showed me a picture of a grand stallion, dressed, and decked in blue and white, like it was leading a precession. The rider was dressed in like manner, with a silver trumpet in His hand and he had on a headdress that was made of long flowing feathers. I asked the Lord what it meant, and He said,

> *"I am about to enter the grand arena of Life, where My body, in My Glory, will parade the Kingdom of Heaven before men. They have been dressed for the occasion. They are covered in the Kingdom. Proclamation is in their hands, and they are called to summon all to My banqueting table. Their head is covered with the nature of my Spirit and the world will see My glory."*

Then He showed me a tall blue curtain that shot up to heaven, so high you couldn't see where it started. It was tied back like the drapes in a house. When I saw it, I understood it to be the veil of the temple that was torn from the top to the bottom. The veil was tied back inviting all to enter in, an invitation, to step into the throne of grace, to gaze into the windows of heaven, to watch as the Lord himself, with the hosts of heaven, step on stage, and take us into this next glorious season in the Kingdom.

The message was so full of hope and encouragement. It breathed life and promise. The beauty of how He spoke to me was just as altering as the words that He spoke. It is forever burned into my spirit. In fact, I can say that every word that the Lord has breathed in my spirit in this way is etched in like manner. I don't care if it was thirty years ago; it is as fresh today as the moment it happened.

## Tears of Healing

During prayer and worship, the Lord brought me into his heart, and I saw the heartstrings of God playing an incredible melody to my soul.

He met me at the bank of a river. It was cloudy and stillness covered the land. The base of the river was like a marshland - Reeds were growing up all around it everywhere, like passive stocks of wheat. They were blowing in the wind and the reeds were rich with substance, stalks full of the water of life – feeding off the water edge. A soft wind was blowing and moving upon the reeds. They almost danced as the breeze rustled the reeds of God. Then Jesus came up beside me and said, "Walk with me."

He touched me and my heart began to melt within me. I knew that this was going to be different, be deep. I knew in my spirit we were going into a deep place. Something inside me was struck with the heaviness of this moment. It was thick, like the clouds, before it rains. Something whaled up inside of me and I started to cry.

Instantly I was in this place. There were pillars like muscles, tendons, and they were vibrating to worship. I felt very unsure of myself. I did not know how to stand in this place. I moved around trying to find my footing. The worship continued and tears continued to come as I moved around, almost trying to hold on. There were many tendons, some wide, some narrow, each moving at different tones of melody. Finely, I reached out and grabbed hold of the biggest muscle next to me and I held on worshiping the Lord. *"God, what is this? What am I seeing?"*

Instantly, I understood I was standing in the heartstrings of Jesus. I was struck with the reality that I did not know how to stand in this place.

There was this incredible melody of love vibrating from within His heart. I walked around in amazement and bewilderment not knowing what to do or how to be here. His heartstrings were playing in waves that overcame me and all I could do was cry. I asked the Lord "What's wrong with me?"

He said, "*You do not know how to rest in My Love.*"

I knew that I did not know how to receive His love. I did not know the depth of His love for me. I did not know how to take-it-in. I was trying but I did not know how. I was trying hard to understand. I was walking around looking, trying to find that place in Him, when I ran into a very big muscle. I looked up and saw how high it went. I could not get around it. I was overtaken by the knowledge that I did not know what to do. I asked the Lord, "*I don't know how to receive Your love, how to love You like I should. What are we going to do? Now what do we do?*"

Then the Lord spoke, graciously, without hesitation, "*I am just going to have to Love you more, more love, more love....*" This time the tears began to flow like a river. My heart was breaking and melting, and throbbing for Him. I felt something changing on the inside.

Then I was gone. He brought me to a river at night. It was a glorious river, full of life. I looked at the river and the life around it, the foliage, and lily pads, flowers, and frogs, and fish. The night sky was incredibly clear with tones of dark blue that became the canvas to the most perfect full moon I had ever seen. The light of the moon glistened upon the waters. I was struck – with the most incredible feeling of peace – just to be with Jesus – looking out at this incredible scene. The serenity, quietness, the cool night breeze, the sounds of stillness, with Him by my side, was breathtaking. Then He reached over and wrapped His arm around me and His very shadow (shadow at night – wow) caused my very nature to want to lean into Him.

Then He said, *"Have you ever walked upon the water under a clear moon light?"* And He embraced me.

That night the Lord did something inside of me that has changed my life forever. The Lord showed me His love nature towards me. For the first time, I saw Him as the LOVER of my soul – in a very deep way.

That was the start of a long love journey. I am still working and resting, learning to trust Him, and let Him love me deeply. I am forever in love with my Lord.

The following Monday the Lord continued this dialog, and it was incredible. I call it temple worship.

## Temple Worship

I was in deep prayer and worship when the Lord took me away. He took me into His temple. I looked and I saw the Glory of His dwelling. There were large pillars of marble, majestic white marble laced with gold, everywhere. I saw myself standing behind a pillar. I was standing there, like a young servant or slave that wasn't sure if he really should be there. I was in the portico in front of the throne room. There was activity happening around the throne. The court of the King was active with His angels moving about as if they were on a mission, as if they were creating battle plans.

The angel that was standing next to Him was tall and slender, almost graceful, if you will. He had a scroll in his hand. There seemed to be a sense of urgency in their dialog. I watched from behind the pillar, as if I was eavesdropping, as if I was listening to things I shouldn't be, like I was in a place of Royalty – and I was but a pauper.

Suddenly, all eyes were fixed on me. It was as if I had knocked something over - and I was found out. I tried to hide behind the pillar but I was drawn to Him, I was drawn to peek from behind my hiding place. Everyone was looking ... smiling at me. There was a joy present that is hard to describe. The place was thick with His joy. The Lord was dressed in a brilliant white robe with blue trimming. He was leaning forward, trying to see me. He had the most incredible smile upon His face. He was beckoning me with His hand to come closer. He was calling me with His smile, He was beckoning me with His eyes. He wanted me to step out from behind the pillar and come to Him.

As I stepped from behind the pillar and began walking towards Him, I was transformed into a child. Instantly, I was a boy cradled in His arms. I was not just a boy; I was like an autistic boy that did not know how to be held. I was squirming about, moving in all directions. In spite of my wiggling, He just kept holding me, until, slowing, I began to change, and His peace filled my being, and I rested in His arms.

And I heard the Lord tell me…

"My people have not learned their abiding place in Me. My people do not know the place of My dwelling ... and the position I have called them into. They have a poverty mindset.... They feel like paupers in the palace of the King. They do not see the depth of My love and the secret place in My Heart for them. Tell them I am calling them to a higher place. I am enlarging their footprint and their place in Me. Tell them I am calling them to a place of sweet comfort, to a place of dwelling - to be seated with Me in the Heavens. Tell them I desire to have them where I am. No longer shall they be called servants – but friends – friends of the Most High God. I am bringing them into My presence – I am bringing them into the place of sonship, that where I am they will be also.

They are of the Royal line – They have access to My throne, not only access, but a dwelling place, a home set within the temple of My heart. Tell them there is a secret place in the temple of the King. There is a place in which I will abide in them, and they will rest in the cradle of My arms. It is there ... that I shall whisper. It is there ... that I will share the deep desires of my heart."

My children do not know how to rest in this place.... They are standoffish ... they are trapped with a spiritual autism ... they squirm and turn and lose their focus. They have not found that quiet place; they have not found the stillness of

*My presence.... The world has imprinted them with preoccupation, hyperactivity has invaded their minds and fear, anxiousness, and impending disappointment has over taken them.*

Then the Lord said,

*"But I am breaking down the walls of their minds – I am renewing their way of thinking, and I will fill them with My peace and My love. I am placing them in the cradle of My arms and speaking life into their hearts. I will hold them – and teach them the depth of My love. But they need to relax, to rest in Me, and to trust Me. I will be their trust. Tell them – it's ok – tell them to – go ahead, press into the door that is set before them. Permission has been granted, and they shall learn the place of Royalty and My joy ... My unspeakable joy.*

*They need to come to Me like a child would come. There are places in Me that they will not know how to stand, or how to settle into. But I shall cover them, and I shall teach them, and I shall be their hiding place – for they shall learn to live and be in me. I know how to comfort My beloved – they can trust in Me."*

Most importantly, I also understood He was talking about me, and I could feel a deep healing in my heart and our love relationship.

Then the Lord stood up and took me by the hand. He walked with me to the most incredible patio. It was circular like an arch wrapped in marble with pillars on either side. It was so incredibly beautiful – and peaceful. The balcony faced the darkness of the night skies of heaven and the heavens were illuminated with the glory and splendor of God.

I stood there overcome with His peace. It was a peace that is so very hard to explain, like you could almost breath it in. We leaned against the balcony staring out at the stars; it seemed like hours of just resting and staring out at the sky. Jesus pointed at various places in the heavens.... *"Look – there,"* He said, and a shooting star would fly by in utter brilliance. *"Look – over there,"* and the swirling mass of stars were dancing in the galaxy....

Then the Lord said as he paned and pointed across the night sky:

> *"Behold – my endless possibilities.... Know the power of My presence – for My hands have embraced the fire of the sun. My chest brushed against the heavens and the lights of Aurora were created."*

I was undone, overwhelmed by the depth and majesty of His desire, and my heart stirred within me.

Then the Lord pointed to a horizon. The sun was coming up in radiant brilliance. Surrounding the sun was a massive wave of clouds that stretched across the horizon and peeked at the center of the sun. He kept pointing at the clouds and the clouds were coming towards us. Like a massive wave of white, bordered in brilliant fiery orange, they kept rolling, faster and larger, and closer towards us – until I was caught up into the clouds.

The clouds were moving so fast and the Lord said: *"Fly away with Me."*

Suddenly, I was flying in the midst of the cloud. The cloud was moving incredibly fast. The cloud was wet with His presence and the wind against my face was incredible. It took my breath away - and the wetness washed me and refreshed me even down to my very pores. Then I heard the voice of the Lord say, *"Follow the cloud – and not the crowd.... Follow the cloud - and not the crowd..."*

Suddenly, the cloud landed, and I was standing in a desert place on a dirt path. In front of me was a mighty pillar of cloud, a la Moses. It turned with the intensity of a tornado. It was massive ... big! I could see the power of the cloud digging into the dirt and the rocks, kicking up a path as it turned and moved.

Then the Lord said:

> *"When you enter the deep places of My heart ... when you enter My temple and embrace your place in Me – then you shall hear the whispers of My heart and you will call forth My desires.*
>
> *When you follow the cloud of My glory and taste the water of My presence – then you shall call that which is in My heart – to come and be on earth, in this place, even now – as it is in Heaven.*

> *The cloud of My glory shall be unto to you like a pillar of My glory and it shall carve out a path of My presence and make straight a highway in the desert. Every valley shall be exalted; every mountain and hill shall be brought low. The crooked places shall be made straight and the rough places shall be made smooth. My Glory shall be revealed, and all flesh shall see it."*

As I looked down towards my feet – I saw the feet of Jesus. They were mighty and strong, bruised, worn, and dusty – calloused as if they had walked this path before. He had sandals on and His feet dug into the ground. I was amazed at the strength in his feet. Then I looked at my hands – and they too were the hands of Jesus – only strong, calloused, and rugged. I stood back in amazement – and I heard the Lord say:

Then I saw the Lord standing in front of the pillar of cloud and He was filled with incredible joy. He began to dance along the path in front of him. In His hands were doves. As He danced, he released the doves, over, and over, one dove after another.

> *"This is abiding ... This is abiding ... When you abide in Me – you will truly be changed, for you will be in Me, and you will be captured by My desires and be thrust into the work of My hands. You will say, "I can't help it – I must, I have to, I need to be about the work His hands – for He has captured my heart – and I am undone...."*
>
> *Lift up your voice with strength; Lift it up and be not afraid. Say to the cities, "Behold your God. Behold, the Lord God shall come with a strong*

> *hand. And His arm shall rule for Him; Behold –*
> *His reward is with Him, and His work before*
> *Him. He is calling you to a higher place...."*

Then, suddenly, in a moment, His face was inches in front of mine – and my breath left me as I stared into His eyes. He was moving so close I thought he was going to move right through me. I was captivated by His look – His eyes. He got so close – like millimeters away and said ... *"And I shall abide in YOU...."*

I was overtaken by His presence, and I could see Him envelope me like a translucent glove – and I was moving in Him and He in me ... and I wondered ... and I was amazed at how deep He was calling and yearning for our presence with Him. I was beginning to understand what it means to abide – but more so – for Him to abide in us.

Then I saw the profile of His eye – large, massive, filling the sky – His eye lashes moved to the sound of worship – and I looked and I saw His hands – and I looked – and saw His feet – and He said very slowly and very powerfully:

*"My eyes..."* then he paused

*"My feet..."* then he paused

*"My hands..."* then he paused

Pausing that seemed to fill the room with expectance between each proclamation. LOUDER this time...

*"My Eyes..."*

*"My Feet..."*

*"My Hands..."*

LOUDER STILL with deep passion…

*"MY EYES…"*

*"MY FEET…"*

*"MY HANDS…"*

I was blown away – I had to abide – I had to let Him abide in me.…

Then I saw Jesus – with the same rugged look and attire as His feet hands, sitting against a well. He was so very strong, but peaceful and confidant … waiting. He had in His hand a cup. He looked at me, extended the cup, and said:

"Drink," pause.…

My heart was racing.

He said it again … "DRINK,"

My heart was really pounding.…

"Drink," a third time he said it with a smile"

Suddenly, I was right in front of Him with the cup to my mouth – and as I began to drink, I was suddenly drawn into the cup – swimming in the deep water of His presence. I was floating and swimming – and I looked up at the surface of the water from inside the cup and saw His reflection – and I was overcome.

Then He said:

> *"Let the water of My presence overwhelm you. Let the reflection of My presence burn deep within your soul. Let it soak you and fill you till water is coming out of your very pores and you can stretch out your hands and be the reflection of My Glory - For I desire to abide in YOU. He who has measured the waters in the hollow of His hands has come unto you - And He shall come again"*

**Even so, Come Lord Jesus, come!**

By sharing these last three encounters I hope to give you not only an understanding of the function of a seer and how visions work within a trance encounter, but also wish to stir your hearts to go deeper with the lover of your soul. I want to cause your hearts to burn for the revelation of His tender mercy and inexpressible love for you and offer the cup of His presence to you – so that you may drink deeply from the Master's hand.

# CHAPTER 5

# Can I See?

*"And when the servant of the man of God arose
early and went out, there was an army,
surrounding the city with horses and chariots.
And his servant said to him, Alas, my master!
What shall we do? So he answered, Do not fear,
for those who are with us are more than those
who are with them. And Elisha prayed, and
said, Lord, I pray, open his eyes that he may see.
Then the Lord opened the eyes of the young
man, and he saw. And behold, the mountain
was full of horses and chariots of fire all around
Elisha."*

- 2 Kings 6:15-17

## How can I tell if someone operates as a seer?

The easy answer is this; Listen to how they introduce their message or word. If they begin by saying, "The Lord showed me" or "I saw" they, more than likely, operate from the seer modality. If they say, "The Lord would say" or "I believe I heard the Lord say," they are operating in the prophetic "hearing" modality. Remember the root word for prophet is *"Nabi"* meaning to "bubble up," a spontaneous impartation of a word from the Lord.

## How can I activate my seer senses?

One of Apostle Paul's main desires in his letter to the Corinthians was that they would not be ignorant regarding spiritual gifts (1 Corinthians 12:1).

> *"Now concerning spiritual gifts, brethren, I do not want you to be ignorant:"*

Paul was interested in activation as well as order. He did not want to hinder their ability to function in the gifts. On the contrary, he encouraged them for he said that they could all prophecy (1 Corinthians 14:31):

> *"For you can all prophesy one by one, that all may learn and all may be encouraged."*

When speaking to Timothy regarding his gifting he encouraged him to activate the gift of God that was in him.

> *"When I call to remembrance the genuine faith that is in you, which dwelt first in your grandmother Lois and your mother Eunice, and I am persuaded is in you also. Therefore I remind you to stir up the gift of God which is in you through the laying on of my hands. For God has not given us a spirit of fear, but of power and of love and of a sound mind."*
>
> – 2 Timothy 1:5-7

The question arises: How do I know I have this gift? They simple answer is to start by asking for it. *"Holy Spirit, release in me the ability to "see" what you are seeing. Activate all my senses so that I may walk in the fullness of all your revelatory communication."*

You see God's desire is for you to communicate with Him in all dimensions, as His is with you. In Ephesians 1:15-18, Paul prays that the Father of glory would give them the spirit of wisdom, and revelation in the knowledge of Him and that the eyes of their understanding would be enlightened.

> *"Therefore I also, after I heard of your faith in the Lord Jesus and your love for all the saints, do not cease to give thanks for you, making mention of you in my prayers; that the God of our Lord Jesus Christ, the Father of glory, may give to you the spirit of wisdom and revelation in the knowledge of Him, the eyes of your understanding being enlightened; that you may know what is the hope of His calling, what are the riches of the glory of His inheritance in the saints,"*
>
> – Ephesians 1:15-18

When Elisha prayed in 2 Kings 6:15-17 for his servants eyes to be open, he didn't pray, *"Lord, if he has the gift of seeing, open his eyes."* No, he simply prayed, *"Lord, I pray, open his eyes that he may see."*

> *"And when the servant of the man of God arose early and went out, there was an army, surrounding the city with horses and chariots.*

> *And his servant said to him, "Alas, my master!*
> *What shall we do?"*
>
> *So he answered, "Do not fear, for those who are*
> *with us are more than those who are with them."*
> *And Elisha prayed, and said, "Lord, I pray, open*
> *his eyes that he may see." Then the Lord opened*
> *the eyes of the young man, and he saw. And*
> *behold, the mountain was full of horses and*
> *chariots of fire all around Elisha."*

I find it interesting in the book of Revelation, when the Lord speaks to the church of Laodicea he says:

> *"Because you say, 'I am rich, have become wealthy, and*
> *have need of nothing'—and do not know that you are*
> *wretched, miserable, poor, blind, and naked—I counsel*
> *you to buy from Me gold refined in the fire, that you*
> *may be rich; and white garments, that you may be*
> *clothed, that the shame of your nakedness may not be*
> *revealed; and anoint your eyes with eye salve, that you*
> *may see."*
>
> - Revelation 3:17-18

In this verse, we see a description, not only of our state before the cross, i.e. wretched, miserable, poor, blind, and naked. We also see His desire for us after salvation. He wants to clothe us in His righteousness, give us spiritual riches beyond measure, and – now get this – trade our blindness by anointing our eyes with eye salve that that we might see. Paul teaches us that that we are to desire spiritual gifts, especially the prophetic, because it can equip and benefit the body of Christ.

*"Pursue love, and desire spiritual gifts, but especially that you may prophesy."*

- 1 Corinthians 14:1

The Greek word for *"desire"* is *"zeloo"* meaning to *"burn with zeal"* or *"to be zealous in the pursuit of something."* In this case, that *"something"* is spiritual gifts. The Greek for *"especially"* is *"mallon"* meaning *"more, to a greater degree, rather."* Ironically, it is the same word found in Luke 11:9-13 where Jesus is speaking about the gift of the Holy Spirit.

*"So I say to you, ask, and it will be given to you; seek, and you will find; knock, and it will be opened to you. For everyone who asks receives, and he who seeks finds, and to him who knocks it will be opened. If a son asks for bread from any father among you, will he give him a stone? Or if he asks for a fish, will he give him a serpent instead of a fish? Or if he asks for an egg, will he offer him a scorpion? If you then, being evil, know how to give good gifts to your children, how much more [mallon] will your heavenly Father give the Holy Spirit to those who ask Him!"*

This is the starting place, ask, seek, knock, desire, and be zealous for your eyes to be open. Clearly, this is the Lords will. All it takes is faith and an open heart.

Second, pay attention. It takes time to recognize God's voice. When you stop brushing aside that small still voice or ignoring that faint image that floats across your mind when you are in worship and pay attention you will beginning to see and hear differently. One of the keys to seeing in the spiritual realm is relearning "how" to think, and "how" to process information. Learn to understand the metaphorical language of God. Ask the Lord to teach you His metaphorical speech. Devour the Scriptures and pay attention to "How" he speaks. Pay attention to the symbolism from your own life experiences.

Learn to rest and be quiet before the Lord. Distraction is the worst enemy to hearing from God. We live in a society where we are inundated with voices and noise. When you learn to block out distraction you have taken the first step in listening. It takes time, but you can train yourself to dial down, focus, and listen or look at what the Lord is saying.

## What if I can't see?

Jim Driscoll, founder of "Stir the Waters" and author of the "Modern Seer" (www.stirthewaters.com), answered this question very well:

> *"Potentially everyone can see. When we can't see, it could be for a few different reasons: Our gifting is dormant, we aren't ready to see yet, we don't realize we already seeing (that the pictures in our heads are from God), something in our bloodline (like a spiritual curse) is keeping out gifts from functioning, or the enemy made us fearful of our giftings when we were young and we responded by shutting them down,"*

As we will discuss later in this volume, seeing is one of the many ways God communicates. It is open to all believers, as a tool to equip them for the work of ministry. It is not necessarily a prophetic gift as much as it is a language. You can see while operating with words of knowledge or wisdom. It can manifest while ministering healing or deliverance. Not everyone is called to be a Seer or Prophet at a highly public level, but everyone is free to embrace the seer gift and see. The Lord is simply speaking. Let's open up the dialog.

Keys to seeing, listening, and activating the seer's gift in your life:

- Start by paying attention, even if what you see does not make sense at the time.
- Evaluate what God seems to be saying.
- Wait for God. Quiet your spirit. Learn to hit the pause button.
- Ask God for clarification. Talk back to God. Dialog is a two way street.
- Pray about it. Look for that inner peace that will resonate in you.
- Realize that God can speak through anything. All your senses are open to listening.
- Sharpen your discernment meter by staying in the Word and through prayer.
- Practice with the Holy Spirit. Jesus said the Holy Spirit would teach you all truth. It is ok to practice.

Doing the things of the Spirit is the surest way to hone your ability to hear. Sharing your experiences with your brothers and sisters in a home group or other safe setting will reinforce your growth in this area.

# CHAPTER 6

# The Language of Visions and Dreams

*"And the whole earth was of one language, and of one speech."*

- Genesis 11:1

*"The heavens declare the glory of God; and the firmament shows His handiwork. Day unto day utters speech, and night unto night reveals knowledge. There is no speech nor language where their voice is not heard."*

- Psalms 19:1-3

*"Then He said, 'Hear now My words: If there is a prophet among you, I, the LORD, make Myself known to him in a vision; I speak to him in a dream.'"*

- Numbers 12:6

Henry Longfellow once wrote, *"Three silences there are: the first of speech, the second of desire, and the third of thought."* From the very beginning, language has been a part of life, as we know it. It works together with all that we know or do. Desires, thoughts, passions, feelings, praise, worship, and prayer, all move in and out of this vehicle called language.

In the Scriptures, God's written language to the world, we see the inception of language for humanity and earthly creation. In the first book of the Bible, we have the story of creation. In this account, God not only speaks creation into existence but also gives names to that which He created. Man, in his attempt to elevate himself to new heights, concluded that developed language came through maturation from a primate to Homo sapiens.

Yet in Genesis, we see that language is part of the very nature of God and that He created man with that same ability to communicate through a symbolic system.

In Genesis we read:

> *"Then God said, "Let Us make man in Our image, according to Our likeness; let them have dominion over the fish of the sea, over the birds of the air, and over the cattle, over all the earth and over every creeping thing that creeps on the earth." So God created man in His own image; in the image of God He created him; male and female He created them."*

> - Genesis 1:26-27

Here we have the impartation of or the reflection of God's image in man. Part of this attribute was the ability to communicate thoughts and ideas, to have emotions and feel love. In fact, the first act of man on this planet was the naming of the animals as seen in Genesis 2:19.

> *"Out of the ground the Lord God formed every beast of the field and every bird of the air, and brought them to Adam to see what he would call them. And whatever Adam called each living creature, that was its name."*

And about Eve he states:

> *"Then the rib which the Lord God had taken from man He made into a woman, and He brought her to the man. And Adam said: "This is now bone of my bones and flesh of my flesh; She shall be called woman, because she was taken out of man."*

> - Genesis 2:22-23

Language has undergone many definitions. Henry Sweet, an English phonetician and language scholar, stated:

> *"Language is the expression of ideas by means of speech-sounds combined into words. Words are combined into sentences, this combination answering to that of ideas into thoughts."*

Bernard Bloch and George L. Trager, both linguists, made this definition:

> *"A language is a system of arbitrary vocal symbols by means of which a social group cooperates."*

The key words in both definitions are *"ideas," "thoughts,"* and *"social group cooperation."* The idea of social group cooperation is so powerful that in Genesis 11:1-9 we read the story of Nimrod the hunter. In this account we read:

> *"Now the whole earth had one language and one speech. And it came to pass, as they journeyed from the east, that they found a plain in the land of Shinar, and they dwelt there. Then they said to one another, "Come, let us make bricks and bake them thoroughly." They had brick for stone, and they had asphalt for mortar. And they said, "Come, let us build ourselves a city, and a tower whose top is in the heavens; let us make a name for ourselves, lest we be scattered abroad over the face of the whole earth. But the Lord came down to see the city and the tower which the sons of men had built. And the Lord said, "Indeed the people are one and they all have one language, and this is what they begin to do; now nothing that they propose to do will be withheld from them. Come, let Us go down and there confuse their language, that they may not understand one another's speech." So the Lord scattered them abroad from there over the face of all the earth, and they ceased building the city. Therefore, its name is called Babel, because there the Lord confused the language of all the earth; and from*

> *there the Lord scattered them abroad over the*
> *face of all the earth."*

In this account, we find humanity in a unified force bound by their ability to communicate and imagine. This unity is so powerful that the Lord changes their language in order to scatter them across the face of the earth. We also see a link between the imagination and imagery and its correlation to language. Creative powers to accomplish that which is envisioned, if they all think, speak, and desire the same thing, so all three linguistic scholars are right to some extent in their definition of language.

Nonetheless, they fall short in that they actually define speech, which is only one kind of language. Take for example sign language used by the deaf around the world. In sign language, we do not have vocal symbols to communicate. The symbols used are hand symbols representing the vocal language of a given culture. We have body language, instrumental language, the language of art, the language of creation, and yes even the dance of the bees.

Language can better be defined as a set of symbolic images, which conjure up ideas and thought patterns to communicate one to another.

In Leanne Payne's book *"The Healing Presence,"* chapter 9 entitled *"Imagery and Symbol: "The Imagery Really Matters"* she states:

> *"...We are mythic beings: we live by and in our*
> *symbols. Man is an animal who symbolizes, who*
> *talks. (To talk is to symbolize. Language itself is*

> symbol.) *Thus, man is set apart from the rest of the natural creation. Symbols bind up reality for us."*

When I speak of the language of visions and dreams, I am not talking about oneiromancy, occult divination by dreams brought on by the demonic world to confuse and twist the hearts of man. Nor am I speaking of Freud's dream analyses and Jung's archetypes, as helpful as they may be in the field of psychoanalyses.

What I am speaking about is the *"Rhema"* of God (God's spoken word to a person at a given moment regarding a specific situation, in contrast to the *"Logos,"* his eternal written Word to humanity) coming to man in pictorial language. As stated earlier, this spoken language from God may come through any of the senses including visionary dreams or visions.

In the crazy fast-paced world we live in, many times we are so preoccupied that it is hard for us to hear God. Yet, God is speaking, and He desires to get or attention. If He cannot get our attention while we are awake, He will get our attention while we sleep and that through dreams. Our Heavenly Father often will use dreams and visions as a vehicle to identify the barricades that are hindering our path to His purpose in our life as illustrated in Job.

> *"In a dream, in a vision of the night, when deep sleep falls upon men, while slumbering on their beds, then He opens the ears of men, and seals their instruction."*

> - Job 33:15-16

Dreams and visions are a major part of the outpouring of God's Spirit in the Last Days!

> *"And it shall come to pass afterward, That I will pour out My Spirit on all flesh; Your sons and your daughters shall prophesy, Your old men shall dream dreams, Your young men shall see visions. And also on My menservants and on My maidservants I will pour out My Spirit in those days."*
>
> - Joel 2:28-29

## Redeemed Imagination

We regard the imagination as our ability to picture, pretend, or envision a given situation. A student sits in a classroom staring out the window, transfixed by thoughts a million miles away and we say he's daydreaming. A little girl playing with her dolls is actively engaged in a conversation with a friend nobody sees, and we say she has an imaginary friend. The mysterious mind with all of its facets is truly a wonder.

Yet, what is the function of pizza dreams, nightmares, daydreams, visual thinking, imagery, dreaming, and alike? How do we rationalize all the workings that involve our imaginations? What was the creative purpose in the eyes of God for this kind of activity before we fell from grace?

When God created man, he put within his mind, the mechanism, or ability to receive pictorially, communication from God. Much like a T.V. receiver man can see what God was speaking into his spirit. Then, at the fall of man, he lost this ability, and the receiver became distorted, opening it to other signals. These signals may come from the emotional pain of one's past, pizza, fleshly pleasure, creative thought, or even the demonic realm.

Yet, it was not until the redemption of man through Christ that this operation of the mind began to function properly, though through a glass darkly (1 Corinthians 13:12), the healing process had begun. In the old covenant, it came through the forward look to the cross.

> *"For now we see in a mirror, dimly, but then face to face. Now I know in part, but then I shall know just as I also am known."*
>
> - 1 Corinthians 13:12

In the new covenant regeneration and the renewing of our minds by the Holy Spirit healed it.

This is the creative working of the living God in the life of the believer, the healing of our broken nature. The casting-down of worldly symbolic thoughts that have invaded our minds and restoring the channel to its intended purpose so that we can listen and receive from God that which He desires to breath into our lives.

A dear friend of mine Lyn Sorensen, a seer in her own right, put it this way:

> *"I see pictures and it's like He (the Lord) connects the dots ... pointing the way or an idea or*

> *something he's saying to the world... I call it*
> *connecting the dots ... some dots are very large,*
> *but some are very small..."*

That is how it works, the regenerative process of hearing what God is saying. All the communicative gifting of God, be it prophecy, the word of knowledge, the word or wisdom, distinguishing of spirits, or preaching as an oracle of God, are the out flow of this healing processes.

James Goll, referring to dreams and visions states:

> *"God is the Master Dream Weaver. Through dreams, God communicates directly with us concerning our destiny as well as the destinies of our families, our nation, and our world. Many people today, particularly in the Western culture, never recognize God speaking to them in this way, because they have been conditioned by a skeptical and sophisticated society to discount the language of dreams. Within our own generation, God is reconnecting us to a vital part of our spiritual heritage."*

There are two very similar Hebrew words used in the Old Testament to refer to *"dreams."* The first is *"chalam"* meaning *"to dream, or dreamer"* as in Genesis 37:19, where the brothers of Joseph call him a *"dreamer."*

> *"And they said one to another, Behold, this dreamer [chalam] cometh."*

The second word is *"chalom,"* meaning *"a dream."* Where either word is used, the Old Testament makes it clear that God is the one orchestrating the dream. He downloads His dreams within us and thereby transforms us into dreamers of His will.

There are three primary words for *"vision"* in Hebrew. The first is *"chazon;"* meaning vision, but carries with it of being in an ecstatic state or trance as seen in 1 Samuel 3:1 (KJV).

> *"And the child Samuel ministered unto the Lord before Eli. And the word of the Lord was precious in those days; there was no open vision.[chazon]"*

The second word is *"mar'eh"* meaning vision or sight, but the emphasis is on the phenomenon, spectacle, appearance, or vision – it is about *"what is seen,"* or the *"power of seeing,"* as seen in Exodus 24:17 (KJV).

> *"And the sight [mar'eh] of the glory of the Lord was like devouring fire on the top of the mount in the eyes of the children of Israel."*

The third word is *"chizayon,"* meaning *"ecstatic vision,"* vision (in the night), or vision, oracle, prophecy e.g., divine communication as seen in 2 Samuel 7:17 (NKJ).

> *"According to all these words, and according to all this vision [chizayon], so did Nathan speak unto David."*

*"Onar"* is the common word for dream in the New Testament. It is the kind of dreaming we all do when we sleep. God can and does use common dreams to communicate with ordinary people. Example is Joseph's dream to wed Mary, in Matthew 1:20.

> *"But while he thought on these things, behold, the angel of the Lord appeared unto him in a dream [onar], saying, Joseph, thou son of David, fear not to take unto thee Mary thy wife: for that which is conceived in her is of the Holy Ghost."*

The second word is *"enypnion,"* meaning a vision or a dream received while asleep. Enypnion stresses a surprise quality that is contained in that dream. It is the kind of dream that carries weight or has a surprising effect as seen in Acts 2:17 (KJV),

> *"And it shall come to pass in the last days, saith God, I will pour out of my Spirit upon all flesh: and your sons and your daughters shall prophesy, and your young men shall see visions, and your old men shall dream dreams [enypnion]."*

and Jude 1:8 (KJV):

> *"Likewise also these filthy dreamers [enypniazomai] defile the flesh, despise dominion, and speak evil of dignities."*

There are three primary words used in Greek for the word *"vision."* The first word is *"horama,"* meaning that which is seen, spectacle, a sight divinely granted in an ecstasy or in sleep, or a vision as seen in Matthew 17:9 (KJV).

> *"And as they came down from the mountain, Jesus charged them, saying, Tell the vision [horama] to no man, until the Son of man be risen again from the dead."*

The second word is *"optasia,"* meaning a vision, an appearance presented to one whether asleep or awake as seen in Luke 1:22 (KJV).

> *"And when he came out, he could not speak unto them: and they perceived that he had seen a vision [optasia] in the temple: for he beckoned unto them, and remained speechless."*

The third word is *"horasis,"* meaning the act of seeing, a vision, an appearance in visible form, or an appearance divinely granted in an ecstasy or dream as seen in Revelation 4:3 (KJV).

> *"And he that sat was to look upon like a jasper and a sardine stone: and there was a rainbow round about the throne, in sight [horasis] like unto an emerald."*

And Revelation 9:17 (KJV):

> *"And thus I saw the horses in the vision [horasis], and them that sat on them, having breastplates of fire, and of jacinth, and brimstone: and the heads of the horses were as the heads of lions; and out of their mouths issued fire and smoke and brimstone."*

The Greek highlights the fact that visions can come within a dream, come in a state of ecstasy, or come in an open vision where the appearance is in visible form.

Wither its dreams or visions, God desires to invade our minds and open the doors of communication so that we my function with Him, by Him, and through Him, in all that we do, that we may be one even as He is one.

The purpose of visual communication is to awaken us to a new dimension in Christ, to quicken us to be alive in Him, and be used by Him, anytime and in any place. Jesus is calling us to put on the mind of Christ and to renew our minds and be changed. He wants to transform our thought processes, so we think in Heavenly mode. He wants us to operate out of a Kingdom mindset and not function in a fallen earthly mode.

As we begin to seek His face and release the symbolic images of our fallen nature to Him, we can replace those images with the Word of God and the eternal truth of His Kingdom. That is where the healing process begins, and our "*receivers*" are honed to tune in to Heaven's channel.

Only then will we hear the Word of God through all that we think and do. His Word will dance upon our minds when we sleep. It will leap upon the mountaintops when we walk through woods enjoying the work of His creative hands. It will move before us in mighty visions as we tread upon serpents in our missionary journeys. It will lead us beside the still waters and comfort us when we are alone. The Word will be active and sharper than any two-edged sword and will pierce asunder the thoughts and intents of the hearts of man.

God desires to baste us in the presence of His Word. He desires to envelope us in the cloud of His Glory so that every dot and title of our life revolves around fellowship with Him. This is the language of visions and dreams, the expansion of a hearing ear through the renewing of a mind that was once fallen.

*"That you put off, concerning your former conduct, the old man which grows corrupt according to the deceitful lusts, and be renewed in the spirit of your mind, and that you put on the new man which was created according to God, in true righteousness and holiness."*

- Ephesians 4:22-24

# CHAPTER 7

# God Speaks

*"But he who enters by the door is the shepherd of the sheep. To him the doorkeeper opens, and the sheep hear his voice; and he calls his own sheep by name and leads them out. And when he brings out his own sheep, he goes before them; and the sheep follow him, for they know his voice. Yet they will by no means follow a stranger, but will flee from him, for they do not know the voice of strangers."*

- John 10:2-5

I find it very exciting to look at creation and examine how God has woven us together, every detail complete in His eternal design. For example, did you know that the nerves leading to the eye are much larger than those leading to the ear? Science tells us that we give twenty-five times as much attention to what we see as to what we hear.

Accordingly, a communication expert for the Army has stated that, *"If you want people to remember what you say, illustrate your talk."* Today we know, in educational circles, that the best way of increasing the retention rate of your students is to blend visual aids with verbalization. When relying on verbalization alone to communicate, an estimated 90% of a message is misinterpreted or forgotten entirely. We learn 10% of what we hear and 83% by what we see. By using both visual in conjunction with verbal, are retention rate is approximately 50%, and if we "*say*" what we "*see*," we retain 70%. However, if we "say" and "*do*," our retention rate climbs to 90%. The Lord has wired us to not only to be "*hearers*" of His Word, but to "*see*" His Word, and once we have "*seen*" to "*speak*" His Word, and finely, to be "*doers*" of His Word (James 1:22-25).

> *"But be doers of the word, and not hearers only, deceiving yourselves. For if anyone is a hearer of the word and not a doer, he is like a man observing his natural face in a mirror; for he observes himself, goes away, and immediately forgets what kind of man he was. But he who looks into the perfect law of liberty and continues in it, and is not a forgetful hearer but a doer of the work, this one will be blessed in what he does."*

It's easy then to understand why the Lord, in His desire to communicate to His children, has chosen a wide variety of creative mediums and has created us to listen from all the spectrums of His creative speech. The power of visionary language paired with the act of proclamation and action results in not only advancing the Kingdom, but also hard wiring the truth of His Word into our renewed minds.

A quick look at some of the resources that God has deposited in our lives causes us to remember the riches we have in communication with Him. One of the greatest of all the gifts that He has given us is the Comforter; that blessed Holy Spirit that descended on the Church, on the day of Pentecost. The Holy Spirit lives in you, and through you. Incredible as it sounds, when you stop and grasp this, it is a very powerful truth; not only this, but the Father Himself abides in you, as well as the blessed Son of the Most High God.

Yet, the Lord did not stop there in His desire to secure a living and breathing relationship with His children, He has given us the inspired Word of God. The entire Scripture is one inspired revelation of God's mind, will, and word communicated to man and bound within the cover of a book we call the Bible. Take a look at these Scriptures:

*"All Scripture is given by inspiration of God, and is profitable for doctrine, for reproof, for correction, for instruction in righteousness, that the man of God may be complete, thoroughly equipped for every good work."*

*- 2 Timothy 3:16-17*

*"And so we have the prophetic word confirmed, which you do well to heed as a light that shines in a dark place, until the day dawns and the morning star rises in your hearts; knowing this first, that no prophecy of Scripture is of any private interpretation, for prophecy never came by the will of man, but holy men of God spoke as they were moved by the Holy Spirit."*

*- 2 Peter 1:19-21*

We know from these Scriptures that this written revelation of sixty-six books, penned in three different languages, by forty different authors, over thousands of years, by men, of all walks of life, is God's complete revelation to humanity. The Bible is perfect and sufficient to bring all the revelation of God that we can comprehend in our present mortality. No further prophetic communication from God is required. Yet God did not stop there in His desire to communicate to His Church.

In the Greek there are two words used for the word "*word.*" The first is "*Logos,*" and the second is "*Rhema.*" Greek scholars and Biblical theologians have debated about whether these words are synonymous. Yet, many believe that the inspired writers chose each word to express the exact meaning that they were trying to get across. Thus we see two words to express God's communication to man. When we refer to the word "*Logos,*" we are referring to the "*Word (Logos) of God,*" the Scriptures, the Holy Bible. Logos also refers to Jesus Christ Himself as seen in John 1:1 and 14.

> *"In the beginning was the Word (Logos), and the Word (Logos) was with God, and the Word (Logos) was God...*
>
> *And the Word (Logos) became flesh and dwelt among us, and we beheld His glory, the glory as of the only begotten of the Father, full of grace and truth."*

The Logos of God is settled and complete, it shall never pass away; it is the same, yesterday, today, and forever and can never be added to. It is God's eternal standard, outlining His eternal plan, principles, doctrines, and decrees, by that we use

THE SEER'S GIFT • 119

to weigh all truth, in its light. However, what of "*rhema*," how is it used in scripture? What role does rhema play in the life of the Christian and how does it operate in God's communication to His Church?

To better understand rhema let's examine the word rhema as defined by W.E. Vine's Expository Dictionary of the New Testament Words.

> "*Rhema denotes that which is spoken, what is uttered in speech and writing: in the singular, a word. The significance of rhema (as distinct from LOGOS) is exemplified in the injunction to take the sword of the Spirit, which is the word (rhema) of God*"

> - W.E. Vine

We see here that the reference is not to the whole Bible but to a single word or truth from scripture that the Holy Spirit brings to remembrance in a time of need. One needs to store the Word (*Logos*) within his spirit so there is something to draw from. So Logos then is like a well of living water and rhema is like a cup of water drawn from that well; It is like that timely, Holy Spirit inspired word from the Logos that brings faith, life, and power to fulfill God's will in a given situation. Romans 10:17 states, "*So then faith cometh by hearing, and hearing by the word (rhema) of God.*" Therefore, we see that the hearer must receive rhema with faith for it to fulfill its desired mission.

## Revelatory Gifts

To understand rhema one needs to understand the various gifts that God has placed within His Church. The gifts of the Holy Spirit are referred to in several places in scripture, one of which is found in 1 Corinthians 12.

The Greek word used there for gifts is the word "*charismata,*" which means "*gifts of grace.*" The whole purpose of giving these free gifts of God to His people is to do the work of the Kingdom, and to move in deeper fellowship with Christ. They are not given to exalt a believer or to be hidden in a closet. These gifts are given so that Christ, through His body, can build up its members and equip the saints, for the work of ministry.

Let's look at a few of revelatory gifts that are considered rhema from God.

**The Word of Knowledge:** Is the speaking or uttering of a truth given to an individual, in a given moment, or a particular situation. This gift is divine illumination or insight from the Holy Spirit; it is a particular disclosure of knowledge and not formed through natural means. The gift is not knowledge but the declaration thereof, a gift of oracular utterance.

**The Word of Wisdom:** Is a manifestation of the Holy Spirit where the supernatural wisdom of God is declared or proclaimed. It is an impartation of depth and understanding regarding the truth of the gospel or a specific situation. This is neither a result of man's wisdom, human elegance, or the work of a great orator. It is an outflowing from the Holy Spirit concerning the depths of God's heart, a revelation of wisdom, in a given situation or moment.

**Discerning of Spirits:** It is the supernatural ability given to an individual to see through the outer-man and discern the spirit of the inner-man. It relates to "spirits" and can involve the distinguishing of the human spirit, demonic spirit activity, or angelic spirit activity. This insight into the spiritual realm can only be made possible through the workings of the Holy Spirit. The purpose is to discern the spirit at work in any activity within the body of Christ, in a region, a city, or within an individual.

**Prophecy:** It is a revelation, given by the Holy Spirit, as with all the gifts it is subordinate to the Word of God. It is communication from God, spoken in the common language, to an individual, to the corporate body at large, or to a nation. It is an expression of the mind and Spirit of Christ. Prophecy can be foretelling-to know the future (Acts 11:28),

> *"Then one of them, named Agabus, stood up and showed by the Spirit that there was going to be a great famine throughout all the world, which also happened in the days of Claudius Caesar."*

or it can be forthtelling-to cause the future (Ezekiel 37:1-10).

Prophecy is for the edification, exhortation, and consolation (comfort) of the believer (1 Corinthians 14:3).

> *"But he who prophesies speaks edification and exhortation and comfort to men."*

Prophecy is for building up and not tearing down. Prophecy can speak to a present situation or future events. Prophecy is to always be weighed and judged (1 Corinthians 14:29).

*"Let two or three prophets speak, and let the others judge."*

Weighed as to the depth of what God is saying, judged as to testing the source, whether it be of the Lord, of the flesh, of the demonic realm, or a combination. In essence, it's the weighing of the significance and the source of what's been said. We know in part and prophesy in part.

**Tongues and Interpretation of Tongues:** A manifestation of the Holy Spirit where one has yielded the ability of speech to the Holy Spirit and is speaking in one of many languages, be it the language of men or of angels, as the Spirit gives utterance. The mind in essence is bypassed and the spirit is directly speaking through the depths of the Holy Spirit in a given moment.

The gift of tongues can be divided into two categories. The first being ministry tongues where the purpose is to speak the mysteries of God to the assembly of the church as a whole. The exercise of this gift, in this context, is for the edification of the body of Christ and is always accompanied by the gift of interpretation of tongues, the latter being the supernatural gift to translate in a given moment what is spoken by the Holy Spirit, to the gathered assembly.

In these situations, the gift operates very much like prophecy. The second category is that of devotional tongues. Used by an individual for either prayer or praise to God. There are no limitations on devotional tongues. When one prays in tongues one's spirit is praying making intercession, with the Holy Spirit who sees the hidden and unknown things of God and searches the heart of God making one's request known to God. Praise in tongues my happen in song or utterance and is used for personal edification or for intersession.

Along with these gifts, we can add to that list some methodology on how they could come to you:

- A small still voice of the Holy Spirit
- An inner witness of the Holy Spirit
- Revelatory Prayer
- Prophetic Song
- Vision or Dream
- Audible voice of God
- A surge of supernaturally knowing
- Angelic Utterance
- Prophetic Action or Event
- Natural Events or Events in Nature

## The Spirit of Revelation

After examining the various ways that God speaks to us, it is imperative that we learn wisdom in handling revelation. We need to learn "how" to test and weigh all that comes in our direction, to move into what God desires to do in our lives. God is speaking today. God is a God of communication. His very name is the "*Word*" and he wants to speak to you today. Dive into the depths of God and listen to all the ways He is speaking to you. God is speaking today. He speaks through the tongues of men and of angels.... He speaks through His Word of pin and quill.... He speaks through His servants, both prophet and preacher.... He speaks through His creation, great and small.... He speaks in a wind or a wee little whisper.... He speaks through a child ... with childlike faith.... He's speaking today ... if you listen, you can hear it. In the book of Ephesians 1:17-18, Paul prays the following:

> "...that the God of our Lord Jesus Christ, the Father of glory, may give to you the spirit of wisdom and revelation in the knowledge of Him, the eyes of your understanding being enlightened; that you may know what is the hope of His calling, what are the riches of the glory of His inheritance in the saints,..."

In this verse he is praying that they may receive the spirit of wisdom and revelation and that the eyes of their understanding being enlightened. The Greek word there for understanding is *"dianoia"* meaning, the exercise of deep-thinking using ones imagination, mind, understanding.

Therefore, Paul is asking the Father to pour out the spirit of revelation upon them and with that revelation infuse them with divine wisdom. He is asking the Father to open their eyes, to let them see, light a spark, and set a fire within their hearts igniting their imaginations and their minds with understanding.

This is my prayer for you, that the Father would pour out revelation upon you and you would be a seer filled with all wisdom and understanding, that your minds would be lubricated and your imaginations be released to see. That you, like Elijah, can infuse that ministry into the lives of those around you.

CHAPTER 8

# Testing and Interpreting Visionary Language

*"For a good tree does not bear bad fruit, nor does a bad tree bear good fruit. For every tree is known by its own fruit. For men do not gather figs from thorns, nor do they gather grapes from a bramble bush. A good man out of the good treasure of his heart brings forth good; and an evil man out of the evil treasure of his heart brings forth evil. For out of the abundance of the heart his mouth speaks."*

- Luke 6:43-45

*"Do not quench the Spirit. Do not despise prophecies. Test all things; hold fast what is good."*

- 1 Thessalonians 5:19-21

This book deals mainly with visionary language. The purpose of this chapter is to explain how to test and

127

interpret dreams and visions, though the principles also apply to the testing of all the "*rhema*" of God.

There are three core components to understanding and implementing a revelation from God. The first is the Revelation itself. The second is the Interpretation of that revelation. The third is the Application of that revelation. Before we dive into the details of these three areas, let's set some groundwork or foundational principles.

The first step in discerning revelation is taking a hard look at your own life, a spiritual survey if you will. You need to do a system check. You need to test your heart and character. Ask yourself various questions to get a spiritual measurement of your walk with the Lord. Take a spiritual pulse-check if you will. This is very important because your discernment is in direct relationship to your abiding in Christ. You were a "fallen" creature that has been saved by grace. Currently you are housed within a mortal fallen body, with all its flaws. It is only by abiding in Him that the spiritual filter of the Holy Spirit can function fully in you. We are in a war and the enemy of our souls will not stop in his efforts to delude and destroy all that God is trying to do in your life. Jesus said,

> "*I am the true vine, and My Father is the vinedresser. Every branch in Me that does not bear fruit He takes away; and every branch that bears fruit He prunes, that it may bear more fruit. You are already clean because of the word which I have spoken to you. Abide in Me, and I in you. As the branch cannot bear fruit of itself, unless it abides in the vine, neither can you, unless you abide in Me.*"

*"I am the vine, you are the branches. He who abides in Me, and I in him, bears much fruit; for without Me you can do nothing. If anyone does not abide in Me, he is cast out as a branch and is withered; and they gather them and throw them into the fire, and they are burned. If you abide in Me, and My words abide in you, you will ask what you desire, and it shall be done for you."*

- John 15:1-7

## System Check

Here are some key questions to ask when doing a spiritual system check.

**How is my devotional life?** Am I regularly reading the Word of God along with studying the Scriptures? It is very important not to just study the Bible, but to devotionally read the Bible, slowly, and meditatively, giving the Holy Spirit an opportunity to breathe His truth into your spirit; Much like dining on the Word of God, savoring every bit, as opposed to studying the recipes, which though very important, do not compare to eating a solid diet of simple reading and extracting all its nutrients.

**Check your prayer life.** How is my prayer life? Do I spend quality quiet time with the Father? Is my prayer life more than corporate prayer or intersession? Do I have quiet fellowship with the Lord? Do I listen as much as I speak? Devotional prayer is just as important as any other kind of prayer. To learn to savor those moments with God on a regular basis will build a lifestyle of abiding.

**Am I having fellowship with other believers?** You need to fellowship within the body of Christ. You need to be a part of a local fellowship. A branch set apart from the vine soon withers. A log removed from a burning fire soon smolders. Ask yourself - how is my fellowship?

**Do I have un-confessed sin in my life?** Jesus said, *"And whenever you stand praying, if you have anything against anyone, forgive him, that your Father in heaven may also forgive you your trespasses."* (Mark 11:25.) The ability to release the issues of life to the Father and confess your sins quickly and expediently unto the Lord is the surest way to stay on the path of abiding. If we confess our sins, he is faithful and true to forgive us our sins, and to cleanse us from all unrighteousness.

**What are my motives?** Do I seek to edify the body of Christ? Am I others oriented? Do I have a humble and contrite spirit or am I filled with pride, religiosity, or one-up-man-ship? God is searching for humble hearts of simple devotion to Him. This trait is often honed in the fire of adversity, trial, and brokenness ... but is one that should be strived for.... The ability to seek His face and not just His hand is the surest posture to take when abiding.

## Listening

Once you have done a system check, and find yourself in a place of abiding, then you are ready to discern, listen, and judge what God is breathing into your spirit. You must understand that it is important to judge and test revelation. In 1 Corinthians we read:

> *"Let two or three prophets speak, and let the others judge. But if anything is revealed to another who sits by, let the first keep silent. For you can all prophesy one by one, that all may learn and all may be encouraged. And the spirits of the prophets are subject to the prophets. For God is not the author of confusion but of peace, as in all the churches of the saints."*

> *- 1 Corinthians 14:29-33*

Testing and judging are the natural outcome of moving in revelatory knowledge. Too many times people want to throw out the baby with the bath water. Because of fear, they despise prophecy, deny the moving of God's Spirit, and turn from God to protect the church from error.

Yet, Paul tells us in 1 Thessalonians 5:19-21:

> *"Do not quench the Spirit. Do not despise prophecies. Test all things; hold fast what is good."*

The command here is proper balance, testing without grieving, judging without despising. One of the difficult problems believers face as they learn to move in revelatory knowledge is to discern what is accurate or inspired by the Holy Spirit or what is inaccurate or fleshly.

To help better understand this let's look at three sources of revelation that can come into your mind. It is critical to our understanding, for Peter tells us that:

*"But there were also false prophets among the people, even as there will be false teachers among you, who will secretly bring in destructive heresies, even denying the Lord who bought them, and bring on themselves swift destruction.*

*And many will follow their destructive ways, because of whom the way of truth will be blasphemed. By covetousness they will exploit you with deceptive words; for a long time their judgment has not been idle, and their destruction does not slumber."*

- 2 Peter 2:1-3

The very fact that false teachers shall arise should move us even more into the direction of abiding, but abiding does not mean abandonment of the gifts that God has given us.

## Sources of Revelation

Now let's look at a few sources of revelation that exist.

### The Holy Spirit

The first and most important source of revelation comes from the Holy Spirit.

In 2 Peter 1:21, we are told:

*"For prophecy never came by the will of man, but holy men of God spoke as they were moved by the Holy Spirit."*

The Greek word here for "*moved*" is "*Phero*," meaning to bear, carry, or borne along. This word is also used in Acts 27:15-17, where Paul, on his way to Rome by ship, was caught in a fierce storm.

> "So when the ship was caught, and could not head into the wind, we let her drive. And running under the shelter of an island called Clauda, we secured the skiff with difficulty. When they had taken it on board, they used cables to undergird the ship; and fearing lest they should run aground on the Syrtis Sands, they struck sail and so were driven."

The winds drove (*Phero*) the ship into the island of Malta where it was shipwrecked. In this instance, we see the same word used for the ship being driven by the wind as was used previously.

This is reminiscent of the rushing wind we see in Acts 2:2:

> "The winds drove (Phero) the ship into the island of Malta where it was shipwrecked. In this instance, we see the same word used for the ship being driven by the wind as was used previously."

On several occasions Jesus, in the book of John speaks of the Holy Spirit and His relationship to the church, let's look at a few of them (cf. John 14:16-17):

> "And I will pray the Father, and He will give you another Helper, that He may abide with you forever—the Spirit of truth, whom the world

> *cannot receive, because it neither sees Him nor*
> *knows Him; but you know Him, for He dwells*
> *with you and will be in you."*

In this passage, we learn four things:

1. He is with us forever.
2. We will see and know Him.
3. He will dwell in us.
4. He is the Spirit of truth.

> *"But the Helper, the Holy Spirit, whom the Father will*
> *send in My name, He will teach you all things, and*
> *bring to your remembrance all things that I said to*
> *you."*

> - John 14:26

Two important keys come out of this verse:

First, He is our teacher. Second, He will cause us to remember. This is the activation of rhema, where the Holy Spirit makes the reservoir of the Logos, stored in our spirit, alive for us in a given situation.

> *"But when the Helper comes, whom I shall send to you*
> *from the Father, the Spirit of truth who proceeds from*
> *the Father, He will testify of Me."*

> - John 15:26

The scripture tells us that the testimony of Jesus is the Spirit of prophecy (Revelation 19:10).

*"And I fell at his feet to worship him. But he said to me,
See that you do not do that! I am your fellow servant,
and of your brethren who have the testimony of Jesus.
Worship God! For the testimony of Jesus is the spirit of
prophecy."*

Here we see the Holy Spirit as the activating force behind the
testimony of Jesus.

*"Nevertheless I tell you the truth. It is to your
advantage that I go away; for if I do not go away, the
Helper will not come to you; but if I depart, I will send
Him to you."*

*- John 16:7*

We see in this verse the urgency, expediency, necessity, and the
heartbeat of Jesus. It is as if He is saying:

I have to go away ... if I don't I cannot pour into you my Spirit.
You NEED me to pour into you My Spirit. He is your
comforter.

*"However, when He, the Spirit of truth, has come, He
will guide you into all truth; for He will not speak on
His own authority, but whatever He hears He will
speak; and He will tell you things to come. He will
glorify Me, for He will take of what is Mine and declare
it to you. All things that the Father has are Mine.
Therefore I said that He will take of Mine and declare
it to you."*

*- John 16:13-15*

This is very powerful. When He, the Holy Spirit, comes, He will get your marching orders from the King and speak those things into your life. He will show you what is to come. He will always glorify Jesus. What He receives from Jesus, He will show you.

Along with the Holy Spirit as a source for revelation, there are two other sources that can invade our minds. The Human Spirit or Soul and the demonic.

A second source for revelation is the human spirit or soul. This is illustrated for us in the book of Ezekiel we read:

> *"And the word of the Lord came to me, saying, "Son of man, prophesy against the prophets of Israel who prophesy, and say to those who prophesy out of their own heart, 'Hear the word of the Lord!'"*
>
> *Thus says the Lord GOD: "Woe to the foolish prophets, who follow their own spirit and have seen nothing! O Israel, your prophets are like foxes in the deserts. You have not gone up into the gaps to build a wall for the house of Israel to stand in battle on the day of the Lord. They have envisioned futility and false divination, saying, 'Thus says the Lord!' But the Lord has not sent them; yet they hope that the word may be confirmed. Have you not seen a futile vision, and have you not spoken false divination? You say, 'The Lord says,' "but I have not spoken."*
>
> *Therefore thus says the Lord GOD: "Because you have spoken nonsense and envisioned lies, therefore I am indeed against you," says the Lord GOD."*

- Ezekiel 13:1-8

This is a perfect example for God's people falling into the delusion of false revelation brought on by their own sinful hearts. The Lord links their delusion with the vanity of their walk, the lack of abiding in Christ and resting in their own prideful ways. Jeremiah also expounds on:

> *"Thus says the Lord of hosts: "Do not listen to the words of the prophets who prophesy to you. They make you worthless; They speak a vision of their own heart, Not from the mouth of the Lord. They continually say to those who despise Me, 'The Lord has said, "You shall have peace"'; And to everyone who walks according to the dictates of his own heart, they say, 'No evil shall come upon you.'" For who has stood in the counsel of the Lord, And has perceived and heard His word? Who has marked His word and heard it?"*

- Jeremiah 23:16-18

It is evident from these passages that the need to stay humble before God, to seek His face and not simply His Hand, and keeping our hearts pure before Him, is the only way to abide. This calls for the fruit of the Spirit in all its meekness, anything less, simply leads to strong delusion. In Colossians Paul tells us that we should:

> *"Beware lest anyone cheat you through philosophy and empty deceit, according to the tradition of men, according to the basic principles of the world, and not according to Christ."*

- Colossians 2:8

Here again we see the role that vanity plays in deception and the pride of human philosophy in the web of deceit. We must be wise and humble in all our ways lest we fall into the pitfall of deception.

The wounded soul is also a source of false revelation. In book two of this series, *"The Seer and Healing,"* we talk about the renewing of the mind and inner healing of the wounded soul. The whole process of healing the wounded soul will help guard against soulish delusion.

## demonic Realm

The third source of revelation comes from the demonic realm. Paul makes it very clear in Ephesians 6, that our warfare is not waged against humanity but the spiritual forces of darkness. Paul further elaborates for us in Second Corinthians the craftiness of the enemy in his pursuit to destroy what God is doing (2 Corinthians 11:3-4; 13-15).

> *"But I fear, lest somehow, as the serpent deceived Eve by his craftiness, so your minds may be corrupted from the simplicity that is in Christ. For if he who comes preaches another Jesus whom we have not p reached, or if you receive a different spirit which you have not received, or a different gospel which you have not accepted—you may well put up with it!"*

> - 2 Corinthians 11:3-4

*"For such are false apostles, deceitful workers, transforming themselves into apostles of Christ. And no wonder! For Satan himself transforms himself into an angel of light. Therefore it is no great thing if his ministers also transform themselves into ministers of righteousness, whose end will be according to their works."*

- 2 Corinthians 11:13-15

A good example of this kind of warfare encounter is found in the book of Acts 16:16-18 were read:

*"Now it happened, as we went to prayer, that a certain slave girl possessed with a spirit of divination met us, who brought her masters much profit by fortune-telling. This girl followed Paul and us, and cried out, saying, "These men are the servants of the Most High God, who proclaim to us the way of salvation." And this she did for many days."*

In this account, we see a woman possessed by a demon of necromancy. The deception that she was using, to infiltrate the church, was not a lie, but a truth that was being proclaimed through a demonic spirit. No doubt, this was to give credence to her divination, and I presume, that her ultimate desire was to secure a position in the church that would ultimately lead to damnable heresies.

However, Paul grieved in his spirit, through the gift of discerning of spirits, saw through this false angle of light, and cast the demon out. Oh, how much more today do we need this gift? I pray that the Lord would richly pour out this gift upon us in these Last Days.

This whole process of judging revelation takes on major elements of warfare and that many times this takes place in our minds. That's why we are commanded to renew our minds and put on the mind of Christ. Take up the helmet of salvation and the sword of the Spirit, which is the Rhema of God. Paul tells us in Second Corinthians that:

> *"For though we walk in the flesh, we do not war according to the flesh. For the weapons of our warfare are not carnal but mighty in God for pulling down strongholds, casting down arguments and every high thing that exalts itself against the knowledge of God, bringing every thought into captivity to the obedience of Christ,"*

> \- 2 Corinthians 10:3-5

The key here lies in taking every thought captive and sifting it through the Word of God. We must keep our hearts in check. For vain imaginations and thoughts that proceed, either from the flesh or the demonic realm, have only one purpose in mind and that is to kill the life of Christ in you, to rob you and the Church of the blessings of the Most High, and to destroy all that God desires to do in this dying world.

We must pray for a humble heart and discern what is of God and what is not. Therefore, as Jesus has stated, we must take heed how we hear....

*"Therefore take heed how you hear. For whoever has,
to him more will be given; and whoever does not have,
even what he seems to have will be taken from him."*

- Luke 8:18

This is truly a call to heart cleansing, for ...

*"With the pure You will show Yourself pure; And with
the devious You will show Yourself shrewd."*

- Psalm 18:26

## Mixture

Many times, revelation will be a mixture of the above. Having a mixture does not necessarily label you as a false prophet, for we are in a fallen world with a fallen nature, not perfect, and must sift out what is good and beneficial and ignore the parts that are not. John Wimber once said, *"I always throw out the bones when I eat chicken."* Sifting unmingled truth is simply tossing out the bones and eating the tender, juicy meat.

Remember Paul's words to Corinth:

*"For now we see in a mirror, dimly, but then face to
face. Now I know in part, but then I shall know just as I
also am known."*

- 1 Corinthians 13:12

Paul also tells us in 1 Thessalonians 5:19-21:

> *"Do not quench the Spirit. Do not despise prophecies. Test all things; hold fast what is good."*

Peter is a perfect example of mixture in revelation. Look at these two events in the book of Matthew:

> *"Simon Peter answered and said, "You are the Christ, the Son of the living God."*
>
> *Jesus answered and said to him, "Blessed are you, Simon Bar-Jonah, for flesh and blood has not revealed this to you, but My Father who is in heaven."*
>
> *Then in just a few verses later, Peter was in a different mode....*
>
> *"From that time Jesus began to show to His disciples that He must go to Jerusalem, and suffer many things from the elders and chief priests and scribes, and be killed, and be raised the third day.*
>
> *Then Peter took Him aside and began to rebuke Him, saying, "Far be it from You, Lord; this shall not happen to You!"*
>
> *But He turned and said to Peter, "Get behind Me, Satan! You are an offense to Me, for you are not mindful of the things of God, but the things of men."*
>
> - Matthew 16:16-17, 21-24

At one moment Peter is receiving divine revelation regarding Jesus' identity, and at another moment the devil is speaking through him with lying revelation. Jesus response to all this is a call to self-denial, seeking the will of God and not selfish ambitions. I would guess that Peter felt proud after Jesus blessed him saying (Matthew 16:18-19):

> *"And I also say to you that you are Peter, and on this rock I will build My church, and the gates of Hades shall not prevail against it. And I will give you the keys of the kingdom of heaven, and whatever you bind on earth will be bound in heaven, and whatever you loose on earth will be loosed in heaven."*

This opened his heart to be deceived and give ungodly counsel. If Peter, can fall into this trap, how much more can we in the church today? The fruits of the flesh are not the only doors to false revelation. Fatigue, sickness, tiredness, stress, certain forms of medication, and depression can all add to the confusion found in receiving Godly revelation.

> *"The words of the Lord are pure words, Like silver tried in a furnace of earth, Purified seven times."*
>
> - Psalms 12:6

Judas, being filled with greed and the need for power, opened up the door to the devil, which lead to the betrayal of our Lord.

> *"And supper being ended, the devil having already put it into the heart of Judas Iscariot, Simon's son, to betray Him,"*
>
> - John 13:2

Proverbs tells us that *"All the ways of a man are pure in his own eyes, but the Lord weighs the spirits."* (Proverbs 16:2). Knowing this we must "*Commit your works to the Lord, and your thoughts will be established.*" (Proverbs 16:3).

This is why fellowship is so important. We must submit ourselves to one another (Ephesians 5:21). For, "*Where there is no counsel, the people fall; But in the multitude of counselors there is safety.*" (Proverbs 11:14).

## Testing revelation

When testing revelation, we must also look for evidences of influences other than the Spirit of God. Examine the heart or center core of your revelation. Do a system check of your spiritual walk.

Following is a list of eleven tests for judging revelation:

- Test your motivation and the purpose in giving the revelation. "*But he who prophesies speaks edification and exhortation and comfort to men.*" - 1 Corinthians 14:3; Ephesians 4:11-12. If your motives are other than those outlined above, your heart is not pure in this regard and the revelation is probably not from the Holy Spirit. The result of all of God's work lies in redemption.
- What is the beneficial purpose? Does it bring conviction or condemnation, or does it strengthen and edify?
- Test it against the Scriptures. Does it agree with the Word of God? (2 Timothy. 3:16, 17; Revelation 22:18-19). Does it line up with the purpose of God's written revelation in the Word? (2 Corinthians 1:17-20)

- Test the content of the revelation (1 Thessalonians 5:19-22). Is the rhema confirming something that God is doing in your life or the life of the person it is for? Does it flow with the Scriptures and is God speaking the something to many people in your fellowship.
- Does it seek to Glorify Jesus Christ? (John 16:14, 15; Revelation 19:10; Daniel 7:1-14.) All rhema from God will woo you to Jesus Christ and seek to lift Him up with praise and honor.
- What is the fruit of the revelation and the resulting fruit in your own life? (Matthew 7:15-18; Ephesians 5:9, 10; Galatians 5:19-26.)
- Does it come to pass? (Deuteronomy 18:20-22; 1 Corinthians 13:9-12)
- Does it draw you away from Jesus? (Deuteronomy 13:1-5)
- Does it produce liberty or bondage? (Romans 8:15; 1 Corinthians 14:33; 2 Timothy 1:7; 2 Corinthians 3:17)
- Does it produce life or death? (2 Corinthians 3:6)
- Does the Holy Spirit attest to the revelation? (1 John 2:27) Is it confirmed in your spirit or the spirits of others?

In conclusion, we must test every spirit, and test the spirit of every revelation (1 John 4:1-6). Testing not only involves discerning if the revelation is from God or not, but once discerned that it is of God then, if a vision or dream, it must be interpreted by God before it can be applied.

## Interpreting

The interpreting of visions and dreams starts with your investment in the Word of God. The richness of time you spend in the Word is in direct correlation to your understanding what God has shown you in pictorial form. Throughout the Word, God has illustrated His truth, and you need the truths of scripture to live deep within your being. When that happens, the Holy Spirit is able to reach down into your spirit and pull the relevant truth to the surface and merge it with your revelation.

Secular bookstores, for years, have sold books on dream interpretation, linking various symbols with their interpretation. These books are carnal and often demonic in nature. There are a few Christian books on dream interpretation, and they are useful to some degree. However, it must be remembered that God's visionary language is creative in nature, individual in purpose, and selective, designed for the one receiving the vision. It can't be mass-produced and handed out to the curious like candy.

The only consistency found in the symbolic language of God's visions and dreams is the richness of the truth it proclaims. We do see commonality at times throughout the body of Christ, but these are not set in stone. Symbolism has its foundation in the Word of God! Many times, God will use symbols found in the Scriptures. On the other hand, he often will use symbols that are relevant to your life experience. God is a creative God. His very nature causes the springing-fourth of creative activity in every move. He will not be put into a box. When God speaks to you through visions or dreams, He speaks very personally.

In the back of this book, I have placed a glossary of symbolism. However, it must be remembered that this list is very general and not fixed. Your best source for understanding metaphorical symbolism is the Word of God. It is so rich it will reach across all spectrums of life and communication. It is simply there as a guide on how to look at symbolic imagery.

## Application

Application not only involves God's timing, place, and method, but also the motives of your heart in the deliverance of the revelation.

Ask God:

- Who is this revelation for? Is it for me, for someone else, or for the whole group?
- How should I give this word?
- When should I give this word? Timing is critical for the fruit of a word to be spoken in power and received by the intended audience.
- What should I do after giving this word? And so on.

Remember, when giving a rhema from God, your heart is always in focus. Abide in Him, stay humble, and seek His face. Dare to be a Daniel and strive for the deeper things in Him. Don't settle for revelation, for the sake of revelation. Seek His face in the midst of revelation and you will overflow with rivers of living water. Then, and only then, will your cup, be a cup of blessings to others around you.

CHAPTER 9

# The Seer and the Gifts

*"Now the boy Samuel ministered to the Lord
before Eli. And the word of the Lord was rare in
those days; there was no widespread revelation.
... So Samuel lay down until morning, and
opened the doors of the house of the Lord. And
Samuel was afraid to tell Eli the vision. ...
So Samuel grew, and the Lord was with him and
let none of his words fall to the ground. And all
Israel from Dan to Beersheba knew that Samuel
had been established as a prophet of the Lord."*

- 1 Samuel 3:1, 15, 19-20

*"As they went up the hill to the city, they met
some young women going out to draw water,
and said to them, "Is the seer here? ...
Samuel answered Saul and said, "I am the seer.
Go up before me to the high place, for you shall
eat with me today; and tomorrow I will let you
go and will tell you all that is in your heart."*

- 1 Samuel 9:11, 19

**T**here are many reasons why I have chosen the term "*Seer*" in describing the one who receives communication from God through visions and dreams. As stated earlier, the foremost reason for this lies in the Hebrew meaning of the word "*Seer*." In the Hebrew, the word "*Seer*" is "*ro'eh*" (roh-ay), meaning a visionary, a seer, or one who sees visions. Ro'eh comes from the root verb "*ra'ah*," which means, "*to see*." In the Old Testament, the word "Seer," was used in interchangeably with "*Prophet*."

In the book of Samuel 9:9 we read:

> "*Formerly in Israel, when a man went to inquire of God, he spoke thus: "Come, let us go to the seer"; for he who is now called a prophet was formerly called a seer.*"

I have chosen the word "*Seer*" in the title of this book, not in the narrow sense of being a prophet, but in the wider sense of one who sees visions and dreams. This may very well include the ministry and/or office of a prophet but it can also include many of the other new covenant ministries within the church.

In the Old Testament, there existed three types of ministries within the theocracy of the nation of Israel. These were the offices of Prophet, Priest, and King. When Jesus came, he fulfilled all those offices as Messiah. He was that Prophet like unto Moses; he is our Great High Priest; and most of all he is the King of Kings and Lord of Lords. Whereas in the Old Testament we saw three ministry offices at work for the people of God, in the New Testament we see three sets of gifts given by the Godhead to His church. This is hinted at in 1 Corinthians 12:4-7.

> *"There are diversities of gifts, but the same Spirit. There are differences of ministries, but the same Lord. And there are diversities of activities, but it is the same God who works all in all. But the manifestation of the Spirit is given to each one for the profit of all."*

From this verse, one could say that the Holy Spirit distributes the gifts; the Lord Jesus assigns the administrative positions; and God the Father lays out the foundational operations within the church. Yet, it is the Triune God that is at work in perfect unity (John 17) and in all the functions of the body. It also can be compared to our governmental system where we have the Administrative Branch, the Legislative Branch, and the Judicial Branch. I wonder where our founding fathers got that idea.

## Tri-unity of Gifting

This tri-unity of gifting is broken down as follows:

### Gifts of the Father

In Romans 12:3-8, we see the gifts of the Father, which speak of our place in God's created order. Their focus appears to be characterized by basic *"motivations,"* or *"inherent tendencies."* These *"gifts"* are foundational to our kingdom makeup and more than likely we are made up with a mixture of these things. Following is a list of the Fathers gifts:

**Prophecy** - Speaking of general prophecy, which belongs to all believers (Joel 2:28).

**Ministry** - Serving others (Matthew 20:26).

**Teaching** - Supernatural ability to expound the truths of God.

**Exhortation** - To entreat, comfort, or instruct (Acts 4:36; Hebrews 10:25).

**Giving** - Out of a spirit of generosity (2 Corinthians 8:2; 9:11-13).

**Leadership** - Being a model by example (Romans 12:8; 1 Corinthians 12:28; Acts 6:1-7; Titus 1:5; Numbers 27:18).

**Mercy** - The spirit of empathy and sympathy for another; related to a burden bearer (Romans 12:8; Matthew 5:7, 9:27, 1:16-24; Acts 9:36; Luke 10:33-35; 2 Timothy 1:15-18).

## Gifts of the Holy Spirit

The gifts of the Holy Spirit are found in 1 Corinthians 12:7-11.

> *"But the manifestation of the Spirit is given to each one for the profit of all: for to one is given the word of wisdom through the Spirit, to another the word of knowledge through the same Spirit, to another faith by the same Spirit, to another gifts of healings by the same Spirit, to another the working of miracles, to another prophecy, to another discerning of spirits, to another different kinds of tongues, to another the interpretation of*

> *tongues. But one and the same Spirit works all these things, distributing to each one individually as He wills."*

Their purpose is to profit or bring together the body of the church. These gifts are available to every believer within the church. You can also view these gifts of the Spirit as the toolbox or arsenal of God.

When the church has a need to be met it is here in this toolbox that you will find a gift to meet the need. The manifestations of these gifts are to be expected within the life of a spiritual healthy church (1 Corinthians 13, 14:1).

> *"Pursue love, and desire spiritual gifts, but especially that you may prophesy."*
>
> - I Corinthians 14:1

The nine gifts mentioned in 1 Corinthians are listed as follows (many of which we have defined previously):

**Word of Wisdom** - Supernatural perspective and/or plan to accomplish God's will.

**Word of Knowledge** - Supernatural revelation about a person in any of a multiplicity of situations.

**Faith** - Supernatural ability to believe God, without doubt.

**Gifts of Healing** - Supernatural healing without human aid.

**Working of Miracles** - Supernatural power to overcome earthly and/or demonic forces; Also applies to the creative regeneration of human body parts.

**Prophecy** - Divinely inspired message or utterance from God to His people, by way of the human element.

**Discerning of Spirits** - Supernatural revelation and insight into the spirit realm, whether human, Holy, or demonic.

**Different Kinds of Tongues** - Supernatural utterance in languages unknown; Can take the form of prayer, praise, song, prophecy, or intersession.

**Interpretation of Tongues** - Supernatural ability to reveal the meaning of a tongue; Works side by side with tongues as a form of prophecy; Could have been one of the any miracles that occurred in Acts 2.

The wisdom of Paul illustrated in Romans 12 highlights the momentum of the gifts in action and our responsibility to be fully engaged:

> *"For I say, through the grace given to me, to everyone who is among you, not to think of himself more highly than he ought to think, but to think soberly, as God has dealt to each one a measure of faith. For as we have many members in one body, but all the members do not have the same function, so we, being many, are one body in Christ, and individually members of one another. Having then gifts differing according to the grace that is given to us, let us use them: if prophecy, let us prophesy in proportion to our faith; or ministry, let us use it in our ministering; he who teaches, in teaching; he who exhorts, in exhortation; he who gives,*

*with liberality; he who leads, with diligence; he who shows mercy, with cheerfulness."*

- Romans 12:3-8

## Gifts of the Son – The Office Gifts

Now we come to the gifts of the Son of God, which are found in Ephesians 4:7-16.

*"But to each one of us grace was given according to the measure of Christ's gift. Therefore He says:*

*"When He ascended on high,*

*He led captivity captive,*

*And gave gifts to men."*

*(Now this, "He ascended" —what does it mean but that He also first descended into the lower parts of the earth? He who descended is also the One who ascended far above all the heavens, that He might fill all things.)*

*And He Himself gave some to be apostles, some prophets, some evangelists, and some pastors and teachers, for the equipping of the saints for the work of ministry, for the edifying of the body of Christ, till we all come to the unity of the faith and of the knowledge of the Son of God, to a perfect man, to the measure of the stature of the fullness of Christ; that we should no longer be children, tossed to and fro and carried about with every wind of doctrine, by the trickery of men, in the cunning craftiness of deceitful plotting, but, speaking the truth in love, may grow up in all things into Him who is the head—Christ— from whom the whole body, joined and knit together by what every joint supplies, according to the effective working by which every part does its share, causes growth of the body for the edifying of itself in love."*

- Ephesians 4:7-16

This section can be referred to as the administrative arm of the church. The purpose of these gifts is to ensure that the other gifts are activated within the church. Their purpose is to place leaders within the church so to cause the body of Christ to grow into maturity. This is seen in Ephesians chapter four.

The office gifts of Christ are as follows:

**Apostles** - Refers to a select group of individuals in the church who have tremendous insight into extending the work of the church, opening new territories to the gospel, and administering over large bodies of believers

**Prophet** - A spiritually proven prophet to the larger body of Christ with a divinely focused message to the church and/or the world

**Evangelist** - A divinely inspired preacher whose main focus is to the lost

**Pastor** - A leader and shepherd to the flock of God. Capable of not only feeding and leading the church but also caring and protecting a body of believers

**Teacher** - A leader within the church with a special anointing to teach the larger body of Christ the truths of God.

It is due to this diversity of manifestations, gifts, and offices, that I use the word seer in lieu of prophet when speaking of people who receive dreams or visions from the Lord. There are many in the body of Christ who consistently receive revelations through the language of dreams and visions that may very well be budding prophets of the Lord.

Yet, there are many more who are simply functioning in the body through various gifts such as receiving words of wisdom, words of knowledge, discernment of spirits, ministry of healing, and intersession; let us not confuse the language of visions and dreams with the office of a Prophet.

All believers are to eagerly desire prophecy. It is called - the greater of the gifts - do to its edification attributes. Yet, not all believers hold the office of a prophet. There are various stages of growing in the prophetic that I discuss in Book three of this series, "The Seer and Prophecy," dealing specifically with the prophetic. Prophecy is not my intended focus of book one. The dynamics of receiving visions and dreams are open to almost all the manifestations of the spirit. This is true because visions and dreams are a kind of pictorial language and not the mission itself. By holding this view, I feel that far more people within the church will benefit from this teaching.

Therefore, to summarize, a "seer," in the context of this book, is a Christian who receives, on a regular basis, visions and dreams. They may function in any of the offices of the church or may be a servant member of a local fellowship. Whichever the case, wither a prophet of the Lord or a servant in the fellowship, their desire is to serve Jesus with all their heart, and see His Kingdom fill the whole earth. It is to these individuals that this book is written.

I want to encourage you to embrace the Seer's Gift. Exercise all your senses. Fellowship with the Lord and Let him speak to you through all the wondrous ways of heavenly dialog. You were created to hear and communicate with your God. As you hone your senses and are cognizant of Him during every waking hour, He will flood your heart with His desires. The Seer's Gift is a gift of intimacy. Jesus craves an intimate relationship with you.

The Seer's Gift is given that you might hear clearly and run the race set before you. For the gifts and callings of God to be truly effective in your life you need to hear from your commander and chief, to need marching orders, clarity of vision, and the ability to dream and envision your destiny. The Seer's Gift will hone your hearing ear and cause you to be effective in your journey with Him.

# CHAPTER 10

# The Seer and Prophecy

*"Saying, 'Do not touch My anointed ones, and do My prophets no harm.'"*

— Psalms 105:15

*"'And it shall come to pass in the last days, says God, That I will pour out of My Spirit on all flesh; Your sons and your daughters shall prophesy, your young men shall see visions, your old men shall dream dreams. And on My menservants and on My maidservants I will pour out My Spirit in those days; and they shall prophesy."*

— Acts 2:17-18

I n light of the hour in which we live, this book excites me the most. We are living in a prophetic time, a season of the ushering forth of the Kingdom of God… a time of the Elijahs of God to take their stand, with golden trumpets of proclamation upon their lips and holy fire in their eyes.

This excitement does not stem from an immature view of fringe supernaturalism. Nor does it stem from the frail hearts of those who run to teachers desiring to have their ears tickled. It lies in the root word of "excitement," which has its essence in the idea of an "exodus." It is this exodus of the church, which so parallels the exodus of the Jews to the Promised Land, that stirs my heart.

To know that we, as members of the body of Christ, are advancing the Kingdom of our God and are forerunners to the dawning of a new order – a Kingdom not made with hands is a wonderful thing. We are partakers and forerunners to the return of our Lord and savior Jesus Christ. Like John the Baptist, we are the voices of many crying out in the wilderness - Prepare the way of the Lord.

We are prophetic people. We are the oracles of the living God and now more than ever, the time has come to proclaim from the mountaintops - behold the Lord is coming with the clouds and every eye shall see Him. For surely our God desires to speak to His church and woo His bride to the wedding feast of the Lamb; to call her garments white, wash her in His blood, and to remove every spot and wrinkle. However, the voice of the bridegroom will not stop at the church. For nations shall hear - Our God Reigns. Truly, the time has come for the Elijahs of God to step forth and introduce the nations to our God.

# Prophecy Defined

Vine's Expository Dictionary of New Testament Words defines prophecy as a noun that:

> "Signifies the speaking forth of the mind and counsel of God. It is the declaration of that which cannot be known by natural means. It is the forth-telling of the will of God, whether concerning the past, the present, or the future."

Dr. Bill Hamon states that:

> "A truly, divinely inspired prophecy is the Holy Spirit expressing the thoughts and desires of Christ through a human voice."

Derek Prince says that:

> "The gift of prophecy is the supernatural imparted ability to hear the voice of the Holy Spirit and speak God's mind or counsel. Prophecy ministers primarily to the assembled group of believers but also to individuals. Its three main purposes are:
>
> 1. To edify, meaning to build up and strengthen, to make more effective.
>
> 2. To exhort, meaning to stimulate, or to encourage, or to admonish.
>
> 3. To comfort or to cheer up.

John Wimber wrote,

*"Prophecy is declaring the message of God to His church for the purpose of edification. It is not a skill, aptitude, or talent. It is the actual speaking forth of words given by the Spirit in a particular situation and season... this may be given in a poetic form or even in a song."*

We can see here various definitions to prophecy, telling us various aspects of the prophetic. Vine's say's that prophecy contains the mind, counsel, and or will of God. Derek Prince points out the purposes of prophecy in the ministry to the church while Wimber brings in the variety of prophetic that includes poetic, oracle, and song. Prophecy is a wonderful gift to the body of Christ. Healthy prophecy in a healthy prophetic has the ability to stir the hearts of God's children and plant destiny into their souls. Prophecy is so important to the church that Paul in 1 Corinthians 14:1-5 says that we are to desire the prophetic gift due to the power of its ability to edify, exhort, and comfort the Church:

*"Pursue love, and desire spiritual gifts, but especially that you may prophesy. For he who speaks in a tongue does not speak to men but to God, for no one understands him; however, in the spirit he speaks mysteries. But he who prophesies speaks edification and exhortation and comfort to men. He who speaks in a tongue edifies himself, but he who prophesies edifies the church. I wish you all spoke with tongues, but even more that you prophesied; for he who prophesies is greater than he who speaks with tongues, unless*

> *indeed he interprets, that the church may receive*
> *edification."*

We see this in action when Paul exhorts Timothy to take heed
to his ministry and calling when he says:

> *"Let no one despise your youth, but be an example to*
> *the believers in word, in conduct, in love, in spirit, in*
> *faith, in purity. Till I come, give attention to reading,*
> *to exhortation, to doctrine. <u>Do not neglect the gift that</u>*
> *<u>is in you, which was given to you by prophecy with the</u>*
> *<u>laying on of the hands of the eldership.</u> Meditate on*
> *these things; give yourself entirely to them, that your*
> *progress may be evident to all. Take heed to yourself*
> *and to the doctrine. Continue in them, for in doing this*
> *you will save both yourself and those who hear you"*

> - 1 Timothy 12-16

Yet for some in the church, prophecy is something to be
feared. They don't understand it and therefore turn their backs
on it, which is contrary the Lord's desire. This is sad really
because a healthy body of believers is one in which all its
members function in unison and health. When all the gifts and
offices are functioning in the church, the church is healthy and
vibrant. Thank God we live in a day where there is good sound
teaching on the subject and the prophetic is being revived in
the church. For Peter's-sake, don't you know the church was
birthed with the promise that its hallmark would be a
prophetic people speaking as oracles of God and proclaiming
what they see through visions and dreams, as declared by
Peter:

*"And it shall come to pass in the last days, says God, that I will pour out of My Spirit on all flesh; Your sons and your daughters shall prophesy, Your young men shall see visions, Your old men shall dream dreams. And on My menservants and on My maidservants I will pour out My Spirit in those days; And they shall prophesy"*

- Acts 2:17-18

In fact, the Lord declares that He does nothing unless He reveals it to His servants the prophets:

*"Surely the Lord GOD does nothing, unless He reveals His secret to His servants the prophets. A lion has roared! Who will not fear? The Lord GOD has spoken! Who can but prophesy?"*

- Amos 3:7, 8

A church that embraces the prophetic is not only healthy it is endowed with reward, as Jesus declared:

*"He who receives a prophet in the name of a prophet shall receive a prophet's reward...."*

- Matthew 10:41

However, to facilitate this desire for a healthy vibrant church I think it would be helpful to glean insight on the nature and personality of your typical prophetic person.

# The Prophetic Person

Let's be honest, prophets are weird, and seers, weirder still. As Loren Sanford said:

> *"Who among those in the charismatic wing of the Church has not found at least some prophetic people to be 'a few French fries short of a Happy Meal'.... They can be wonderful, but they can also come across as confusing, extreme, crusty, unbalanced, defensive and moody."*

I think church leaders struggle the most with prophetic people. They have a hard time learning how to pastor this kind of gift or personality. The regular folks in the church usually fall in two camps.

In the first camp you will find people that are overly attracted to them because of their supposed spirituality and its potential benefit to them, and in the second camp you will find people who are repelled by them for reasons they barely understand. Real acceptance is rare and when it happens, it is precious.

Loren Sanford, in his book "Understanding Prophetic People," Chosen Books (available on Amazon.com), points out some common characteristics found in prophetic people:

**Rarely Content** – at least until they have served long and made peace with their gift. Seasoned prophetic people who have persevered over time in seeking the presence and heart of God and have allowed suffering to affect their character changing it in ways it was intended to, come at last into a deep abiding peace and joy that are not easily shaken.

**Burden Bearing** – All prophetic people are burden bearers. They deeply feel everything in the hearts of people around them. Some feel it for nations, some for regions or the church, but they all feel. Without growth and understanding of what it means to bear burdens of the Lord, a prophet can become depressed or even isolated. They may think the emotions they are experiencing are their own and spin out in guilt or confusion. Only growth and maturity on how this gift functions will balance the roller coaster ride of feelings. They need to remember that Jesus is the burden bearer and not the prophet. Prophets are just servants co-laboring with Christ.

**The Gift of Weakness** – Often the path of a prophet is filled with bliss comingled with pain. It is in the painful places that Christ develops character. Paul said it best in 2 Corinthians 12:7-10:

> *"And lest I should be exalted above measure by the abundance of the revelations, a thorn in the flesh was given to me, a messenger of satan to buffet me, lest I be exalted above measure. Concerning this thing, I pleaded with the Lord three times that it might depart from me. And He said to me, 'My grace is sufficient for you, for My strength is made perfect in weakness.' Therefore, most gladly I will rather boast in my infirmities, that the power of Christ may rest upon me. Therefore, I take pleasure in infirmities, in reproaches, in needs, in persecutions, in*

> *distresses, for Christ's sake. For when I am weak,
> then I am strong."*

**Eccentric Personalities** – Prophetic folks are a bit strange. They don't think, feel, or act like the rest of the church. They are often misunderstood, and even rejected. At times, they don't even understand themselves. A church that has built a prophetic culture, allows room to grow and love prophets nurturing a space that values all the giftedness within the body of Christ.

**Self-Protections** – This can be a very harmful place to be in. Rejection can lead to the sin of protectionism, which can result in seeing through the eyes of mistrust, thus filtering all that God is saying. When this happens it can lead a prophetic person to reject the very fellowship that would be so healing to his soul. This desire to protect by running away may feel like a safety net but in fact will bring about isolation and despair.

**Loneliness and Isolation** – Prophetic folks will often ask questions about life and faith that do not seem to matter to others, and they begin to wonder off into dreamland, as the rest of the world passes them by. They are impatient with things they deem shallow. Their quest consumes them, and they may seem aloof. Because of the lack of common perspective, they have trouble relating to people and peers. They live as forerunners. They are usually one-step ahead of the rest of the body of Christ, and when the rest of the body of Christ catches up and are filled with joy of being in this new season, the prophet has moved on to that next place. Because of this, a prophet may feel alone. If the prophetic person is unbalanced in their maturity of this gift, it will lead to isolation and deeper loneliness. This is a dangerous place to be, and prophets need to guard their hearts in this regard.

**Unusual Experiences** – When I first was saved, I thought all Christians experienced what I was experiencing. I didn't grow up in church, so my idea of Christianity came for the Scriptures and my own experiences. It would take me years to come to grips with the fact that not everybody sees or experiences what I do. Let's face it; trances, visions, dreams, burden bearing, contortions, strange healing modalities, and such are not typical for most people. Although, I sense this is changing in the body of Christ. People, in general seldom relate to these experiences. As a young prophet I walked alone, still do most of my time, but today it is in the right context, and within a healthy relationship in my church and family. A prophet needs balance, love, and correction from those who walk in other gifts.

**Awareness Deficits** – Prophetic people rarely think about how their actions, weird behavior, and the way they communicate are viewed in the eyes of other people. In general, people have a hard time understanding why prophetic folks what do they do. Just examine the lives of John the Baptist and Ezekiel and you will understand that God's view of normal is much different from that of society. Normal folks would never do what the prophets of old would do.

**The Fruit of Rejection** – Prophetic people will face rejection. They always have. Jeremiah was thrown down a well. Elijah fled for his life to escape death at the hands of Jezebel. His brothers sold Joseph as a slave. Prophetic people who have not made peace with their calling and have not honed their life balance through the healing hand of God can appear to be angry and defensive, geared up to take on the next assault. They will misread and misinterpret what people are saying. Prophetic people, like all of us, are a work in progress. It is extremely important for the prophet to be as forgiving as Jesus, and let love be their guiding motivation. Compassion and understanding always wins the day. Listen to the words of Jeremiah.

*"O Lord, You induced me, and I was persuaded; You are stronger than I, and have prevailed. I am in derision daily; Everyone mocks me. For when I spoke, I cried out; I shouted, "Violence and plunder!" Because the word of the Lord was made to me a reproach and a derision daily.*

*Then I said, "I will not make mention of Him, nor speak anymore in His name." But His word was in my heart like a burning fire shut up in my bones; I was weary of holding it back, and I could not. For I heard many mocking: "Fear on every side!" "Report," they say, "and we will report it!" All my acquaintances watched for my stumbling, saying, "Perhaps he can be induced; Then we will prevail against him, and we will take our revenge on him."*

- Jeremiah 20:7-10

Life-Threatening Events – It is not uncommon for those that have a high calling of God on their lives to be born in some type of trauma, especially as children. The enemy of our souls has a stake in cutting off our destiny before it can happen, especially if that destiny will affect the lives of many. It has always been that way. Just read "Fox's Book of Martyrs" or DC Talk's "Jesus Freaks" and you will get a glimpse at the warfare struggle.

**Too serious about Life** – Prophetic people are always serious. Everything has a sense of urgency to it. They are driven by destiny and urgency all of their lives. Consequently, life balance is difficult for them. They never seem to find time to play or room to laugh. It is only after years of being seasoned in what I do that I have learned to enjoy life in all its fullness.

## How to deal with and nurture prophetic people

In light of this it is imperative that prophetic people be mentored and blossom in a church that has a prophetic culture of honor and love. Pastors and leaders must nurture prophetic people with gracious understanding, without taking offense at their quirks or brokenness. Prophetic people need loving friends, folks that will drive them to balance, laugh with them and teach them to play. The church also needs prayer warriors – watchmen on the wall, who hold up the prophets and other leaders in the church and cover them with intersession.

Finely, the church needs to foster a prophetic culture. A prophetic culture is one where the prophecy is as normal as the rest of the gifts and offices are. It does not elevate it nor dismiss it. Weighing and testing happens naturally at a grass-roots level. There is a culture of peace and not fear or confusion. It encourages growth and mentorship. Equipping the saints for ministry is a high core value. The body is alive with worship and their only goal is to seek the face of Jesus and love Him.

# Types of Prophetic People

Often, there is confusion regarding how much authority prophetic gifted people carry. People often ask, "Doesn't the prophetic add to the scripture and if so, isn't that wrong?" The simple answer is no. Let's look at the Scriptures and examine the activity of the prophets and their ministry to get a clearer understanding of this answer.

## In the Old Testament

In the Old and New Testaments, we find two levels of the prophetic given. We see the ministry of certain prophets in the Old Testament and Apostles in the New Testament whose ministry was used to give us the Scriptures. These men spoke the very Words of God. On the other hand, we see the ministry of certain prophets in the Old Testament and prophets in the New Testament who ministered to fellow members of the community. These men spoke a message from God to one another, but their words were the words of men inspired by God.

In the Old Testament, the prophets who spoke the very words of God were messengers sent by God. This is seen in the following verses:

> *"Then Haggai, the Lord's messenger, spoke the Lord's message to the people, saying, "I am with you, says the Lord."*

> - Haggai 1:13

*"The vision of Obadiah. Thus says the Lord GOD
concerning Edom (We have heard a report from the
Lord, and a messenger has been sent among the
nations, saying, 'Arise, and let us rise up against her for
battle.')"*

- Obadiah 1:1

*"And He sent word by the hand of Nathan the prophet:
So he called his name Jedidiah, because of the Lord."*

- 2 Samuel 12:25

You can see from these verses that God divinely sent these men
to the people. They were called messengers and ambassadors of
the Lord God. We also know that their very words were God's
words. In Deuteronomy 18:18 the Lord says:

> *"I will raise up for them a Prophet like you from
> among their brethren, and will put My words in
> His mouth, and He shall speak to them all that I
> command Him."*

And in Jeremiah 1:9:

> *"Then the Lord put forth His hand and touched
> my mouth, and the Lord said to me: "Behold, I
> have put My words in your mouth."*

In Ezekiel 2:7 we read:

> *"You shall speak My words to them, whether they
> hear or whether they refuse, for they are
> rebellious."*

These men spoke the very words of God. Their mission was to be the very mouthpiece of the Lord.

In addition to being sent by God as messengers of the Lord and speaking the very words of God, their words carried absolute divine authority. In Deuteronomy 18:19 we are told that the Lord required obedience to the words spoken by this kind of prophet, for they were God's words, and in rejecting the words of the prophet, you are rejecting God (1 Samuel 8:7). The disobedience of the people to the Lord's prophet often brought judgment and the wrath of God (2 Chronicles 25:16; 18:1-34).

In addition to the prophets that spoke the very words of God and give us the Scriptures, there were other prophets in the Old Testament who spoke with the words of men (that is to say their words did not generate scripture.)

A good example of this is found in the ministry of Elijah and Elisha in the books of Kings. The record of their ministry shown in the Kings is there to illustrate the use of the prophetic in the Kingdom of God. It is a historical narrative of the Kings from Solomon to Zedekiah, from a Kingdom in tranquility to the fall of Judah and exile to Babylonia. We see the ministry of these men as they interact with the Kings of this nation and the nations of others.

We also see in this historical narrative, there were companies of prophets at various locations (1 Samuel 10; 2 Kings 2:3, 5, 7; 4:38; 6:1).

> *"Now the sons of the prophets who were at Bethel came out to Elisha, and said to him, "Do you know that the Lord will take away your master from over you today?"*

*And he said, "Yes, I know; keep silent!"*

*Then Elijah said to him, "Elisha, stay here, please, for the Lord has sent me on to Jericho."*

*But he said, "As the Lord lives, and as your soul lives, I will not leave you!" So they came to Jericho.*

*Now the sons of the prophets who were at Jericho came to Elisha and said to him, "Do you know that the Lord will take away your master from over you today?"*

*So he answered, "Yes, I know; keep silent!"*

- 2 Kings 2:3-5

These prophets, found in the book of Kings, were there when Elijah was taken to heaven. They watched as the mantle of anointing was passed to Elisha. In this, we also see a hierarchy in prophetic authority. It appears that the prophetic ministry of Elijah and Elisha were greater than that of the other prophets. They appear to be the elders or teachers to the sons of the prophets as illustrated in the following verses.

*"Now when the sons of the prophets who were from Jericho saw him, they said, "The spirit of Elijah rests on Elisha." And they came to meet him, and bowed to the ground before him."*

- 2 Kings 2:15

*"And Elisha returned to Gilgal, and there was a famine in the land. Now the sons of the prophets were sitting before him; and he said to his servant, "Put on the large pot, and boil stew for the sons of the prophets.""*

- 2 Kings 4:38

*"And Elisha the prophet called one of the sons of the prophets, and said to him, "Get yourself ready, take this flask of oil in your hand, and go to Ramoth Gilead."*

- 2 Kings 9:1

Here we see the prophets not only giving reverence to the ministry of Elisha but taking orders and being directed by the prophet Elisha. The younger prophets ran errands for Elisha (2 Kings 9:1-13). Yet the Lord tells us that he used the ministry of all the prophets to speak to the nation of Israel, and Judah, as seen in the following verse.

*"Yet the Lord testified against Israel and against Judah, by all of His prophets, every seer, saying, 'Turn from your evil ways, and keep My commandments and My statutes, according to all the law which I commanded your fathers, and which I sent to you by My servants the prophets.'"*

- 2 Kings 17:13

We also see that Nathan delivered messages from God (2 Samuel 12:1-14) and that David had court prophets, which were in his service, to help him make decisions (2 Samuel 7:1-17). Baalim was also a prophet who got messages from God for the people (Numbers 22-25). Prophets of less stature are throughout the Scriptures. We have Ahijah who prophesied against Jeroboam (1 Kings 14:1-18), and the man from Judah who prophesied against the altars at Bethel (1 Kings 13:1-32).

In the Old Testament we see traveling Prophets, who were Seers of the Lord, i.e., Samuel, Elijah, and Elisha. We also see Temple Prophets such as Ezekiel and Jeremiah; and Court Prophets, Nathan, Gad, Asaph, Heman, Jedthun who were David's Seers. Finely we see the Free Prophets who held no priestly or court office, such as Amos, Hosea, Micah, and Isaiah.

## In the New Testament

In the New Testament, we see Apostles whose function was similar to the same as the Old Testament prophets who gave us the Scriptures. These men were messengers of Christ (John 20:21; Acts 22:21; 2 Corinthians 5:20). They spoke the very words of God (Galatians 1:11-12; John 14:26; 16:13-14; 2 Peter 3:2; 1 Thessalonians 2:13; 2 Peter 3:15-16). The level of gifting from God in their lives was to complete the cannon of Scriptures and lay the foundation that the church would be built on.

In addition to the Apostles, we also see another kind of prophetic activity found in the New Testament. These prophets ministered to the church speaking the heart of God through the words of men. Their purpose was not to give us the Scriptures but to operate in the body of Christ.

In Acts 11:27-29 we have Agabus predicting a famine in Antioch.

*"And in these days prophets came from Jerusalem to Antioch. Then one of them, named Agabus, stood up and showed by the Spirit that there was going to be a great famine throughout all the*

*world, which also happened in the days of Claudius Caesar. Then the disciples, each according to his ability, determined to send relief to the brethren dwelling in Judea."*

We also see in Acts 21:9-11 where Agabus warns Paul about impending persecution from the Jews in Jerusalem.

*"Now this man had four virgin daughters who prophesied. And as we stayed many days, a certain prophet named Agabus came down from Judea. When he had come to us, he took Paul's belt, bound his own hands and feet, and said, "Thus says the Holy Spirit, 'So shall the Jews at Jerusalem bind the man who owns this belt, and deliver him into the hands of the Gentiles.'"*

Prophetic gifting is also found in relationship to the commission of Paul and Barnabas for a special mission (Acts 13:1) and with Judas and Silas at Antioch (Acts 15:32). The Prophets predicted Paul's trials (Acts 20:32), and warned Paul of trouble at Jerusalem (Acts 21:4). Phillip's daughters are said to be prophetess (Acts 21:9), and Timothy learns of his gifts through prophecy (1 Timothy 1:18).

*"This charge I commit to you, son Timothy, according to the prophecies previously made concerning you, that by them you may wage the good warfare,"*

And in 1 Timothy 4:14-16 we read:

> *"Do not neglect the gift that is in you, which was given to you by prophecy with the laying on of the hands of the eldership. Meditate on these things; give yourself entirely to them, that your progress may be evident to all. Take heed to yourself and to the doctrine. Continue in them, for in doing this you will save both yourself and those who hear you."*

It is evident in scripture there are varying degrees of authority attributed to different levels of prophetic utterance. The New Testament Apostles were functioning in a similar role as that of the Old Testament prophets that gave us the Scriptures. Yet, in the Scriptures, we also see another level of Prophetic activity that occurs in both the Old and New Testaments, these were the prophets that spoke the words of men. Their prophetic activity was initiated by the Spirit of God, was spoken through human words or actions, and was a mixture of the Spirit and humanity. These prophets who spoke the words of men did not leave us the Scriptures. Their purpose was on the day-to-day activity of the church in the lives of individuals. Agabus, Silas, Judas, Phillip's daughters, and the prophets in the church at Corinth demonstrate this.

For the Church today, prophecy operates at the second level. The prophets and Apostles handed down to us the Scriptures that were the very words of God and have supreme authority in the church. Prophecy spoken today does not carry the same degree of authority as the Scriptures.

# CHAPTER 11

# Prophetic Layers

*"Surely the Lord GOD does nothing, unless He reveals His secret to His servants the prophets. A lion has roared! Who will not fear? The Lord GOD has spoken! Who can but prophesy?"*

- Amos 3:7, 8

*"For there is nothing hidden which will not be revealed, nor has anything been kept secret but that it should come to light. If anyone has ears to hear, let him hear. Then He said to them, 'Take heed what you hear. With the same measure you use, it will be measured to you; and to you who hear, more will be given. For whoever has, to him more will be given; but whoever does not have, even what he has will be taken away from him.'"*

- Mark 4:22-25

The gifts and callings of God come from Him. He is the one that calls and distributes as He wills. Jesus illustrated this when He told His disciples:

*"You did not choose Me, but I chose you and appointed you that you should go and bear fruit, and that your fruit should remain, that whatever you ask the Father in My name He may give you."*

- John 15:16

It is Christ that gives the ascension gifts:

*"Therefore He says: "When He ascended on high, He led captivity captive, and gave gifts to men."*

*... And He Himself gave some to be apostles, some prophets, some evangelists, and some pastors and teachers, for the equipping of the saints for the work of ministry, for the edifying of the body of Christ,"*

- Ephesians 4:8, 11-12

This is further elaborated on in Paul's letter to Corinth:

*"And God has appointed these in the church: first apostles, second prophets, third teachers, after that miracles, then gifts of healings, helps, administrations, varieties of tongues."*

- 1 Corinthians 12:28

We are told to desire Spiritual gifts and to desire the gift of prophecy, yet it is God who places the offices in the church.

Mike Bickle, in speaking about contemporary prophetic ministry gifts, identifies four levels of prophetic ministry. His outline of the prophetic is very helpful in identifying the ingredients of development in prophetic ministry. This four-level framework is simply a starting place to look at the function of the prophetic within the church today. Mike Bickle clearly states that this is just a starting place and after further research, it may become apparent that more levels are needed.

## Simple Prophecy

The first level is that of Simple Prophecy, that is someone who speaks something that God brings to mind. This kind of prophecy is illustrated in Acts:

> *"And it shall come to pass in the last days, says God, that I will pour out of My Spirit on all flesh; Your sons and your daughters shall prophesy, your young men shall see visions,*
>
> *Your old men shall dream dreams. And on My menservants and on My maidservants I will pour out My Spirit in those days; And they shall prophesy."*
>
> - Acts 2:17, 18

Paul adds to this where he says that:

> *"For you can all prophesy one by one, that all may learn and all may be encouraged."*
>
> - 1 Corinthians 14:31

This level of gifting is from the Holy Spirit to equip the church for edification, exhortation, and comfort, to one another (1 Corinthians 14:3.) This gift is available to all believers.

## Prophetic Gifting

The second level is that of Prophetic Gifting. This gift falls into the same category as level 1 of simple prophecy but it differs in that the person operating in this gift is beginning to bud forth more of a prophetic anointing. This level is the starting point of the separation of simple prophecy, available to all, and the Gift of Prophecy is exercised on a regular bases. An individual moving in this realm should be honed for leadership and be discipled and nurtured on a regular base. His main purpose is still to edify, exhort, and to comfort.

## Prophetic Ministry

The third level is that of Prophetic Ministry. These are individuals who have been released by the church for ministry. Their gifting is much broader than that of the 1 Corinthians 14 model for in this level there is a measure of authority within the local assembly, but they may travel outside the local church to minister to other members of the body. Often those moving in this level also will operate with many of the other sign gifts, i.e., healing, miracles, and deliverance. In addition, there is strong insight into directional and correctional ministry.

## Office of Prophet

The fourth and final level is that of the Office of Prophet. These individuals have a far-reaching ministry to the body of Christ. Their influence is more international, and natural signs (as in the Old Testament) often confirm their words. Their words carry much authority and they often move in the signs and wonders gifts. They have a current flow of revelation to include angelic visitation, and open visions. At times, they will speak of things that are not spiritual, i.e., natural events and things that speak to the nations. There is also revelation regarding future events and moves of the Holy Spirit worldwide.

## Growing as a prophet

Learning to grow in your prophetic gift involves more than simply hearing and seeing, it involves lifestyle change and a Godly character built upon the word of God. Here are a few keys to your success.

**Immersed in the Word** - To grow as a prophet of the Lord it is imperative that you be filled with the word of God. Study the Scriptures. Meditate on the texts concerning prophecy. This takes a disciplined lifestyle.

**Prayer** - There needs to be strong emphases on prayer and intersession.

**Character** - Your Christian character is very important. The words of a prophet are first judged by the fruits of a prophet. Learn to weigh prophecy, both yours and others. Ask God to grant you wisdom (James 1:5). You must desire to walk blameless before all men letting your light shine forth as outlined in 1 Timothy and Titus.

**Correctable and teachable** - You must be correctable, teachable, and fall under the leadership of your church or governing body. It is very important to be in a learning environment such as a home group at your church. Search out elders within your church who will help you grow up in your gift. Recognize the value of prophecy in the church (1 Corinthians 14:3).

**Seek and Release** - Ask God for the gift of prophecy. We are encouraged to seek after and desire to prophecy (1 Corinthians 14:1,39). Ask your pastor to lay hands on you to receive the gift of prophecy (Romans 1:11; 1 Timothy 4:14; 2 Timothy 1:6). Finely you must be in love with Jesus Christ. Be obedient if God releases prophecy to you. Respond to the Holy Spirit.

# Forms of Prophecy

*"So Samuel grew, and the Lord was with him and let none of his words fall to the ground. And all Israel from Dan to Beersheba knew that Samuel had been established as a prophet of the Lord. Then the Lord appeared again in Shiloh. For the Lord revealed Himself to Samuel in Shiloh by the word of the Lord."*

- 1 Samuel 3:19-21

In the bible, we see various forms of the prophetic. Like a painter's palate the rainbow of colors in which God expresses Himself to His people reflect His divine creative nature. The colors are as vast with variety as the personality traits found in His people.

## The Prophetic Oracle

In Isaiah 49:5-7, we see "The Prophetic Oracle."

*"And now the Lord says, who formed Me from the womb to be His Servant, to bring Jacob back*

> *to Him, so that Israel is gathered to Him (For I shall be glorious in the eyes of the Lord, and My God shall be My strength), Indeed He says, 'It is too small a thing that You should be My Servant to raise up the tribes of Jacob, and to restore the preserved ones of Israel; I will also give You as a light to the Gentiles, that You should be My salvation to the ends of the earth. Thus says the Lord, the Redeemer of Israel, their Holy One, To Him whom man despises, To Him whom the nation abhors, To the Servant of rulers: "Kings shall see and arise, Princes also shall worship, Because of the Lord who is faithful, The Holy One of Israel; and He has chosen You."*

This can also be seen in the New Testament in Acts 13:1-3.

> *"Now in the church that was at Antioch there were certain prophets and teachers: Barnabas, Simeon who was called Niger, Lucius of Cyrene, Manaen who had been brought up with Herod the tetrarch, and Saul. As they ministered to the Lord and fasted, the Holy Spirit said, "Now separate to Me Barnabas and Saul for the work to which I have called them." Then, having fasted and prayed, and laid hands on them, they sent them away."*

The word "oracle" in the Greek is the word "Logion." It is a diminutive of the word "logos" meaning a word, narrative, or statement and it is divine in that it is a message from God to

His people. In the New Testament the use of the word "oracle" can be seen in 1 Peter 4:10-11.

> *"As each one has received a gift, minister it to one another, as good stewards of the manifold grace of God. If anyone speaks, let him speak as the oracles of God. If anyone ministers, let him do it as with the ability which God supplies, that in all things God may be glorified through Jesus Christ, to whom belong the glory and the dominion forever and ever. Amen."*

Here we see oracle and its relationship to the full council of God, or totality in teaching. This I would say is the call for walking and living a life founded upon the Logos thereby causing the Rhema of God to come forth. This is not an addition to scripture as we discussed earlier. Let's look at a Prophetic Oracle found in the book of Acts.

> *"Now in the church that was at Antioch there were certain prophets and teachers: Barnabas, Simeon who was called Niger, Lucius of Cyrene, Manaen who had been brought up with Herod the tetrarch, and Saul. As they ministered to the Lord and fasted, the Holy Spirit said, "Now separate to Me Barnabas and Saul for the work to which I have called them."*

> \- Acts 13:1, 2

## Prophetic Exhortation

In Isaiah 12:1-6 and Acts 15:30-35, we have an example of "The Prophetic Exhortation." The meaning of exhortation denotes the idea of calling one to one's side, to entreat, an appeal, encouragement, and consolation. Let's look at these two examples of the "Prophetic Exhortation."

> *"And in that day you will say: "O Lord, I will praise You; Though You were angry with me, Your anger is turned away, and You comfort me. Behold, God is my salvation, I will trust and not be afraid; 'For YAH, the Lord, is my strength and song; He also has become my salvation.'" Therefore with joy you will draw water from the wells of salvation. And in that day you will say: "Praise the Lord, call upon His name; Declare His deeds among the peoples, make mention that His name is exalted. Sing to the Lord, for He has done excellent things; This is known in all the earth. Cry out and shout, O inhabitant of Zion, for great is the Holy One of Israel in your midst!"*

> - Isaiah 12:1-6

Here the prophet is giving a prophetic word of encouragement, hope, and future blessing. We can also see this type of prophetic word in the book of Acts.

> *"So when they were sent off, they came to Antioch; and when they had gathered the multitude together, they delivered the letter. When they had read it, they rejoiced over its encouragement. Now Judas and Silas, themselves being prophets also, exhorted and strengthened the brethren with many words. And after they had stayed there for a time, they were sent back with greetings from the brethren to the apostles.*

*However, it seemed good to Silas to remain there. Paul and Barnabas also remained in Antioch, teaching and preaching the word of the Lord, with many others also."*

- Acts 15:30-35

In this example, we also get an explanation of the impact of Judas and Silas's words "exhorted and strengthened the brethren."

## The Prophetic Prayer

In Nehemiah 9:6-37 we have an outstanding picture of "Prophetic Prayer." This kind of prayer is an anointed prayer where the Spirit of God steps in as intercessor and bubbles forth the heart of God. Linked to Prophetic Prayer is the prayer of intersession. When intersession is combined with Prophetic insight, it becomes much more powerful, cutting through the heart of the matter and cries out God's solutions to a given situation. Let's look at Luke 1:67-69 for an example of Prophetic Prayer.

*"Now his father Zacharias was filled with the Holy Spirit, and prophesied, saying: "Blessed is the Lord God of Israel, for He has visited and redeemed His people, and has raised up a horn of salvation for us in the house of His servant David,"*

## The Prophetic Song

Now let's look at prophecy in the form of a song. The song of Moses, found in Deuteronomy 32:1-43, is a beautiful example of "The Prophetic Song." Paul tells us in 1 Corinthians 14:15, "What is it then? I will pray with the spirit, and I will pray with the understanding also: I will sing with the spirit, and I will sing with the understanding also." Moreover, in Ephesians 5:19 "Speaking to yourselves in psalms and hymns and spiritual songs, singing and making melody in your heart to the Lord"; In Deuteronomy 31:30 we see that Moses sang to the people of God. "And Moses spake in the ears of all the congregation of Israel the words of this song, until they were ended." In Isaiah 42, we see the prophet Isaiah break into song in the midst of prophecy.

> *"Sing to the Lord a new song, and His praise from the ends of the earth, you who go down to the sea, and all that is in it, you coastlands and you inhabitants of them! Let the wilderness and its cities lift up their voice, the villages that Kedar inhabits. Let the inhabitants of Sela sing, let them shout from the top of the mountains. Let them give glory to the Lord, and declare His praise in the coastlands. The Lord shall go forth like a mighty man;*
>
> *He shall stir up His zeal like a man of war. He shall cry out, yes, shout aloud; He shall prevail against His enemies."*

> - Isaiah 42:10-13

## Personal Prophecy

There is also an aspect of prophecy that takes the form of "Personal Prophecy." The "Personal Prophecy" is not only very popular today but controversial as well. I believe this kind of ministry is very important to the body of Christ. Yet, like anything else there needs to be balance. "Personal Prophecy" is a prophetic Rehma word from God to an individual. "Personal Prophecy" may cover topics concerning gifts, callings, ministries, God's will in a situation, romance or marriage, births, geographical moves, or simply your walk with God.

A good prophetic culture creates guidelines for how to administer personal prophecy and frowns upon what we call "parking lot" prophecies. Like all prophecy, the word needs to be judged and confirmed in the body of Christ with the understanding that "Personal Prophecy" is always "in part" and not the whole picture. And it always will stir a witness of the Holy Spirit in the heart of the receiver. Let's look at 2 Samuel 12:1-7 where we have an example of "Personal Prophecy."

> *"Then the Lord sent Nathan to David. And he came to him, and said to him: "There were two men in one city, one rich and the other poor. The rich man had exceedingly many flocks and herds. But the poor man had nothing, except one little ewe lamb which he had bought and nourished; and it grew up together with him and with his children. It ate of his own food and drank from his own cup and lay in his bosom; and it was like a daughter to him. And a traveler came to the rich man, who refused to take from his own flock and*

*from his own herd to prepare one for the wayfaring man who had come to him; but he took the poor man's lamb and prepared it for the man who had come to him."*

*So David's anger was greatly aroused against the man, and he said to Nathan, "As the Lord lives, the man who has done this shall surely die! And he shall restore fourfold for the lamb, because he did this thing and because he had no pity."*

*Then Nathan said to David, "You are the man! Thus says the Lord God of Israel: 'I anointed you king over Israel, and I delivered you from the hand of Saul."*

- 2 Samuel 12:1-7

Here we see Nathan giving a personal prophecy of correction to David. He does so through the vehicle of a story. In it God draws shows David the depth of his sin. In the book of Acts 21:9-11 we have, another "Personal Prophecy" combined with "Prophetic Action." Let's read.

*"Now this man had four virgin daughters who prophesied. And as we stayed many days, a certain prophet named Agabus came down from Judea. When he had come to us, he took Paul's belt, bound his own hands and feet, and said, "Thus says the Holy Spirit, 'So shall the Jews at Jerusalem bind the man who owns this belt, and deliver him into the hands of the Gentiles.'"*

- Acts 21:9-11

## Prophetic Action

The "Prophetic Action" is found all throughout the Old Testament. This kind of Prophetic communication is a physical acting out what the Lord is saying. It is dramatic and is always done at the Lord's command and not at the whim of an individual. In Jeremiah 13:1-11 we have a good example of the "Prophetic Action."

> *"Thus the Lord said to me: "Go and get yourself a linen sash, and put it around your waist, but do not put it in water." So I got a sash according to the word of the Lord, and put it around my waist. And the word of the Lord came to me the second time, saying, "Take the sash that you acquired, which is around your waist, and arise, go to the Euphrates, and hide it there in a hole in the rock." So I went and hid it by the Euphrates, as the Lord commanded me.*

> *Now it came to pass after many days that the Lord said to me, "Arise, go to the Euphrates, and take from there the sash which I commanded you to hide there." Then I went to the Euphrates and dug, and I took the sash from the place where I had hidden it; and there was the sash, ruined. It was profitable for nothing.*

> *Then the word of the Lord came to me, saying, "Thus says the Lord: 'In this manner I will ruin the pride of Judah and the great pride of Jerusalem. This evil people, who refuse to hear My words, who follow the dictates of their hearts, and walk after other gods to serve them and worship them, shall be just like this sash*

*which is profitable for nothing. For as the sash clings to*
*the waist of a man, so I have caused the whole house of*
*Israel and the whole house of Judah to cling to Me,'*
*says the Lord, 'that they may become My people, for*
*renown, for praise, and for glory; but they would not*
*hear.'"*

- Jeremiah 13:1-11

Prophetic Action is drama. It is parabolic in nature and demonstrates the word of God metaphorically. Jeremiah is a perfect example of this in action. His action with the sash was parabolic to the nation's condition and God's word to them - "For as the sash clings to the waist of a man, so I have caused the whole house of Israel and the whole house of Judah to cling to Me,' says the Lord, 'that they may become My people, for renown, for praise, and for glory; but they would not hear."

# CHAPTER 12

# Prophetic Dreams & Visions

*"Then the Lord came down in the pillar of cloud
and stood in the door of the tabernacle, and
called Aaron and Miriam. And they both went
forward. Then He said, "Hear now My words: If
there is a prophet among you,
I, the Lord, make Myself known to him in a
vision; I speak to him in a dream."*

- Numbers 12:5, 6

*"He sought God in the days of Zechariah, who
had understanding in the visions of God; and as
long as he sought the Lord, God made him
prosper."*

- 2 Chronicles 26:5

As you can see, the prophetic word of God can come in many forms, shapes, and sizes. I would like to zoom in on the use of visions and dreams in the prophetic. Prophetic visions and dreams are all throughout the Scriptures. In Deuteronomy 13:1 a Prophet is referred to as a "Dreamer of Dreams." In Numbers 12 we read:

*"Then the Lord came down in the pillar of cloud and stood in the door of the tabernacle, and called Aaron and Miriam. And they both went forward. Then He said, "Hear now My words: If there is a prophet among you,*

*I, the Lord, make Myself known to him in a vision; I speak to him in a dream."*

- Numbers 12:5, 6

---

## Prophetic Seeing

A good example of "Prophetic Seeing" is found in Isaiah 6:1-8. Let's read:

*"In the year that King Uzziah died, I saw the Lord sitting on a throne, high and lifted up, and the train of His robe filled the temple. Above it stood seraphim; each one had six wings: with two he covered his face, with two he covered his feet, and with two he flew. And one cried to another and said: "Holy, holy, holy is the Lord of hosts; The whole earth is full of His glory!" And the posts of the door were shaken by the voice of him who cried out, and the house was filled with smoke. So I said: "Woe is me, for I am undone! Because I am a man of unclean lips, and I dwell in the midst of a people of unclean lips; For my eyes have seen the King, the Lord of hosts." Then one of the seraphim flew to me, having in his hand a live coal which he had taken with the tongs from the altar.*

- Isaiah 6:1-8

Another example of "Prophetic Seeing" is found in the book of the Prophet Daniel. Let's look at Daniel's dream (Daniel 7:1-15).

> *"In the first year of Belshazzar king of Babylon, Daniel had a dream and visions of his head while on his bed. Then he wrote down the dream, telling the main facts. Daniel spoke, saying, "I saw in my vision by night, and behold, the four winds of heaven were stirring up the Great Sea. And four great beasts came up from the sea, each different from the other. The first was like a lion, and had eagle's wings. I watched till its wings were plucked off; and it was lifted up from the earth and made to stand on two feet like a man, and a man's heart was given to it.*
>
> *"And suddenly another beast, a second, like a bear. It was raised up on one side, and had three ribs in its mouth between its teeth. And they said thus to it: 'Arise, devour much flesh!' "After this I looked, and there was another, like a leopard, which had on its back four wings of a bird. The beast also had four heads, and dominion was given to it. "After this I saw in the night visions, and behold, a fourth beast, dreadful and terrible, exceedingly strong. It had huge iron teeth; it was devouring, breaking in pieces, and trampling the residue with its feet.*
>
> *It was different from all the beasts that were before it, and it had ten horns. I was considering*

*the horns, and there was another horn, a little one, coming up among them, before whom three of the first horns were plucked out by the roots. And there, in this horn, were eyes like the eyes of a man, and a mouth speaking pompous words.*

*"I watched till thrones were put in place, and the Ancient of Days was seated; His garment was white as snow, and the hair of His head was like pure wool. His throne was a fiery flame, its wheels a burning fire; A fiery stream issued and came forth from before Him. A thousand thousands ministered to Him; Ten thousand times ten thousand stood before Him. The court was seated, and the books were opened. "I watched then because of the sound of the pompous words which the horn was speaking; I watched till the beast was slain, and its body destroyed and given to the burning flame. As for the rest of the beasts, they had their dominion taken away, yet their lives were prolonged for a season and a time.*

*"I was watching in the night visions, and behold, One like the Son of Man, coming with the clouds of heaven! He came to the Ancient of Days, and they brought Him near before Him. Then to Him was given dominion and glory and a kingdom, that all peoples, nations, and languages should serve Him. His dominion is an everlasting dominion, which shall not pass away, and His kingdom the one which shall not be destroyed. "I,*

> *Daniel, was grieved in my spirit within my body,*
> *and the visions of my head troubled me."*

## Illustrative Examples

Now let's look at a few personal examples of visions and dreams, relating to various aspects of Prophetic Ministry.

### Illustration One: Personal Prophecy

Not too long ago while praying with Debbie, a friend of mine, the Lord gave me a vision. In this vision, I saw a wooded area with a stream running through it. Debbie was running along the side of the stream, shooting, and darting through the woods. The look on her face was intense and urgent.

Next to her in the river was a salmon swimming upstream. As I looked at Debbie running, she suddenly stopped, as if she was in pain. She reached down and took hold of her foot. She was wearing a pair of moccasins. I noticed there was a hole in the bottom of one of her moccasins. Debbie had a rock or something in her moccasins that was causing her to stumble.

As I began to share this vision with Debbie, the presence of God was all over me. I began to speak as the Lord gave me utterance.

> *"Child you have sought Me with all your heart and you*
> *have ran the race that I have set before you with*
> *diligence and perseverance. Yet every time you stumble,*
> *you beat yourself up with condemnation feeling that I*

*have rejected you. Yet it is this rejection and pain that I have come to heal.*

*For I have not rejected you, says the Lord. I have purchased you for a price more precious than Gold, I have paid for all the pain and the hurt, and I have come to give you life and that more abundantly. I have come to take away the pain of that which causes you to fall and give you a new pair of shoes, fitted for you and the race that I have called you to.*

*For as the salmon swims up stream to give birth to that which I have put in him, so you shall run and give birth to that which I have put in you. For your feet shall be as hinds' feet, set upon a Rock. That Rock is the Rock of your salvation. No longer shall the stubble of this thing, cause you to stumble, for I have broken the curse that has clung to your path, and has given you new shoes to run in, says the Lord."*

The outcome of this personal prophecy to Debbie was truly a point of breakthrough for her. Over the following months, this word from Lord had revitalized her walk with Him. The Lord had healed the spirit of rejection that weighed her down and given her a new vigor. Today she works full time in ministry with Mercy Chefs.

## Illustration Two: Personal Prophecy

Let me share with you another example of a personal prophecy that will help to illuminate visions and the prophetic. A few years back while ministering personal prophecy at a church in

Richmond Virginia, during one of their School of the Holy Spirit nights, I received a vision for a gentleman in the church.

In this vision, I saw a boat floating on a lake. The boat had several life preservers along its side. This man was trying to sit in a lounge chair and relax but every time he began to sit down the waves of the lake began to rise up and he could never sit.

I shared the vision with this brother and the Lord gave me this word to give to Him:

> *"All your life you have been a protector to your children. You have taught them the ways of the Lord and have given them My light that they may serve Me. Just as you have been a life preserver to them in a time of trouble, so I AM to you. Trust Me to be your Father. Trust Me to be that life preserver that takes care of all of you. For surely, I shall watch over your children. I shall protect them and help them in a time of need. Yet know I have come to help you, says God. I have come to refresh your soul and give you a season of rest from the worry that rises up against you. Trust Me O child of mine and I shall be your skipper, your anchor, and your quiet place. Now be refreshed. Be released from so much responsibility; and know this, that I, the Lord, today, have given you rest. Receive my Spirit and know that my peace shall refresh your soul, says God."*

As I shared this word to this dear brother, I could see waves of the Spirit refresh him, as tears rolled down the sides of his face. God desires to speak to His children. He desires to touch them right where they are, and give them abundant life in this hard world that we live in.

## Illustration Three: Personal Prophecy

One final example of personal prophecy will suffice for our purposes here. One day several years ago while ministering to a group of employees at CBN the Lord gave me a vision for a dear lady named Lola. In this vision, I saw the hand of the Lord upon Lola. On His hand, he was wearing a ring with various stones in it. In His other hand, He held a scepter with sparkling jewels that shined forth-tremendous light. Lola was standing with her head down sadness filled her countenance.

The Lord spoke to my heart and said,

> *"This ring on My finger is Lola's family and every stone within it are the birth stones of her children."*

I shared this vision with Lola and then the Lord gave me this word to give her.

> *"Daughter of Mine, I am the lifter of your head, the God of your salvation, the Lord of Comfort in your time of need. You have worried about the destiny of your children, whether they will serve me or serve the fallen one, and sadness has filled your heart. Know this, that I am for you, says the Lord, and I have heard the tears of your sorrow. For with every tear that falls to the ground I have caused it to water the seed that is*

*within your children. Do not fear for their souls for My hand is upon them even as My hand has been upon you. I have placed them upon the ring of My finger and with My scepter I have upheld the desires of your heart.*

*For the jewels on My finger have become the jewels on your crown, for you are my faithful one and your children are set into sockets of pure gold tried in the fire and they shall illuminate the light of My glory. Remember My ways are not your ways; but know this that the way that I have chosen is truly the best way for I am the way the truth and the life, and today I have given you a crown of promise to cover your household. So lift up your head and behold the God of your salvation."*

With teary eyes, Lola lifted her head in praise unto God. The power of His presence pierced through hopelessness and despair, bringing about faith in the author and giver of life. Oh, how wonderful are His ways, how majestic is His name among those who love Him.

## Prophecy and Directional Seeing

Directional seeing is the process in which the Lord shows you something that is specifically related to gaining understanding regarding direction. This may be for you or for someone else.

### Illustration One – Directional Seeing

Let me use this example to illustrate directional seeing. In 1980, I was attending fellowship at Calvary Chapel of Costa

Mesa in California. Every Friday night Pastor Chuck Smith would host a Christian concert through Maranatha Music to minister to the youth. One night, after the concert was over the lead singer for the band made a call to all who would like to participate in "One Day at a Time Prison Ministries." The Lord touched my heart so powerfully that I shot out of my chair and went up to volunteer for that ministry. Over the next several weeks we went to local jails and prisons, ministering to those incarcerated. During that time I met a gentleman, I'll call Bob (not his real name). Bob was a professional businessman and was very involved in the political arena and revitalization projects in Orange County. Bob and I became good friends.

My time in prison ministry was cut short when the Lord called my wife and me to Canada to open a hotel. The next six months we spent our time in the icy cold of Canada. When we returned from Canada, the Lord placed it upon my heart to get a hold of Bob. For the next few weeks, I looked for Bob, and finally I left a message at his office. A few days later, the Lord gave me a dream. In this dream, I saw the architect drawings or blueprints of Orange County Airport. They were very detailed and written across the drawing were the words "John Wayne International Airport." I woke blown away by this dream.

I was standing in the kitchen of my mother's house telling her about the dream when the phone rang. Mom answered it. She looked at me and said, "It's for you. Do you know someone by the name of Bob?"

"Yes," I said. I took the phone and said, "Bob, how are you doing? I have been trying to reach you."

"Good Fred, good, what can I do for you?"

"Well," I said, "I'm not really sure.... I had this dream last night." I proceeded to tell Bob about the dream, when we got in town, and how the Lord had placed him on my heart.

"Praise God," Bob said, "You know I sit on the board of the County Commissioners her in Orange County? Well, I have been seeking the Lord's guidance regarding something. You see – we are looking at rebuilding Orange County Airport and it has been recommended that we rename the airport to 'John Wayne International Airport.' I have been praying if this is the right thing to do. Praise God brother, I believe God just gave me the green light."

I was so blown away at what transpired I just stood in my mom's kitchen praising the Lord, and today, if you fly into Orange County, an eight-foot bronze statue of John Wayne will greet you as you pass through the gates of "John Wayne International Airport."

So, what's the lesson here? One brother is praying for guidance. Another brother is 1,000 miles away driving down the coast heading back to California. God stirs my heart to get a hold of that brother, but not knowing why. After multiple attempts – it was the night before he reached me that the Lord spoke via a dream regarding this brother's situation. It was all - so very naturally supernatural. This is the simplicity of the language of visions and dreams. The Father desires to move in our day-to-day lives. He wants the freedom to pour out the spirit of revelation and understanding in very practical and common ways. He is looking for hearts that are not bound up by a religious spirit but hearts set free to walk with him in simplicity. The God of the everyday is speaking every day.

# Prophecy and the Gathered Assembly

Often times the Lord desires to speak to His people as a group. This is different from what He proclaims in a personal prophecy. When prophesying to the gathered assembly it is very important that all things are done decently and in order (1 Corinthians 14:40). Order deals with timing and the leadership of your church can let you know what is acceptable to your specific church. Remember that the spirit of the prophet is subject to the prophet (1 Corinthians 14:32). That means that you control the "when" and "how" of prophesy. Be teachable and open to correction. Assembly prophecy should fallow the 1 Corinthians 14:3 purpose. Remember that revelation given to you by God while you're at church does not mean that the revelation is necessarily for the whole group. With every revelation there needs to be an interpretation and an application. It is God's application that let's you know the "who," the "where," and the "when," of a revelation.

## Illustration One – Prophecy and the Gathered Assembly

Let me now share with you some examples of prophetic vision from my own experience. In August of 1990, during CBN's "Seven Days Ablaze," I was in worship in front of the studio headquarters building when the Lord gave me this vision.

The Lord spoke to me very loud and clear saying,

> *"What I am doing in the church today is world-wide and I am calling My people to be trees of righteousness, a planting of the Lord, and all My trees shall clap their hands."*

Then I saw this vision.

I was looking up to heaven praising Him. The presence of the Lord was truly overwhelming. All of a sudden, I saw the throne of God, high and exalted. Around about the throne were the trees of the Lord. They were blowing in the wind, moving, and swaying in worship to the Lord. Then I saw a White Mountain of solid rock, like marble, or jasper. It filled the whole earth, as it shot up into heaven in brilliant splendor. There were large crevasses in the sides of the mountain. As I looked, I was overcome with the splendor of the shape of this mountain. As I looked up, I realized that the crevices in the sides of this mountain were the creases in the majestic robe of the Lord Jesus Christ. Then the Lord said,

> *"My trees shall be petrified trees of solid rock. Trees planted not of this world, but trees planted on Me."*

Then I saw these trees planted on the mountain of the Lord and the mountain was Christ. Trees of stone, hallelujah! Then I was standing next to a tree, a tree that shot up so high in the mountain. As I was looking up into the tree, I saw the Holy Spirit, as a dove, flying up over the top of the tree. Then the Lord said,

> *"Look at the place I've called you to. Look at the place I've called you to."*

Then I opened my eyes and I saw the mountain of God surrounding the place where we were standing, it was surrounding everything, everywhere, and the Lord said,

*"BEHOLD THE MOUNTAIN OF THE LORD AND THESE TREES SHALL BE PLANTED UPON THIS MOUNTAIN!"*

The Spirit of the Lord was all over Me.

Pat Robertson sensed that some people had received a word from the Lord and asked if we would like to share. Then I shared parts of this vision to the crowd gathered at this assembly, as the Lord had led. The following day Pat spoke on the book of Daniel and "the Mountain, cut without hands."

This vision had a threefold purpose. Part of it was for the gathered assembly, part was to Pat, possibly confirming his message for the following day, and part of it was a personal word to me. In this setting, the Lord would only have me share that which was for the group and for Pat.

## Illustration Two – Prophecy and the Gathered Assembly

Let me now share with you one more vision that deals with public prophesies to gathered assemblies. On night, a few years ago, I attended a small group meeting at a friend's house. During worship at this meeting, the Lord gave me the following vision.

In this vision, I saw the oceans of the world at dusk. There were naval ships moving across the face of the waters coming from all directions. Then I saw a ballerina beginning to dance across the floor. Her beauty and purity was uncanny. Her stature was as an Olympian with perfectly toned muscles and her face had a look of intense seriousness about it. With every move she made there was a sense of perfect form and balance. Then the Lord spoke,

*"BEHOLD THE DANCE OF THE BRIDE!"*

As He was speaking, I saw the Earth suspended in clear blue space. This ballerina was standing at the top of the Earth in a starting stance with her hand held up to the heavens. Then I saw the Hand of the Lord reach down and take hold of the ballerina's hand. With perfect orchestration, He began to spin the bride in a dance. Faster and faster, He spun, moving the bride across the globe. Then He said,

*"BEHOLD THE DANCE OF THE BRIDE!*

*For surely, she shall dance and surely I shall come. For the dance, that I have called her to is a dance of holiness and power, to shake the foundations on which this world stands. Like a mighty army my bride shall come. From the north even to the south, and from the east to the west, so she shall dance. For greater things than these shall ye see. For my table is set and my wedding shall be - but the dance of my bride this world shall see, for I am coming for the Holy ones. I am coming - GOD THE SON!"*

At the end of this word, we experienced an outpouring of the Spirit that was truly over whelming. We read in Revelation 19:7, 8:

> *"Let us be glad and rejoice and give Him glory, for the marriage of the Lamb has come, and His wife has made herself ready." And to her it was granted to be arrayed in fine linen, clean and*

> *bright, for the fine linen is the righteous acts of the saints."*

And in Hosea 2:19, 20:

> *"I will betroth you to Me forever; Yes, I will betroth you to Me in righteousness and justice, in loving kindness and mercy; I will betroth you to Me in faithfulness, and you shall know the Lord."*

And finally in Isaiah 62:5:

> *"For as a young man marries a virgin, so shall your sons marry you; And as the bridegroom rejoices over the bride, so shall your God rejoice over you."*

So, Paul adds to this in Ephesians 5:32 where he has been expounding on marriage says:

> *"This is a great mystery: but I speak concerning Christ and the church."*

The bride of Christ shall prepare the way for the return of her Husband. She shall get her house in order and sweep through this planet with Holy fire as the extended arm of the Lord. The power of God shown the church during apostolic era has not ended. As a matter of fact the dance of the bride shall be like nothing before it, For as one man ushered forth the proclamation of His first coming, a company of believers shall bring in his second coming. For this is the time of the bridal shower - where the later rains shall mingle with the former rains - bringing down a shower that will flood the earth. Like a title wave of His presence the earth shall again be flooded but this time with the rain of His glory.

---

## Gifts and Callings

Often times the Lord will prophetically confirm the gifts and callings to an individual through prophecy. This is illustrated by Paul, in Romans 1:11:

> *"For I long to see you, that I may impart to you some spiritual gift, so that you may be established."*

Paul adds to this idea when he addresses Timothy in 1 Timothy 4:14:

> *"Do not neglect the gift that is in you, which was given to you by prophecy with the laying on of the hands of the eldership."*

Later Paul tells Timothy in to stir up that gift was given him:

> *"Therefore I remind you to stir up the gift of God which is in you through the laying on of my hands."*

> *- 2 Timothy 1:6*

In 2 Samuel 7:8-17 we have a good example of this kind of prophecy.

> *"Now therefore, thus shall you say to My servant David, 'Thus says the Lord of hosts: "I took you from the sheepfold, from following the sheep, to be ruler over My people, over Israel. And I have*

*been with you wherever you have gone, and have cut off all your enemies from before you, and have made you a great name, like the name of the great men who are on the earth.*

*Moreover I will appoint a place for My people Israel, and will plant them, that they may dwell in a place of their own and move no more; nor shall the sons of wickedness oppress them anymore, as previously, since the time that I commanded judges to be over My people Israel, and have caused you to rest from all your enemies. Also the Lord tells you that He will make you a house.*

*"When your days are fulfilled and you rest with your fathers, I will set up your seed after you, who will come from your body, and I will establish his kingdom. He shall build a house for My name, and I will establish the throne of his kingdom forever. I will be his Father, and he shall be My son. If he commits iniquity, I will chasten him with the rod of men and with the blows of the sons of men. But My mercy shall not depart from him, as I took it from Saul, whom I removed from before you. And your house and your kingdom shall be established forever before you. Your throne shall be established forever.*

*According to all these words and according to all this vision, so Nathan spoke to David."*

## Illustration One

Let me now share with you a personal experience that will illustrate how visions relate to this kind of prophecy. One night while ministering prophecy at a church in Virginia the Lord gave me a vision for a young lady sitting in the congregation.

In this vision, I saw this young lady standing on a dusty dirt road. The road looked like it was in Jerusalem. In her hand was a bowl of milk. She knelt down in the center of the street and placed the bowl of milk on the ground. All of a sudden, I saw little kittens from all over the city running up to this bowl to get milk. They were all huddled around that bowl, lapping, and drinking all they could get. Then I saw this young lady standing on this road surrounded by children.

I shared this vision with that young lady and the Lord gave me these words to give to her.

> *"Daughter of mine I have placed a sweet anointing of My Spirit within you, and I have called you and chosen you to be a missionary and teacher to My children. For the milk, that I have placed within you is true milk indeed, sweet, and pure. For this milk shall draw all that I put in your path to come to you. You shall be a refuge to the children and nourishment to their souls. For I know, Daughter, that you shall go wherever I send you. It shall be even as kittens are drawn to milk so these children shall be drawn to you, says the Lord God."*

We all then prayed for this young Lady and called down God's blessing and anointing upon her. As we prayed, the presence of

God was all over her and she was slain in the Spirit (meaning falling down due to the presence of God), falling to the ground with His sweet presence. I later found out her father was a pastor and that she had been seeking God about being a missionary and going to Israel. God had confirmed the desires of her heart, and in fact had placed that desire within her, Himself.

---

## Summary

Prophecy can touch many accepts of our lives. The Lord desires to speak to our day-to-day needs even as He desires to plant hope for our future and bring us into the gifts and callings of our lives. I have seen God speak to people regarding geographical moves, major decisions, business endeavors, romance, pregnancies, financial endeavors, and future events. God at times has even spoken words of correction and though this is rare, it is always spoken in love, nonetheless it happens for whom the Lord loves He also chases and chastises. The Lord desires to woo His bride unto himself. Jesus is jealous for His own and He will not share His bride with the spirit of this world.

The bible speaks very clearly about prophecy in the scripture. We are told not to despise prophecy or give it a lesser role than is appropriate. At the same time, we are commanded to prove all prophecies, and hold fast to that which is good (1 Thessalonians 5:20, 21).

Even beyond all this, we are commanded to desire and earnestly covet the prophetic ministry:

*"But earnestly desire the best gifts. And yet I show you a more excellent way. ...*

*Pursue love, and desire spiritual gifts, but especially that you may prophesy....*

*Therefore, brethren, desire earnestly to prophesy, and do not forbid to speak with tongues"*

- 1 Corinthians 12:31; 14:1, 39

To respond properly to the prophetic, it is important that we learn to judge properly what has been said. But more importantly is to judge a prophet as a person by the quality of his life. This entails the fruit of his ministry, his message, the maturity in his life, the methods he employees, his moral character, and motives of his heart. Motives are high on God's discernment list. Samuel declared that when anyone manipulates prophecy for his or her own gain, that person is guilty of the sin of witchcraft (1 Samuel 15:22-23).

## It takes faith

Responding to something that God has given you takes an element of faith. In Hebrews 4:2 we read:

*"For indeed the gospel was preached to us as well as to them; but the word which they heard did not profit them, not being mixed with faith in those who heard it."*

If a prophetic word is received with an attitude of faith and acceptance, then the rhema that is heard will create faith for the fulfillment of that word. In Romans 10:17 it states that:

> *"So then faith comes by hearing, and hearing by the word of God."*

In the Greek, the "word" here is "rhema." A word from God quickened to you for that moment. Faith is foundational. Without faith, it is impossible to please God. However, with faith all things are possible.

True faith produces the ability to obey, and obedience is better than sacrifice. James tells us to be doers of the word, and not hears only. And in Deuteronomy 29:29 we read:

> *"The secret things belong to the Lord our God, but those things which are revealed belong to us and to our children forever, that we may do all the words of this law."*

And in Romans 2:13 it is the doers of the law that shall be justified and not just the hearer. So, James tells us in 4:17:

> *"Therefore, to him who knows to do good and does not do it, to him it is sin."*

Finally let patience, humility, meekness, and submission be the foundation on which you respond to a true word of prophecy. Humble obedience is the ignition key that starts the fulfillment of what God has spoken to you. Let the prophets of God arise and proclaim this world for the Kingdom of our God!

# CHAPTER 13

# Guidelines for Prophetic Ministry

*"Having then gifts differing according to the
grace that is given to us, let us use them: if
prophecy, let us prophesy in proportion to our
faith; or ministry, let us use it in our
ministering; he who teaches, in teaching; he who
exhorts, in exhortation; he who gives, with
liberality; he who leads, with diligence; he who
shows mercy, with cheerfulness."*

- *Romans 12:6-8*

Guidelines are not laws etched in stone. They are guardrails that keep us on a path of etiquette and peace, where the fruit of the word can flourish. Kris Vallotton, an incredible prophet with Bethel Church in Redding, California, said it well:

> *"Guidelines are intended to give some banks to the river. Without banks, the river becomes a flood. In a flood, the water typically does more damage than good."*

A prophetic culture creates riverbanks so the water can flow freely. The Scriptures say clearly in 1 Corinthians 14:39-40 that:

> *"Therefore, brethren, desire earnestly to prophesy, and do not forbid to speak with tongues. Let all things be done decently and in order."*

As I shared earlier what the Word stated, "the spirits of the prophets are subject to the prophets" (1 Corinthians 14:32). What that means that you are in control of discerning the "who, when, where, and what." Your motivational guidepost is edification. In 1 Corinthians 14:26 we read:

> *"How is it then, brethren? Whenever you come together, each of you has a psalm, has a teaching, has a tongue, has a revelation, has an interpretation. Let all things be done for edification."*

Kris Vallotton, in his book "Basic Training for the Prophetic Ministry" outlines the following examples to illustrate when it is inappropriate to give a prophetic word.

**Out of anger** - When we are angry or have strong, negative emotional feelings toward the person or people for whom we have a prophetic word.

**Personal platform** - When we use prophecy as a "platform" to validate our personal doctrines or belief system. Example: "I, the Lord, say to you tonight thou shall not go to the movies!"

**No relationship or accountability** - When we have no relationship or accountability to the person or group of people receiving our prophecy. It is important for prophetic people to have relationship with the people to whom they are ministering. Too often people have an "us" and "them" attitude toward the people they are ministering to. This is unhealthy and dishonoring. Healthy relationships build bridges for effective ministry.

When delivering a prophetic word it is important to speak in your normal voice, through your personality. Some folks invoke the "King James" language to validate the word. This is silly. Talk normal and in humility. Dial down; let the peace of God carry your mood. Like my wife always says, **"breathe."** The essence of your language and demeanor should be equal to the Holy Spirit's.

It is seldom necessary to yell or raise the level of our voice, as if that will increase its authority. Authority comes from God and what God initiates; God validates. The tone we communicate with says just as much as the words we use. Using phrases like "Thus says the Lord" or "I the Lord say to you," really aren't necessary. Follow your churches guidelines in delivering a prophetic word. Remember love should be at the center of all we do.

Love and ethics in prophetic ministry are so incredibly important I thought this would be a good place to insert a document produced by a dynamic team of prophetic leaders to guide the church in the area of the prophetic.

# Convergence Council's Principles, Ethics, and Protocols

*Originally compiled by John Paul Jackson and Marc Dupont with editorial guidance from: John Paul Jackson, Marc Dupont, Loren Sandford, John Sandford, Jim Goll and Bobby Connor, this document outlines prophetic protocol for those involved in the prophetic ministry.*

Use these guidelines as a foundation tool for the prophetic ministry in your church. The work is well thought out and gives Godly guidance to those who desire to serve from a heart of love, compassion, and accountability.

**Biblical Principles Concerning Ethics and Protocols Relating to New Testament Prophetic Ministry**

## The Preamble

Within the contemporary church the term, "prophetic ministry," can mean a great many things. Therefore, we have attempted to outline a brief description of biblically based values and practices for New Testament prophetic ministers and prophets. The following are intended primarily for those called to trans-local ministries to the church at large. However, we also acknowledge many of these principles can be applied to individuals whose prophetic work does not extend beyond their local church.

Some persons labeled as "prophets" may be more accurately categorized as "prophetic ministries." While they may minister to the church at large, they primarily operate within the occasional "charisma" gift of prophecy. Others are called to bear the ministry of a prophet consistently as a primary calling.

An established prophet will not only operate in the gift of prophecy but will carry seasonal prophetic burdens and messages from God the Father to the wider church, and sometimes even to nations. His or her emphasis may be much more "the word of the Lord," as opposed to "words from the Lord." They may, at times, even give a prophetic rebuke or warning to the church, which should always be a message of grace, postured within the Father heart of God.

Our heart in preparing and submitting these values is neither to police, nor to correct any known individuals or situations. Rather, we are simply endeavoring to articulate biblical standards that can help ensure long-term fruitfulness both for prophetic ministries and the recipients of those ministries. Revelation 19:10 states: "The testimony of Jesus is the spirit of prophecy." Therefore, we wholeheartedly believe that the overriding theme, goal, and vision of any biblically based New Testament prophetic ministry should be to make known the Person and ways of Christ Jesus. And while a prophetic ministry may often be accompanied by revelatory words, signs and wonders, healings and miracles, a true prophet will always seek to champion the Person of Christ, the gift-giver, more than the gifts.

Because God's will is for each disciple of Christ to be conformed to the image of Christ, we believe, as well, that God calls those who represent His will, voice, and ways to be living testimonies of Christ-like integrity, lived out within the context of healthy relationships that provide accountability.

The goal of our presentation is Christ-like love and service from a pure heart. We do not present these principles and protocols from an assumed posture of authority or elitism. The spirit in which we present them is two-fold; Firstly, we desire to offer this as an appeal for Christ-centered unity of purpose among current prophetic ministries. Secondly, we wholeheartedly desire to see our co-laborers bear witness to who Jesus is in every facet of ministry as they seek to prophetically serve the Body of Christ.

## Biblical Principles Concerning Ethics and Protocols Relating to New Testament Prophetic Ministry

### I. Concerning Beliefs and Practices

1. The Bible, as the perfect revelation of Jesus and the infallible word of God, is the absolute standard for weighing and assessing all revelation (2 Timothy 3:16, Colossians 2:18-19, John 1:14).

> A. While I treasure spiritual experiences from the Holy Spirit, I will not place subjective experiences and discernment above the Bible (Revelation 19:10; Colossians 2:18-19).

> B. I will not allow my emotions or pride to rob me of utilizing the Bible as my standard for weighing a revelation and any interpretation I may attach to a revelation.

C. I will always speak a Bible-centric message.

D. I will seek to draw all who hear me toward a greater relationship with the Father through Jesus, and to make the name of Jesus known in a biblical way.

2. God values His Word as the expression of His name and nature (Psalms 138:2). Therefore, we hold truth as a necessity in prophecy.

A. I will always try not only to speak truth, but to speak prophetic words in a way that reflects the loving heart of God.

B. I will determine to always speak prophetic correction lovingly—in such a way as to avoid condemnation toward those who receive the prophetic word.

C. I will intend to always communicate hope for change through the transforming power of Jesus.

D. I commit to reflect the nature of my God by loving people more than my gift.

E. Prophecy is a word from God. I will try to speak it with both humility and confidence.

F. While fearing God, I will not fear man. Whenever God directs me to release revelation I will not hold back through fear of man, fear of offending those with whom I am in relationship, or fear of losing popularity and/or opportunities to minister (Galatians 1:10, Proverbs 29:5).

G. I commit to God's call on my life to proclaim the ways and will of God ahead of the "success" of my ministry in the eyes of man or the church.

3. I believe that prophetic accuracy is essential. I believe that the method and manner of delivery (the heart) of a prophecy is also important.

A. I understand that voicing words from God is a responsibility not to be taken lightly. I aspire to have 100% accuracy in all I say.

B. I will admit when I am wrong and take steps to acknowledge, repent and make restitution for my error in a prophecy or its delivery, in a manner appropriate to correct the error and the reason for the error.

C. Repentance and restitution must also be appropriate to my sphere of influence and the scope of the prophetic word (Psalms 138:2).

4. If I do give an errant prophecy, I commit to full repentance. This will include:

A. An apology. If I gave the prophecy to a private party, my apology must be to that party. If the prophecy was given to a group such as a church or the public, the apology must be given to that group.

B. Biblical repentance does not mean saying, "I'm sorry" only to God, but also to those I have hurt. Most importantly, I must communicate that I am deeply concerned about the harm I have done or the hurt I have inflicted, and I will do whatever else is needed to help heal the wounds I have caused.

C. With the help of wise counsel, I will seek to find if there is anything in my heart that caused this error, and deal with it through confession, repentance and action.

D. I commit to continuing in accountability to a safe and loving authority whom I believe will support me and help me walk in integrity. I will not remove myself from this process even if painful to me and/or it seems that those to whom I am accountable are not treating me fairly.

E. I believe there are consequences to all actions. If my error is particularly serious or repeated, I will be willing to take time off from prophetic ministry until I and those in authority over me have discerned that I am ready to resume ministry.

5. Concerning supernatural manifestations, I will not substitute the seeking of angels, angelic activity, or other supernatural manifestations, over the seeking of God, His presence, and the truths contained in Scripture. The source of all truth is the Holy Spirit (2 Corinthians 11:14; Colossians 2:18-19).

A. I believe that the character of Christ in me is more important to the Kingdom than my gift. It is the application and manifestation of God's Word in my life.

B. I will not fall prey to idolatry by seeking to generate, initiate or exaggerate supernatural manifestations, no matter what may be expected by the church culture in which I speak.

C. Likewise, I endeavor to allow the Holy Spirit to initiate how and when He releases supernatural manifestations and/or ministry through me.

D. If God does speak to me through angels, or causes certain manifestations, or gives particular types of revelation, I will communicate what I hear and see only as God directs. I will do so without elevating myself, my experience or revelation in any way that might detract from the Person of God Himself.

6. Understanding a prophetic word is vital to its implementation. Therefore, I commit to being open to discuss, with appropriate leaders within the Body of Christ, the prophetic words I receive and interpretations of those words. I will endeavor to do so because prophetic gifts are given to serve the people, not to promote the one who prophesies.

7. Words from God should encourage, train, and equip the Body of Christ to conform to the image of Christ (Ephesians 4:11-16). I will endeavor to always help the Body of Christ perceive the Person of Christ more clearly and to hunger for Him and His ways (Colossians 1: 8-10, Ephesians 1:17-18).

8. Ephesians 4 ministries are to equip the Body of Christ to receive, develop and mature, rather than to cultivate an audience of spectators for our gifting. Thus, we hold in high

regard the priesthood of each believer in Christ (1 Peter 2:5; Romans 8:14; Isaiah 61:6).

A. I commit to preaching sound doctrine rather than dividing the Body of Christ through non-scriptural doctrines designed to amaze my audience and develop a following (2Tim 4:3-4).

B. I will not use the gift God has given me in a reckless manner that might cause others to stumble or misunderstand God and His ways (Jer. 23:32).

C. I commit to help Christian leaders and trainers discern between the operation of God-given spiritual gifts and human psychic abilities (Daniel 2:27-28; 4:8-9).

D. I commit to help train the Body of Christ to discern between true, Holy Spirit-inspired revelation and mere human intuition, New Age pseudo-spirituality or psychic abilities (1John 4:1).

E. I will intentionally try to communicate revelation and the interpretation of revelation in ways that encourage strengthen and comfort the recipient(s) of the word (1 Corinthians 14:3).

F. I will seek to avoid prophesying anything that controls or manipulates the lives of others.

G. When giving a prophetic word, I will seek to always encourage hearers to biblically and prayerfully weigh it, rather than to take it without consideration (1 Corinthians 14:29).

9. I commit to help train the Body of Christ to discern between genuine encounters with God and other pseudo-spiritual experiences, as well as to help the Body of Christ understand the various degrees of revelation and their relative levels of importance.

10. I commit to refusing to prostitute the revelatory gifting God has given me by attaching a fee to a prophetic word* (Micah 3:11).

> A. I will not use a prophetic word or prophetic ministry to manipulate people to give financially to me, and or the ministry I lead (2 Peter 2:15).

> B. I will not lead people to believe that the prophetic word will be triggered or influenced by a gift.

> *Accepting honorariums, gifts or travel remuneration is acceptable. This is different than prophesying for an agreed amount of money and is equivalent to a pastor receiving a salary.

## II. Concerning My Life in Representing Christ Jesus Prophetically

1. I commit to living, modeling, and championing the character of Christ. I believe Christ-like character to be more important than operating out of gifting (2 Corinthians 7:1).

> A. I choose to consistently promote and model the ways of Christ more than simply communicate revelation.

B. When it comes to representing Christ Jesus, I believe that I not only have a message, but that I am the message.

2. I believe that wisdom from above is "reasonable and peaceable." I will place high value on Christ-like humility and shun prophetic arrogance (James 3:17).

3. I commit to having an accountability group in place to whom I will hold my lifestyle, marriage, and ministry accountable.

A. I commit to living a life free of substance abuse, love of money, extra-marital sex, pornography, pride, and unforgiveness/bitterness.

B. I commit to living out God's high value of love and covenant emotionally, spiritually, and physically with the "spouse of my youth," to the best of my ability.

C. I will guard my heart and make a covenant with my eyes not to look upon another in a lustful manner.

4. I commit to being free from both the love of money and the love of appearing successful in the eyes of man. I commit to choosing venues to host my ministry, based on the leading of the Holy Spirit as opposed to the size of the crowd or financial remuneration.

5. I commit to being not only a person of prayer and worship but a continual student of the Bible and the ways of God.

6. I commit to honor the Lord by honoring and strengthening His delegated authority in the Body of Christ.

A. I will honor and strengthen local pastors and church leaders as God's-appointed shepherds and gatekeepers for their local congregations.

B. I will not usurp the authority of the local leadership in the Body where I am called to speak.

7. I commit to perceiving myself as a servant to both the church at large and the local church as God gives me opportunity.

A. I will not view congregations and other ministries as mere platforms, or tools to facilitate my vision and calling.

B. I will not steal another leader's people or leadership in order to build my ministry.

8. I commit to financial, ethical, and moral purity, and will not use the Body of Christ to advance my ministry nor build my own empire. My endeavor is to imitate Jesus' example of servanthood, and only do as I see the Father doing.

III. The Nature of Authentic Prophetic Ministry

**Bible-centric** — Bare witness, expose, declare, and establish the truth of Scripture.

**Salvation-centric** – Declare, teach, and demonstrate the gospel of the Kingdom of God with signs and wonders following (Mark 16:20).

**Jesus-centric** – Edify, comfort, encourage and exhort believers and the church in the way to Jesus as well as the way of Jesus.

**God-centric** - Demonstrate in word, deed, and manner the character of the Father: love, righteousness, justice, compassion, mercy, majesty and holiness.

**Sovereignty-centric** - Bring glory to God alone. His name, His acts, and His Glory are inseparable. He exercises His will through His Omniscience, Omnipotence, Omnipresence, Immutability, and Eternality, as He chooses.

I agree

> *I, (insert YOUR name) agree with the Convergence Council's Principles, Ethics, and Protocols as written by John Paul Jackson and Marc Dupont and the editorial team of Loren Sandford, John Sandford, Jim Goll and Bobby Connor.*
>
> *I join my agreement with my other brothers and sisters in prophetic ministry:*

- Don Wayt
- Robert Fetveit
- Andrea Bareither
- Scott Evelyn
- Aaron Evans
- Jeannine Rodriguez
- Giulio Gabeli
- Dan Mosely
- Marc Lawson
- Brendan McCauley
- Stacey Campbell
- TOV Rose
- James Goll

- Howard Espie
- Shannon Tolbert
- Shelton Davidson
- Duncan Graham
- John and Ruth Filler
- Patricia King
- Rod and Marie Holt
- Tom and Jean Blasi
- Rick and Cynthia Hayes

# CHAPTER 14

# Words to the Church

*"Your ears shall hear a word behind you,*
*saying, 'This is the way, walk in it,' Whenever*
*you turn to the right hand Or whenever you*
*turn to the left."*

- Isaiah 30:21

*"Having then gifts differing according to the*
*grace that is given to us, let us use them: if*
*prophecy, let us prophesy in proportion to our*
*faith; or ministry, let us use it in our*
*ministering; he who teaches, in teaching; he who*
*exhorts, in exhortation; he who gives, with*
*liberality; he who leads, with diligence; he who*
*shows mercy, with cheerfulness."*

- Romans 12:6-8

## Introduction

The purpose of this book is to cause change. The purpose of this writing is to help equip the saints for the work of ministry. The purpose of the book is to illuminate an aspect of God's communicative workings that seldom receive attention. Paul said, "...that which we know we declare unto you," that which I know I share with you, that you will run, and having run, obtain. For truly our work has only begun.

As I come to the last section of this book, my heart burns within me, not because of the words contained in this section but because of the work God has laid out before us. The following chapters are devoted to **demonstrating** the language of visions and dreams and how the Seer's gift operates. I will do this by sharing words, visions, and dreams the Lord has given me. I have also selected words that speak to the heartbeat of our Lord Jesus and His passion for this generation and the call of the hour.

As you read the following chapters, let your hearts be stirred. Look for the nuggets of revelation that spark your hearts with fire. Revelation 19:10, reminds us *"the testimony of Jesus is the Spirit of prophecy."* What that means for you, is you can hear the word of testimony and claim that word for yourself. By taking hold of a word that ignites your heart, you can say, "**that word is for me!**" If it blesses you and lights a fire in your soul, and your life and heart is marked by change and a revived passion, then I have accomplished what I have set out to do. Be blessed, in His precious name.

# CHAPTER 15

# Season of the Corn

*"Proclaim ye this among the Gentiles; Prepare
war, wake up the mighty men, let all the men of
war draw near; let them come up: Beat your
plowshares into swords and your pruning hooks
into spears: let the weak say, I am strong...
Put ye in the sickle, for the harvest is ripe: come,
get you down; for the press is full, the fats
overflow; for their wickedness is great.
Multitudes, multitudes in the valley of decision:
for the day of the LORD is near in the valley of
decision."*

- Joel 3:9, 10, 13, 14

*"Ask ye of the LORD rain in the time of the
latter rain so the LORD shall make bright
clouds, and give them showers of rain, to grass
in the field."*

- Zechariah 10:1

*"Also I heard the voice of the Lord, saying,*
*Whom shall I send, and who will go for us? Then*
*said I, Here am I; send me."*

- Isaiah 6:8

O We are living in a prophetic day, an hour when the Spirit of God is moving within His Church with incredible urgency. We have seen the fires of revival burn on the landscape of Africa. We watched in amazement as the Spirit of God rose against the walls of communism and opened the doors to people that were shut out by a political stronghold. We have seen the blind receive their sight, the deaf hear, and the lame leaping for joy. All of these miracles, signs, and wonders are just the beginning of the outpouring that God desires to rain down upon us.

Nonetheless, we as a people, in the midst of tremendous grace and wanting more, have fallen into a type of spiritual complacency. We have grown accustom to the little rain we have received and settled in thinking that where we are at is good enough, it will sustain us.

Yet, God would say,

*"This is not rain but a mist, a sprinkling of My*
*presence."*

You see, God wants so much more than anything we can imagine. His desire for the church of this age is so far beyond or ability to think and imagine. That is why the Lord refers to this current season as a mist. There's more church. There is so much more.

A while back, when I started to prepare for this chapter the Lord gave me a vision. In this vision I saw a landscape, parched with dryness, similar to the soil of a riverbed that was once flowing and alive, but now dry, hard, and cracked, because of the lack of water and the intensity of heat. In the horizon sat the sun, flaming red, as if at sunset. As I looked, all of a sudden, the land began to quake, and the ground opened up with flames of molten lava clinging to its sides. From the midst of the crack, people began to come forth. Their eyes upward, and faces aglow with the glory of God, they began to march out of a hell that bound them to eternal darkness.

I asked the Lord what this meant. He replied,

> *"The time has come for a quaking in the Land, not as in the day of Korah's rebellion. For surely, I will cause a quaking to come, not a quaking unto judgment, but a quaking of release…, I will set free them that are bound and call forth the dead of this age… bringing life to those held captive by the evil one."*

All of a sudden, the horror of those headed for the gates of hell paralyzed me. I thought of the sadness that fills the heart of God when he looks upon those enslaved by the devil. That is when I heard the Lord say,

> *"I, the Lord, have come to set the prisoners free."*

The purposes of God are always Kingdom purposes. His gifting has not come to tickle our ears at a weekly prayer meeting. He did not send His Spirit that we should sit in pews, week after week, waiting for the next thrill, or the next guest speaker, or the next healing, or the next prophecy. He sent His

Spirit into the world that the Kingdom of our God would invade the kingdom of this world. That He would usher in the fullness of the kingdom to come. For in truth, there is an ending in the Bible. There is a time of the consummation of all things, when our God will fill the whole earth even as the train of His robe, now, fills the temple. Let it fill our temple God!

God is calling us to a new maturity. God is seeking people weaned from foundational milk – He's looking for meat seekers. He is looking for the framers to build on a foundation already laid (Hebrews 6:1). For the time is coming when the plowman shall overtake the reaper, and the treader of grapes, him who sows seeds... for the eyes of the Lord are upon us. Even now - the former and latter rains are merging to become one and the reception of that rain will only come to a lamp-trimmed-bride without spot or wrinkle. God is calling forth an army for these last days. The Lord is fulfilling what He spoke to the Prophet Joel 2:1-3, 11:

> *"Blow the trumpet in Zion, and sound an alarm in My holy mountain! Let all the inhabitants of the land tremble; For the day of the Lord is coming, for it is at hand: A day of darkness and gloominess, a day of clouds and thick darkness, like the morning clouds spread over the mountains. A people come, great and strong, the like of whom has never been; Nor will there ever be any such after them, even for many successive generations. A fire devours before them, and behind them a flame burns; The land is like the Garden of Eden before them, and behind them a desolate wilderness; Surely nothing shall escape*

> *them. ... The Lord gives voice before His army, for His camp is very great; For strong is the One who executes His word. For the day of the Lord is great and very terrible; Who can endure it?"*

There is a quaking in the land, our God is shaking us to wake-up to *the call of the Bride, to hear the voice of the Bridegroom as he beckons her to the dance...*

> *the Dance of the Bride that will fill the whole earth. For the trumpet shall sound, and the flute shall play, and the Bride shall dance in these final days.*
>
> *As we stand by listening, we hear the prophet sing, crying out, and urging the Lord's Bride to be. What is this voice that I hear, Words of prophecy - loud and clear...! It is the voice of our God heard throughout the land - It is the voice of the Lord, when He begins to stand - to take back creation from the fallen one. It's a time of possession. His time has begun!*

As I sat writing this heaviness rested on my heart. I didn't understand it so I cried out to God. As I cried, I looked out at the clouds above my patio and saw written in the heavens, "Prophecy to My people." At that moment the Lord said to me,

> *"What I whisper in your ear - shout it from the roof tops. What I reveal in your heart proclaim upon the mountaintops. I have called you to be a prophet to my people, a watchman on the wall."*

After He spoke those words, I saw the Wailing Wall around Jerusalem and I was standing at the entrance of a gate. I looked and saw people, lame and crippled, going in and coming out through the gate. Around them were God's people, watching, but doing nothing. Then I remembered Peter at the Gate Beautiful and I cried, "**God change me!**"

God is breathing life into a new generation of Christians whose eyes have been turned upward, whose ears have been honed by the Holy Spirit to listen to what the Spirit is saying to the churches, and whose voices have been oiled with the sweet anointing of proclamation.

Lately, the Lord has been showing me pictures of corn, ears of corn, as far as the eyes can see. Everywhere I look, when my mind is searching and reflecting on the majesty of the Lord of all Glory, I would see stalks, tall and full of rich sweet corn. My mind would wonder as I explored the concept of corn, *the maize, meaning life*, as the Indians called it.

Suddenly I saw Jesus standing tall in a field or mighty valley. He was taller than the mountains that spanned the background of this image. Jesus had been walking the length of the valley. He had a nap-sack over His shoulder and in His hands were seeds. As He walked through the valley, he was sowing seeds. Everywhere he walked, He scattered seeds. Then He stood at the base of the mountain, looked up towards heaven, and **called for the rain... and it rained. Then He called for the sun... and it shined brighter than the noonday. Then He called for the wind... and there arose a breeze from heaven that blew across the landscape of the valley.** It wasn't a mighty wind but a soft wind. Its force was more like a mother hen nurturing her chicks as the soft breeze brushed away the surface dirt across the landscape.

Then Jesus stood, taller than the mountains. He started to bend over. In slow motion, I saw Him bending down. He was bending over looking at a single blade of a leaf in the dirt. It was so small compared to His size, how big He was. He was looking at it with such intensity, as if He was searching for life from the scattered seeds of His labor. He was looking to see what was sprouting. When He saw that single blade breaking forth from the ground, He reached down to examine it more closely. Then I saw that leaf turn into a large ear of corn, thick, rich, and plentiful. Then He spoke to the earth and more leaves sprang up and instantly they were transformed into corn. Rows and rows of corn filled the valley where He stood.

As I sat there pondering the ears of corn I heard a mighty popping sound. The ears of corn began to pop like popcorn. Then the Lord said,

> *"These ears of corn that you see are ears to hear, and the sound that your hear are nuggets of revelation exploding into fulfillment upon the landscape of humanity."*

I understood that these kernels were indeed the rehma of God ignited in the hearts of His children.

Then the Lord spoke this into my spirit,

> *"I am calling for the harvest of the corn - the ears of my body - to stand up and proclaim all that I have birthed within them. The day of the corn has come – and all my corn is ripe for the popping – exploding upon the scene of humanity - white nuggets of proclamation from My throne, eagerly waiting for the day of their destiny.*

*I have planted them. I have watered them. I have caused My glory to shine upon them and I am the one who calls for the wind and the rain. They have been prepared for the day of proclamation. They have been drenched in the butter, from the altar of my presence.*

*These kernels of mine have been prepared for a moment such as this. My desire is to fill the earth with the sound of My Spirit and the popping that you hear in the land is the beginning of my proclamation for I am turning up the heat – and releasing the "Kernels," – those who are ready – waiting to explode - explode upon the sea of humanity. I have come so that you will hear the sound of my call, and usher into the frying pan of My altar, an altar whose coals have been burning from the foundation of all creation.*

*This altar, My altar, is a place where the tongue is touched by the fire of My desire and lips are sealed into the covenant of praise and proclamation. It is a place where dross is removed and what is left is refined into pure silver, a ring for My finger that will touch all that I touch... pure gold, a garment for My raiment – a coat of many colors... colors of promise and purpose.*

*Yes My corn is not "yellow" – it does not retreat at the sound of My popping – it plunges in, passing through the fire, reaching out for all that I desire - it is like the maize – Indian corn of many colors accomplishing all that I desire and require.*

*Yes, I am the keeper of the corn. I am He, who whispers in your ears and causes you to hear all that I speak into it. More than that, I am He who brings life to My proclamation - for the I AM – I AM the LOGOS - I AM the Son of God – I AM the whisper in your ear and as a hand full of kernels fills a bag of popcorn to overflowing so My word shall not return to Me void but will fill abundantly more.*

*He who has ears to hear – let him hear what the Spirit is saying to the churches.... Today is the Day of the Corn."*

# CHAPTER 16

# Let it Rain

*"And I heard, as it were, the voice of a great*
*multitude, as the sound of many waters and as*
*the sound of mighty thunderings, saying,*
*"Alleluia! For the Lord God Omnipotent reigns!*
*Let us be glad and rejoice and give Him glory,*
*for the marriage of the Lamb has come, and His*
*wife has made herself ready."*

- Revelation 19:6, 7

As I write this my eyes keep glancing out the windows of my office to the horizon, I see flashes of lightning and thunder. Now, in the natural, it is a lovely day, 80 degrees and sunny, but in my spirit I see storm clouds coming, great and mighty storm clouds, unlike any day the world has ever seen before, nor shall ever see again. I sense a day upon us unlike any time in history. It is a season of transfiguration, a time of the kingdoms of this world to collide with the Kingdom of our God! A rapid moving of the consummation of all things is at hand. I can hear the beckoning of the Lord Jesus crying out,

*"Come My children, for truly the harvest is plentiful but the laborers are few. Come to Me My children, for this is the hour that My prophets spoke of - A time of the end of all things, as you know them. A new season has begun and the balances are in My hands, to weigh the hearts of my children.*

*No longer will you say it is the beginning of spring and we have plenty of time until winter falls upon us, for I tell you that today is the day of the winter storms of Heaven. Today is the day of the early rains of spring. Now is the time for the latter rain of My presence! Walk with Me in this rain - or you will be washed away by the foolishness of your willful hearts. For no longer shall I wait to heal the dryness of this earth, prepare for the rain of God!"*

After Jesus had walked with His disciples for nearly three years and was reaching the end of His redemptive mission here on earth, He spoke these words to His disciples,

*"For the Son of Man will come in the glory of His Father with His angels, and then He will reward each according to his works. Assuredly, I say to you, there are some standing here who shall not taste death till they see the Son of Man coming in His kingdom."*

- Matthew 16:27, 28

He then took three of His disciples, Peter, James, and John and brought them to a high mountain where He was transfigured before them. His face begun to shine like the brilliance of the sun and His raiment was as white as light. Then He said to His disciples, "Arise, and do not be afraid."

> "Lord, have mercy on my son, for he is an epileptic and suffers severely; for he often falls into the fire and often into the water. So I brought him to Your disciples, but they could not cure him." Then Jesus answered and said, "O faithless and perverse generation, how long shall I be with you? How long shall I bear with you? Bring him here to Me." And Jesus rebuked the demon, and it came out of him; and the child was cured from that very hour."

- Matthew 17:15-18

When I read this scripture, I asked myself; what was Jesus saying? This sounds like a strong rebuke coming from the Lord. What does He mean when He says, "...How long shall I be with you?"

This is what I believe Jesus was saying here. After nearly three years of intensive training, demonstrating for them the works of the kingdom and teaching them how to move in the Spirit, to heal the sick, raise the dead, and cast out demons, he arrives at the final chapter of His life here on earth. He is transfigured in front of their eyes while having a conference with the Father, Moses, and Elijah, regarding I suppose, the weeks that lie ahead, and the cross. He proclaims to them His impending death and resurrection. He tells them about the glory of His second coming and the end of the age.

Then, He is confronted with the progress of His disciples. Its report card time and Jesus being dissatisfied over the outcome, cries out, "...How long shall I be with you?" In other words, don't you realize the hour in which we live? My time is short. You have been with Me for over two years and still you do not know how to operate in the Kingdom. Class is over kids and the time for kingdom advancement is now. Where is your faith? This is their wake-up call. This is a hearts cry to stand at attention and pay attention. This is exactly where we are today.

We are at a time such as this, and God is wooing the bride to awake from her sleep. How long does it take us to be trained? How long does it take us to move out in Kingdom power and resurrect this dead world? God is calling us to stand, to listen, and to learn. In the global economy of God's timing, School is almost over. Individually, if it has not begun, it needs to start now. If it has, then we need to move beyond head knowledge and start doing the works of the kingdom. You might be asking yourself; how do I know if I'm ready?

That's easy. The prerequisite to doing the works of the kingdom are outlined by Jesus comments after His rebuke in Matthew 17:

> *"...I say to you, if you have faith as a mustard seed, you will say to this mountain, 'Move from here to there,' and it will move; and nothing will be impossible for you."*

> - Matthew 17:20b

He is looking for recipients of mustard seed faith. He is looking for servants that have tilled the soil of the hearts and prayed **"God plant that seed in me."** He is looking for folks that will take what they have and be "doers" of the kingdom.

The heart cry of Jesus is that whatever measure we have been given – we would spend it all and be spent by Him. It is in the doing that the increase comes. By spending the measure of faith, we have, He will fill us with more. It takes a little action to get a reaction. He is looking for saints that see the big picture and in seeing... they will discover the power of His resurrection and the Kingdom of heaven. This is a small investment... to do such mighty works... a little seed can move mountains.

It doesn't get much easier than that. We have become too professional in our outlook of the church. If Peter waited to graduate from seminary to do the works of the kingdom, we would have never read about Peter in the Scriptures. We have to get back to the simplicity that is in Christ Jesus and leave big business and professionalism to the rulers of this world. Remember the greatest in this Kingdom are those that have become as little children.

For the last several decades, the church has been anticipating a tremendous harvest for the Kingdom of God. We have looked upon the landscape of this world spinning out of control - and prayed, "Father, send us revival...." We watch as the separation of light and darkness draw lines in the sand and the culture war wages on... lashing out at values that were once the norm. We bow our knees in prayer as we see the horror of global terrorism, war, and the crisis of the Middle East. We pray all the more, as this world quakes its way towards destruction. We grab hold of each other, searching for the hem of His garment as earthquakes, tsunamis, hurricanes, and natural disasters... shake this planet, all the while the world seems to be heading down a path of no-turning-back.

Yet, through it all we press in and press on, knowing that Our God Reigns. So we call out for the rain of His presence... we cry out for the Latter Rain of His Glory, and we, in Holy Spirit desperation, pray "Father, THY KINGDOM COME... on Earth, now, as it IS in Heaven!" We are looking for that End Times breakthrough... that only the Lord of all Glory can bring.

You know, in the fall and winter months, the Mediterranean world reverberates with excitement and anticipation of the olive harvest. As they should, olives take time to grow. The average tree can take up to seven years to produce enough fruit to yield a harvest... and even then, each tree only produces three to four quarts of oil. That's the buzz... You can hear it in the streets, "the olives are ripe, and abundant... the Harvest is at hand...." You want to shout it from the rooftops.

Listen dear saints, dear keepers of the oil, prepare your hearts for the harvest... for today the olives are ripe for the pressing.... Yet, remember dear ones, dear keepers of the oil, each tree will only yield enough oil for itself. Be mindful, be fruitful, and keep your jars full, wicks trimmed, and hearts set ablaze, for the groom is about to leave His chamber to embrace His bride, and the bride He desires to embrace is an "extra" virgin bride whose decanter is full and whose light is set ablaze.

Yes, we are very much like the olive grower waiting for that final harvest. We watch as the orchard moves and sways to the changes in the weather. We cry out to God when drought is upon the land for fear that the harvest won't come. We cringe, and then pray, asking the Lord of the harvest to send forth the spring rains. We wait and we fertilize, crying out for the winter rains....

Yet, through the years of waiting, we are suddenly struck with that promise from Heaven…

> *"…Let us now fear the LORD our God, who gives rain,*
> *both the former and the latter, in its season. He reserves*
> *for us the appointed weeks of the harvest"*

> - Jeremiah 5:24

Therefore, we press on and pray the more…. We can sense, in the Spirit, the times they are a changing, so we stand with the words of Joel:

> *"Fear not, O land; Be glad and rejoice, for the Lord has*
> *done marvelous things! Do not be afraid, you beasts of*
> *the field; For the open pastures are springing up, and*
> *the tree bears its fruit; The fig tree and the vine yield*
> *their strength. Be glad then, you children of Zion, and*
> *rejoice in the Lord your God; For He has given you the*
> *former rain faithfully, and He will cause the rain to*
> *come down for you—The former rain, and the latter*
> *rain in the first month. The threshing floors shall be full*
> *of wheat, and the vats shall overflow with new wine*
> *and oil."*

> - Joel 2:21-24

That is what we are waiting for… we are waiting in anticipation for a Holy Spirit outpouring like no other… a Latter Rain visitation of Jesus upon this earth. I hear constantly, "the rain, we so long to see, is coming…." You can feel it in the air, like the stillness before a storm, the moisture level has risen, the barometer is off the charts, and the climate is changing before our very eyes. We all want revival, we all want the Word of God to go forth in power and transform the lost and the destitute in a final wave of His presence.

Yet the Lord would say *there is a precursor to the out-pouring of this rain.* Jesus is so full of rain it coming out His pores… like the great drops of blood bursting through His flesh in the Garden. Nonetheless, to the breaking of His heart, He holds back the rain…. Though the waters are ready to burst through the heavens – He says – *Not yet, Hold back a little longer… the time is now but My bride, she's not ready.*

You see, for several days, every time I went to pray the Lord kept showing me this picture. In this vision, I saw a massive stone wheel; slowly turning… the picture was so vivid I could almost hear the sound of crushing as I watched the intensity of this stone wheel turn. I asked the Lord what it was. He spoke these words into my heart:

> *"The hour has come for My anointed ones…. My olives, which stand before me, are now, this day, ripe for the crushing. The season of new oil is upon you and you shall go forth and pour yourselves out upon this land; for I have seen the agony of My people – I have heard the cries of My saints. Within their bosom lies the fruit of My labor - To birth in them a tsunami of My presence… and in their labor they shall birth the deluge of My deliverance and My love.*
>
> *Their labor has reached its final hour and the birth of this out-pouring is that of New Oil… Golden Oil from*

*the olives of My Latter Rain, for know this day, that I have called you to a new place.... I have called you to lie beneath the stone of my pressing. I have watered My olive trees with visions of My Latter Rain and now they have grown ripe with the hope of My outpouring. This day I have begun the shaking.*

*This day I have begun to gather My olives. For at My feet lie olives, ripe for the pressing. Now, this day, My Spirit will begin to gather.... So listen to Me now... your services are needed. Come with Me... lie down upon the floor of My alter... come with Me... lie down beneath the Stone of my pressing.... For the oil from this press will usher in My Latter Rain."*

As I pondered upon His words, I saw again that massive stone... and then the picture zoomed out and I saw a spigot or gutter extending out from the base of the stone. Out of the stone, dripped Golden Oil. As the stone wheel turned, the oil went from dripping to pouring.

Below the spigot was a bucket. It had become so full it was overflowing. The flow soon turned into mighty splatters. Looking from above the bucket, I saw the heavens and the earth below – then the bucket burst open, releasing its contents upon the face of the earth. Then I saw the legs of people standing upon the earth. They were looking down at their feet in amazement. They all were standing in this Golden Oil... and the oil began to rise... amazed they looked up to Heaven, eyes beaming with the Glory of God.

Then the voice of the Lord spoke,

> *"A new glory is rising and shall cause your feet to be transformed from bronze to iron."*

That was when I saw a new strength enter the people of the Lord... and then I saw Jesus rise above all and begin to walk through the Land. His stature was mighty, and His body filled the whole earth.

## The Call of Jesus in this Hour

God is calling us into a new day. He has planted within our heart the desire to see His glory. He has placed within us the cry and the prayer to call forth the Latter Rain – to usher in the deluge of His presence. However, there is something vital that needs to happen in this ushering.

He is not only calling us to press in... **but to be pressed, crushed, under the presence of His Holiness.** You see, without the complete yielding of our hearts to Him, the Oil cannot come, and it is the Oil that brings forth the rain and the rain becomes as golden oil. So what does it mean to be pressed, to yield us to Him completely?

Just yesterday, the Lord spoke to my heart and said,

> *"The fire you desire is My desire, but that torch is only lit on Heaven's alter of worship."*

You see pressing happens in His presence. When we press in and worship the lover of our souls we are crushed by the incredible nature of His love for us. Worship is a lifestyle. Worship is adoration. Worship is a lover pressing into to Him with such urgency, because she can't do anything else, she has to be with her Lover. Jesus adores you. Jesus is so in love with you that He wants you to be with him and the door to His kingdom is worship. Worshipers are lovers; they are so sold out to be in His presence that they constantly have their eyes upward looking for Him and His presence. Worshipers are like the Shulamite bride of the Song of Solomon.

> *"Let him kiss me with the kisses of his mouth—For your love is better than wine. Because of the fragrance of your good ointments, Your name is ointment poured forth; Therefore the virgins love you. Draw me away!"*
>
> - Song of Solomon 1:2-4

The kisses of the King draw us. The heartbeat of His presence changes us. Through intimacy with our Lord, we can proclaim, like the Shulamite, **"The king has brought me into his chambers.... He brought me to the banqueting house, and his banner over me was love."** You see Jesus is looking for a people so hungry for Him, so thirsty for Him, so desiring Him, that they are as lovesick as He is, and when they hear the sound of His voice their hearts leap inside of themselves. Listen to the words of the Shulamite.

> *"The voice of my beloved! Behold, he comes leaping upon the mountains, skipping upon the hills. My beloved is like a gazelle or a young stag. Behold, he stands behind our wall; He is looking through the windows, gazing through the lattice. My beloved spoke, and said to me: "Rise up, my love, my fair one, and come away. For lo, the winter is past, the rain is over and gone. The flowers appear on the earth; The time of*

*singing has come, and the voice of the turtledove is heard in our land. The fig tree puts forth her green figs, and the vines with the tender grapes give a good smell. Rise up, my love, my fair one, and come away!"*

- Song of Solomon 2:8-13

Since our destiny is set to be the bride adorned in white and married to the King of all creation, we might as well start now, adorn ourselves with His presence, and pursue Him. It is only in worship and adoration for Him that will bring us into the hour of great anointing. He invested everything, His very life is to create a people that are lovers, that will be an extension of His hands, doers, that will see what He sees and march out, full of the Holy Spirit, and heal this land.

I had a dream, in the dream I was standing on the beach with some folks, and it was dark, like a red sky. All around us were zombies, the walking dead, trying to devour us and kill us. The tide came in. It was a red tide. We were splashing water with an oar on the zombies. As soon as the water touched the zombies they began to dissolve. I saw the red tide cover the beachhead and thousands of zombies started dissolving into the sea. Then I heard the voice of two zombies dissolving in the waters. One said, "I can feel the Holy Spirit's presence."

Then the other said, "Well that makes sense, He created us."

Then I watched as the tide receded, like a tsunami inhaling, drawing back to the belly of the ocean. When it did, I looked at the beach and more zombies popped up out of the ground, attacking and aggressively pursuing us. In a panic, we started running for our lives. I looked to the left and saw soldiers running as well, some were riding Segways, and others were simply running. Everyone was running towards a wall trying to jump over. Then I saw a man with no legs riding a motorcycle. He was trying to help a child over the wall but couldn't because he had no legs. Then I woke.

As soon as I woke, I heard the Holy Spirit say,

> *"Not by might, nor by power, but by My Spirit says the Lord."*

You see a powerless church has no legs to stand on. When the tide of His presence recedes for a season, if we aren't filled with His presence, with living water, with the golden oil of anointing, we cannot stand. Our fight is weak and tiring. We spend more time running for our lives than we do changing the lives of the walking dead.

It's important to get this. The very DNA of humanity was designed to respond to the presence of the Holy Spirit. They will melt in the heart of His presence when they feel the red tide upon them. We are in warfare, and this fight is not against flesh and blood, but against principalities, powers, and forces in dark places.

The Lord has positioned each of us in strategic places around the planet. Whether individually, or as an organization, we are encamped like clusters of grapes, being prepared to engage in this Holy battle. However, it is only in Him and through Him that hearts, souls, and minds of this world will be changed. This is not a political fight. It is a spiritual fight. We are called to bring life to the walking dead. However, know this, a tide that recedes, recedes only for a season, and the tide that is coming back, is a tsunami of Christ's blood that will flood and saturate the land.

## God's strategy: You

Awhile back, the Lord spoke to my heart about the strategic planting of His people in strategic places upon a battlefield. I was in a trance, and the scene that I saw was, as one would see if they were watching an old civil war movie, watching a camp of Union soldiers strategizing their advancement into battle. These outposts of His kingdom were placed strategically about at various locations, waiting for their next move to engage the enemy. Even now I can see the white tents clustered together with soldiers moving about, lighting fires to warm their coffee, and preparing their weapons for battle as the morning sun begins to rise and the dew lifts from the landscape.

Suddenly, the Lord showed me the valley of the battlefield. I was looking up at the skies above the valley and saw massive storm clouds covering the sky like a powerful blanket, shaking, and moving with incredible intensity. Then the Lord spoke to me very powerfully and said,

*"Call to the winds."*

Then the sky began to move, and He said,

*"Call to the North, Call to the South, Call to the East, Call to the West."*

Then the skies began to move, and blow, and thunder.

So, I cried out to the winds. I cried out to the North winds, and the South winds, and the Winds of the East and the West. I cried – "Lord, send your power," and the sky began to turn like the development of a mighty hurricane.

Then the Lord showed me a lake that was overshadowed by the storm. Then he showed me a massive drop of rain hitting the lake. When it hit, mighty ripples flowed out from it, and the Lord said,

*"Call to the rain!"*

And I cried out, "Send your rain oh God." I kept crying out, "I call to the wind, I call to the rain, I call to the North, the South, the East and the West. Send your rain oh God." Then the Lord showed me the hurricane that was building above the valley and out of the hurricane came forth-small cyclones, waterspouts. Suddenly these tornados landed upon His people, individually, like little cyclones spinning in the hearts of men.

Then the Lord said,

*"Speak to the rivers and the streams, call to the ground*
*to release the waters of My presence."*

And I saw people standing on the ground and suddenly, water came forth from the earth like what would happen if someone squeezed a wet sponge, and the people were getting soaked, and the water turned into a stream, into a river unstoppable.

Then the Lord showed me a Bell Tower. It was a like an old Spanish mission bell tower... (like Taco Bell) and the Lord was standing next to the bell tower with a staff in His hand. He took His staff and began to hit the bell. With incredible force and rhythm he hit the bell, and the sound of the bell went out throughout the Land.

Then I heard a voice say,

> *"Blow a trumpet in Zion, sound an alarm upon My*
> *Holy mountain. Call for the elders, let the saints come*
> *out of her chamber. Blow a trumpet across the land."*

Then I heard the Lord say as He swung and hit the bell.

> *"This is My mission bell and I am on a mission, I have*
> *a mission to complete."*

Poppa loves you dearly. He wants to rain down His presence upon you and move in the lives of your families, communities, and the region you live in. The Lord has called and placed churches and people around various regions around the world like outpost of the Kingdom of Heaven, strategic outposts positioned with purpose to advance His plan in this day and hour. There is a great outpouring on the horizon. The Lord is on a mission to bring about a great work.

The Lord would say to us,

> *"Listen Sweet Vine, Sweet Vineyard of mine, you are*
> *the winds..., you are the mighty winds of change," and*
> *the Lord would say to you, if you rally to His heart's cry*
> *and respond to the sound of the mission bell, "I the*
> *Lord, the King of Heaven, will blow upon you with such*
> *a sweet, sweet, fragrant wind that you will become*
> *(collectively) the force that I will use to usher in the*
> *hurricane of Heaven upon this land."*

Please know that today is a day of refreshing. Today is a day for setting the captives free. The Lord is looking for the bride to come together in a unified force and call for the rain of God. His promise to you is to:

> *"Ask for rain in the time of the latter rain. The Lord will make flashing clouds; He will give them showers of rain, grass in the field for everyone."*

- Zechariah 10:1

When you call, He will answer. "Yes!" He will respond with massive drops, one for each of you. Then He will cause a rippling to take place. The cyclone will be His passion - His power - the ripples will be the outflow of His love, and this outflow will become a highway in the midst of dry land and the people will begin to hear a sound – a fresh sound in their ears, a tune and a melody from heaven designed especially for them. For He is about to paint the landscape in living color, He is about to paint the land with His glory and play a melody of mercy to this generation.

The Lord is saying,

> *"Arise you elders, you tribes, arise, and come to My sanctuary. Say to the mountains, 'Bow before the Lord of Glory.' Call to the rivers, Call to the streams – Release the waters of salvation, release the waters stored up for this hour. For I have a plan and a purpose, my flower, I have a plan for power in this hour."*

Press in this day to the pressing of the Lord. Only then will we walk with Him in this final hour. The promise is that of a new filling, a new glory. When we yield, He will not only release this anointing, He will trade our feet of brass (representing the need to be cleansed and healed all the time) for feet of iron (representing His strength, where we transition from the healed to the healers). We will become a people ready to walk in this final hour.

Zechariah, in chapter four, when desiring to see the restoration of Judah and the temple, was caught-up in a vision. An angel approached him, awakened him from his sleep, and said, "What do you see?" Zechariah responded, telling the angel what he saw, and then he asked the angel what it meant:

> "Now the angel who talked with me came back and wakened me, as a man who is wakened out of his sleep. And he said to me, "What do you see?"
>
> So I said, "I am looking, and there is a lampstand of solid gold with a bowl on top of it, and on the stand seven lamps with seven pipes to the seven lamps. Two olive trees are by it, one at the right of the bowl and the other at its left." So I answered and spoke to the angel who talked with me, saying, "What are these, my lord?"
>
> Then the angel who talked with me answered and said to me, "Do you not know what these are?"
>
> And I said, "No, my lord.'
>
> So he answered and said to me: This is the word of the Lord to Zerubbabel: Not by might nor by power, but by My Spirit, Says the Lord of hosts"

- Zechariah 4:1-6

Now the angel was taken back, he should have known what olive trees and the golden olive oil were, but he didn't. The angel said, "...Do you not know what these are?"

Admittedly, Zechariah said, "No, my lord."

Then the Angel said, "**Not by might nor by power, but by My Spirit, Says the Lord of Hosts.**"

You see we have something that Zechariah did not have. We have the Holy Spirit, the resurrected Lord of all glory, and the Father of all creation living inside us. You see, the lesson form Zechariah is, unlike an oil lamp, an olive tree has an endless living supply of oil, forever producing, forever replenishing. Our desire is the same – only bigger.

Let's not stand before the Lord and ask, what are those olive trees? If we are going to press in we must be pressed in His presence. Only then we shall watch as the Lord anoints His tabernacle (Exodus 40:9-11) and fulfills the words of Jesus, as we proclaim His kingdom to the ends of the earth (Acts 1:4-8). For the call to His church, in this last hour, is to have lamps filled with oil, lamps that burn without ceasing (Exodus 27:20; Mathew 25). This is what all of creation is groaning for (Romans 8:22-27). Consider the words of Jesus, and ponder and pray regarding these things. Seek His face.

> "*Then the kingdom of heaven shall be likened to ten virgins who took their lamps and went out to meet the bridegroom. Now five of them were wise, and five were foolish. Those who were foolish took their lamps and took no oil with them, but the wise took oil in their*

*vessels with their lamps. But while the bridegroom was delayed, they all slumbered and slept.*

*And at midnight a cry was heard: 'Behold, the bridegroom is coming; go out to meet him!' Then all those virgins arose and trimmed their lamps. And the foolish said to the wise, 'Give us some of your oil, for our lamps are going out. But the wise answered, saying, 'No, lest there should not be enough for us and you; but go rather to those who sell, and buy for yourselves.' And while they went to buy, the bridegroom came, and those who were ready went in with him to the wedding; and the door was shut.*

*Afterward the other virgins came also, saying, 'Lord, Lord, open to us!' But he answered and said, 'Assuredly, I say to you, I do not know you.'*

*Watch therefore, for you know neither the day nor the hour in which the Son of Man is coming."*

- Matthew 25:1-13

Now is the time to look up!" A new season has begun. God is on the move, and He is searching for His bride to take her place and arise... to be the voice of one crying out in the wilderness, Prepare ye the way of the Lord, for the Kingdom of God is at hand! It is time to move-on folks.

CHAPTER 17

# Mercy Drops are Falling

*Then He said, "I will make all My goodness pass
before you, and I will proclaim the name of the
Lord before you. I will be gracious to whom I
will be gracious, and I will have compassion on
whom I will have compassion."*

- Exodus 33:19

A while back, the Lord kept showing me a picture. it wasn't a dream or a trance. It was simply one of those panoramic visions. In the vision I saw a massive drop of golden liquid hanging in the air. It was translucent and glistening, and it was rich thick like honey. As I walked into worship and began to sing and pray, the Lord gave me the following vision. I was looking up to the heavens and suddenly the sky above me was covered with a sheet of honeycomb. The honeycomb stretched from one end of heaven to the other and the pockets of honey were vibrating to the sound of worship. Then, as I was looking in anticipation, the Lord changed my perspective, and I was watching the honeycomb from heaven's side.

As I was looking at the throne room, I saw Jesus standing there in Kingly attire. The entire room was filled with His glory and draped in golden light, as if everything was made of translucent gold. Jesus was standing on the backside of the honeycomb. It was as if a sea of honeycomb stretched across the heavens. He had a golden staff in His hand, and He took His staff and pounded the honeycomb floor three times.

Suddenly, I was back, watching the honeycomb from the ground. The sky started to shake and then, with a massive thrust, the combs burst open and sky began to rain down massive drops of golden honey. I watched as people began to be covered with honey. Joy fell upon all as they lifted up their eyes and began to rejoice over the richness of the outpouring. They were reaching out and touching others. The honey was sticky and clung to everyone it touched. Like a golden impartation, the honey was distributed to all. Much like "pay it forward" – the commission was to reach out and touch somebody, sweeten their lives, and let the anointing stick to them and draw them to Him.

I asked the Lord what the honey was and He said,

> *"The honey is my sweet tender Mercy. Just as Moses sought to seek my face and to see my glory, I made all my GOODNESS pass before him, and I proclaimed My name before him. For I am gracious upon whom I am gracious and I will have compassion on whom I have compassion. For I am clothed in tender mercy, and my kingdom stands upon that mercy, for I am good all the time and My goodness is starting to pour out.*
>
> *Mercy drops are falling, are falling – yes,*

*Mercy drops are falling, are falling.*

*I will drape you with tender mercy. You will go out and come in with sweet mercy upon your lips – and you will take My mercy to the streets, to the highways, and byways, and My mercy will flow. My mercy is endless. My grace is more than sufficient for you. My desire is that you would be vehicles of My peace and power – that you will touch the downcast and the broken hearted and release My tender mercy.*

*The people are rigid; they don't see Me as the lifter of their heads. My Mercy is endless; it sets free them that are bound. They need to see Me in all My goodness, for I Am GOOD all the time and My mercy is from everlasting to everlasting. I laid down My life so that My honey would fall and fill the earth with My glory.*

*Mercy drops are falling, are falling....*

*And this drop is for you."*

The cry of the Lord in Isaiah 49:8-13, amplifies His heart and mercy:

> *"Thus says the Lord: "In an acceptable time I have heard You, and in the day of salvation I have helped You; I will preserve You and give You as a covenant to the people, to restore the earth, to cause them to inherit the desolate heritages; That You may say to the prisoners, 'Go forth,' To those who are in darkness, 'Show yourselves.'*

*"They shall feed along the roads, and their pastures shall be on all desolate heights. They shall neither hunger nor thirst, neither heat nor sun shall strike them; for He who has mercy on them will lead them, even by the springs of water He will guide them. I will make each of My mountains a road, and My highways shall be elevated.*

*Surely these shall come from afar; Look! Those from the north and the west, and these from the land of Sinim." Sing, O heavens! Be joyful, O earth! And break out in singing, O mountains! For the Lord has comforted His people, and will have mercy on His afflicted."*

Let Your mercy fall upon us. Let our hearts be merciful. To know the love nature of God is to know the heartbeat of mercy. God is love. **God is good. He is good ALL the time.** If grace is getting what we don't deserve, mercy is not getting what we do deserve.

Mercy is a two-sided coin. On one side, we have our own testimony of God's mercy and grace towards us, how we were once blind, but now we see. On the other side, we have the responsibility to give away what we have received, the love of God and His mercy. When we, as a people, learn to embrace the love nature of Christ and move out in a non-judgmental way, radiating the love of Christ, the world will take notice. They will see that we aren't looking to manipulate them into the Kingdom. **Love will draw them.**

Jesus is calling us to be the "Love Feast" for the world to dine. When they see honest love in action, they will taste and see that He is good. We will be sticky like honey bringing sweetness to the lives of those around us. In these last days, our Lord wants a bride that is fragrant with His nature. Love releases the Kingdom.

God is calling us to a new place, a higher place, and nothing we have known from the past will be sufficient for this new season. We are moving into a place much like Moses was in Exodus 33. Moses lived his first forty years in royalty in the house of Pharaoh and forty years tending sheep on the backside of the desert. At 80 years of age, he was confronted by God and commissioned into his life mission. This reluctant, stammering, excuse-making fugitive was called back to Egypt to lead the Hebrews out of captivity. Now this broken-down sheepherder became the man of the hour and for the next forty years, he would see the mighty hand of God deliver a ragtag motley assembly of complaining, unbelieving, and rebellious tribesmen into a nation.

From the beginning, the very nature of Moses' relationship with God was one of "**presence.**" From the days of the burning bush to the heights of the unveiling of the law on Mt Sinai, Moses would have a face-to-face relationship with God. His relationship with God was unlike any before him in scripture. He witnessed the miraculous deliverance of Israel from the grip of the Pharaoh. He saw the grand exodus take place and the power of the Passover blood on the doorposts of God's children turn the page of Pharaoh's 430-year grip on Israel. Now it was ending. He witnessed the miraculous journey to Sinai, with deliverance at the Red Sea, provisions of manna and quail provided in their desert wanderings, and protection from the hostile Amalekites. He had encounters with God, so powerful, that his face literally glowed with the Glory of God.

Then in Exodus 33 we see the heart of Moses revealed when the Lord commands him to depart from Sinai and go to the Promised Land.

> *"Then the Lord said to Moses, "Depart and go up from here, you and the people whom you have brought out of the land of Egypt, to the land of which I swore to Abraham, Isaac, and Jacob, saying, 'To your descendants I will give it.'"*

> - Exodus 33:1

Moses is promised that God would send His angel before him. Here's the catch, God said He would not go himself lest He wipe out this stiff-necked people from His presence.

> *"And I will send My Angel before you, and I will drive out the Canaanite and the Amorite and the Hittite and the Perizzite and the Hivite and the Jebusite. Go up to a land flowing with milk and honey; for I will not go up in your midst, lest I consume you on the way, for you are a stiff-necked people."*

> *And when the people heard this bad news, they mourned, and no one put on his ornaments. For the Lord had said to Moses, "Say to the children of Israel, 'You are a stiff-necked people. I could come up into your midst in one moment and consume you. Now*

*therefore, take off your ornaments, that I may know what to do to you.'" So the children of Israel stripped themselves of their ornaments by Mount Horeb.*

*Moses took his tent and pitched it outside the camp, far from the camp, and called it the tabernacle of meeting. And it came to pass that everyone who sought the Lord went out to the tabernacle of meeting which was outside the camp. So it was, whenever Moses went out to the tabernacle, that all the people rose, and each man stood at his tent door and watched Moses until he had gone into the tabernacle.*

*And it came to pass, when Moses entered the tabernacle, that the pillar of cloud descended and stood at the door of the tabernacle, and the Lord talked with Moses. All the people saw the pillar of cloud standing at the tabernacle door, and all the people rose and worshiped, each man in his tent door. So the Lord spoke to Moses face to face, as a man speaks to his friend. And he would return to the camp, but his servant Joshua the son of Nun, a young man, did not depart from the tabernacle."*

- Exodus 33:2-11

Moses was grieved in His heart. All he knew of God was birthed in His presence. The very thought of God taking them into the next season of their destiny without the presence of the Almighty, was too much to bear. He moves in closer to God. He starts to pull on His heartstrings. From the depth of his being Moses says in Exodus 33:12-14:

> *"...See, You say to me, 'Bring up this people.' But You have not let me know whom You will send with me. Yet You have said, 'I know you by name, and you have also found grace in My sight.' Now therefore, I pray, if I have found grace in Your sight, show me now Your way, that I may know You and that I may find grace in Your sight. And consider that this nation is Your people."*
>
> *And He said, "My Presence will go with you, and I will give you rest."*

Moses, in essence is drawing a line in the sand. His heart is aching for more of God. He had been to the mountaintop and his face had radiated with the glory of God. He walked with God like no other, yet in this moment he is relentless, saying, "If Your Presence does not go with us, do not bring us up from here." His desire to live in the presence moved the Lord to relent and give Moses the desire of his heart (Exodus 33:15-17).

> *"Then he said to Him, "If Your Presence does not go with us, do not bring us up from here. For how then will it be known that Your people and I have found grace in Your sight, except You go with us? So we shall be separate, Your people and I, from all the people who are upon the face of the earth."*
>
> *So the Lord said to Moses, "I will also do this thing that you have spoken; for you have found grace in My sight, and I know you by name."*

Even at this, Moses is not satisfied. His hunger for God is unstoppable. His mind is not on the mission ahead or the future promised land. He is not thinking about his call or his duty. All he wants is more of God. He wants to see Him in all His glory. It is at that moment that God is moved to answer the heart cry of Moses and show him His glory. Only the surprising thing is, when God responds to Moses about His glory He points him to His nature, He says (vs 19):

> *"Then He said, "I will make all My goodness pass before you, and I will proclaim the name of the Lord before you. I will be gracious to whom I will be gracious, and I will have compassion on whom I will have compassion."*

In essence, God is saying,

> *"My identity, My nature, who I am, reveals My glory, and that is My goodness, that is My name, it is the revelation of the understanding who I am, and the love nature of My being that displays My glory. When you see and understand that, you are ready."*

The Exodus story continues (33:18-23):

> *"And he said, "Please, show me Your glory."*
>
> *Then He said, "I will make all My goodness pass before you, and I will proclaim the name of the Lord before you. I will be gracious to whom I will be gracious, and I will have compassion on whom I will have compassion." But He said, "You*

> *cannot see My face; for no man shall see Me, and live." And the Lord said, "Here is a place by Me, and you shall stand on the rock. So it shall be, while My glory passes by, that I will put you in the cleft of the rock, and will cover you with My hand while I pass by. Then I will take away My hand, and you shall see My back; but My face shall not be seen."*

At that moment, Moses is given a gift, and the gift is the revelation of the nature of God, His name, His goodness, and His overflowing compassion. God takes him and places him in the cleft of the rock-of-our-salvation. He is hidden, as it were, in Christ, and then, when God removes His hand, he sees the back of God.

I would suggest to you that the back he saw was the back of Jesus himself, scourged on Calvary at the whipping post. It is that place of complete surrender and desire to see God face to face, knowing that nothing else matters in life but that one desire is the platform for God to draw him in.

God is bringing us to that place. He is changing our desires and drawing us to a place of transformation. Each one of us, personally, is at a crossroad. Do I go to the left, and settle for His angelic covering as I move forward in life? Or, do I stop and say, *"God, I can't go anywhere, unless you go with me. I need to know You completely, in all Your fullness. I need to see Your glory. Father, reveal to me Your nature and Your name. Let me be saturated with the knowledge of Your incredible love and compassion."* You see, when His love nature and goodness burns inside us, we can change the world.

The Lord hinted at His nature when He gave Moses the schematics of the tabernacle in Exodus 25. What's interesting in this set of instructions is that God does not start with exterior of the tabernacle and work inward. He instead starts at the most Holy place of all, the "Holy of Holies."

The first furnishing of that place is the Ark and the Mercy Seat. The Mercy Seat was the cover that rested on top of the Ark. It was made of pure gold and had two golden Cherubim that bowed on each end.

The Mercy Seat was more than a covering for the Ark, it was the place of His presence, for between the Cherubim, the cloud and fire of His presence would hover just above the Mercy Seat. It was the space between the Cherubim, which represented God's presence among the people.

This seat of pure gold, could not be controlled by man. It was a Holy place. The Mercy Seat conveyed to the Israelites the idea that God was in their midst. The Ark then becomes a foundation of the Mercy Seat and the place where His presence rests.

However, we don't get a full revelation of this until the resurrection of Christ. John's record of this is very interesting. We read in chapter 20 a very unusual encounter Mary has at the tomb.

*"But Mary stood outside by the tomb weeping, and as she wept she stooped down and looked into the tomb. And she saw two angels in white sitting, one at the head*

*and the other at the feet, where the body of Jesus had lain. Then they said to her, "Woman, why are you weeping?"*

- John 20:11-13

It is here, and nowhere else in the gospels, we see the actual Mercy Seat, mentioned in Exodus 25. Mary peers into the tomb and she stops down and sees the spot where Jesus had been laid. At each end of that space were Angels, one at His feet and one at His head. At this moment, the essence of the Holy of Holies and the Mercy Seat becomes clear.

From the time that Moses built the tabernacle, and the Priests carried the Ark of the Covenant before the people, what they were actually carrying was a living prophecy of the Lord Jesus Christ, their Messiah, resurrected on Easter morning. The space between the Angels was indeed the place where Christ raised from the dead, and in His resurrection, He conquered sin and death and brought us into His presence and into the Holy of Holies. This is a powerful revelation. When God gives Moses the schematics of the tabernacle, He starts with a picture of the resurrected Lord.

The first act of Mercy on that Easter morning, 2,000 + years ago was a presence encounter with Mary. Like Moses, Mary was hungry for her Lord. She was disheartened. Her Jesus was gone. The man who freed her from seven demons, the one who healed her heart, and forgave her of all her sins, was gone. She woke that morning, crying inside. She had to be with Him, even in His death. She took off running, probably before dawn and ran to the tomb. It was probably still dark outside. Didn't matter, she had to be with Him. And when she arrived she found herself at an empty tomb, face to face with the Mercy Seat.

"Where have you laid Him," she cried.

Nevertheless, the tomb was still empty. That empty tomb is the place we find ourselves today. When all of our preconceived ideas and thoughts about God's nature are placed in the tomb, crucified if you will, then we are in a position to, like Mary, hear Him call out our name, and like Mary, we shall see Him for who He really is. He will show us His love nature. His love nature will bring about the change we are seeking. He will bring us into that Holy place. His love nature will transform us into a Bride ready for a wedding.

> *"Now when she had said this, she turned around and saw Jesus standing there, and did not know that it was Jesus. Jesus said to her, "Woman, why are you weeping? Whom are you seeking?"*
>
> *She, supposing Him to be the gardener, said to Him, "Sir, if You have carried Him away, tell me where You have laid Him, and I will take Him away."*
>
> *Jesus said to her, "Mary!"*
>
> - John 20:14-16

You see, everything we are, and everything we do is wrapped up in the resurrection of our Lord. At the heart of the sacrificial act lies the tender heart of the Father and His Mercy towards us. His incredible love and mercy draw us. It is His undying commitment to forgive us, woo us, and draw us into His presence that sustains us. We go from glory to glory in His love. With every step we take, the revelation of His loving kindness takes us deeper into Him. This deepness is always birthed out of resurrected mercy and love.

It is also interesting that the Hebrew name for the Mercy Seat is "kapporeth," which is best rendered in English, "propitiatory," meaning - having power to atone for or offered by way of expiation or propitiation. In other words, the very name points again to the atonement and the redeeming power of Christ's forgiveness extended to us.

The first time my eyes were opened to the truth of how much the Father perpetually loves me happened thirty years ago. I was a young Christian, still carrying luggage from my past on my back. I had sinned, I had gotten in an argument with my wife, and the weight of my guilt was crushing me. Up to this point in my life, I had felt that salvation was something I had to work at, as if it was fragile, and I needed to toe the line, or it was over.

I was feeling so dreadful. I felt ashamed. The shame in my heart was smothering me. I couldn't even talk to the Lord about it. I was driving home from work along a road that parallels the mountains, along the desert, from Palm Desert to Palm Springs, California. The sun was starting to set, and the sky was starting to turn orange. I was crying inside. Then, without thinking about it, I mumbled to the Lord, "I feel like dirt."

Suddenly, in a moment, I was in a trance. You have to understand I was driving. The Lord must have had some angel take over at the wheel, because I was caught up in the most incredible vision. Here's what I saw:

I was standing in the middle of a field on a farm. Jesus was standing in front of me. His long hair was blowing in the wind. He was dressed in overalls. He looked at me intently. Then, very gently, He reached down and scoped up some dirt in the palm of His hand. He brought His palm up close to His mouth, staring at the dirt. Then He stretched His arm out, palm facing up, and spun around. As he was spinning, He began to blow upon the dirt in His hand. Instantly, the dirt flew out of His hand and scattered across the land like seeds being scattered. Instantly, as the dirt hit the ground, crops began to shoot up, as far as the eyes could see. Then looked at me with soft tender eyes, very close, and said,

*"Boy, what I can do with dirt."*

I was blown away, crying my heart out. He, in a moment, when I expected rejection and the firm hand and discipline of a father, He showered me with love and favor. Like Mary, I wanted to run to Him and cling to Him. I had found my Lord in the midst of my pain. I came to, still driving, and cried and praised Him all the way home. His love nature drew me in. His tender mercy and compassion caused me to want to go deeper. I knew one thing, His love for me was unshakable, and it caused me to love Him even more.

When we get this, we will truly be able to show the world the love of Jesus Christ. The resurrection is wrapped up in love and mercy. Like the sons of Aaron, we are called to carry the Ark of resurrection and presence before us in battle. That Ark is, in essence the Ark of tender mercy and love wrapped up with His presence and His power. Paul reminds us of this very thing when he says in 1 Corinthians 13:1-10:

*"Though I speak with the tongues of men and of angels, but have not love, I have become sounding brass or a clanging cymbal. And though I have the gift of prophecy, and understand all mysteries and all knowledge, and though I have all faith, so that I could remove mountains, but have not love, I am nothing. And though I bestow all my goods to feed the poor, and though I give my body to be burned, but have not love, it profits me nothing. Love suffers long and is kind; love does not envy; love does not parade itself, is not puffed up; does not behave rudely, does not seek its own, is not provoked, thinks no evil; does not rejoice in iniquity, but rejoices in the truth; bears all things, believes all things, hopes all things, endures all things. Love never fails. But whether there are prophecies, they will fail; whether there are tongues, they will cease; whether there is knowledge, it will vanish away. For we know in part and we prophesy in part. But when that which is perfect has come, then that which is in part will be done away."*

The last day's bride is a lovely bride. She will move out with incredible grace, mercy, peace, and love. She is so lovely that she will literally draw the Lord of Glory to return for her. Be lovers dear children. Seek what Moses sought. Be as eager as Mary, and lay your preconceived ideas at the doorstep of the tomb. Embrace Him like John the beloved at the last supper. Be clothed by Him like Gideon of old. Run to Him and don't stop until you have a life changing love encounter with Him.

Only then can you be His eyes, hands, feet, and heart to this dying, hungry planet. He needs your loveliness.

CHAPTER 18

# The House of Bread

*"The average church has so much machinery
and so little oil of the Holy Spirit that it squeaks
like a threshing machine when you start it up in
the fall after it has been out in the field all year."*

- Billy Sunday (1862–1935)

The problem with many churches today is the same problem we see in many of our restaurants. The French were the first to coin the word "Restaurant." In the Dictionnaire de Trevoux, in 1771, defined the word restaurateur:

> *"Someone who has the art of preparing true broths, known as 'restaurants', and the right to sell all kinds of custards, dishes of rice, vermicelli and macaroni, egg dishes, boiled capons, preserved and stewed fruit and other delicious and healthy-giving foods."*

It wasn't until 1786 that the word restaurant was used to describe an eating-house. The simplicity of the early eating-houses was nothing like the restaurants of today. They were the local hangouts – places that served comfort food – honest and homemade, at a value that was friendly to the common folk. What started out as a simple house-of-bread suddenly became more complex.

Today, restaurants are big business and we are inundated with them. Like merchant-booths in an ancient marketplace, waiting for the crowds to sample their wares, we have them on every street corner and every inch of space between. These cookie-cutter concepts unfold, pop-up, and spread out across the landscape like settler's tents across the prairie planes. No longer is the sole-proprietor standing at the door to greet you. No longer do you walk into a neighborhood café and have intimacy with the owner and your neighbors as well. The corporate Big Buck and the bottom line drive it all.

The days of the independent owner who had only one goal in mind, to fill the place with well nourished, extremely stuffed, and happy consumers is over. It doesn't matter what you call it... a Café, Bistro, Brasserie, Tavern, Diner, Coffee Shop, or Restaurant, if there's one on every street corner you can be guaranteed that the menu as well as the experience is carved out of the boardroom and not from the heart of a chef proprietor.

The days of the community restaurant beating with the heart-felt passion of an independent neighborhood owner is gone in most communities. In times past, the independent owner saw their restaurant as a place with purpose.... People would come in; they'd eat and be satisfied beyond their expectations. Their experience is so fulfilling, so wonderful, that they leave feeling full and content. They want to come back again. Not only do they come back – they become a marketing-campaign unto themselves. They tell their friends, their neighbors, anyone who will listen… what a grand experience they had in your restaurant.

The sad reality is that many independent restaurants today struggle to survive. They strive while going up neck to neck with the big boys. They can't compete with the glitz and glitter of the well-staged cookie-cutter concept of their corporate counterpart. The corporate giants on the other hand have it down pat. They have the educated experience, corporate marketing, project planning, a solid infrastructure of controls and training, with a so-called pulse on the consumer, and the corporate cash to back up their enterprise. They have done their homework, and they know the demographics of the area where to put their hot branded concept. The problem with these corporate institutional giants is not their expertise and business acumen… the problem is passion.

Without passion, even though you have all the ingredients of success, you will soon become a whitewashed tomb of a restaurant. You will be a colorful balloon – bright and shiny on the outside – but inside – full of hot air serving up dribble to a consumer that has lost their ability to taste real food. They have bought into the picture on the billboard with its thick and juicy representation of a dish that in reality is not even close to the picture. Thank heaven for glitz and glitter… if you spin it right, strong theme, lots of energy and glitzy decorative elements to distract them from the product – maybe the folks won't notice… and the sad thing is – most don't.

A while back, Jan (my wife) and I were sitting around trying to decide what to eat for dinner... when, like a moment of marital oneness; we looked at each other and said, "Breakfast." That was it, nothing like breakfast for dinner. We hopped on my motorcycle and shot over to a nearby chain coffee shop that had recently opened. The building and design package of the facility was nice. They had all the extra consumer hooks one would anticipate these days, retail merchandising at the entrance, walk-up to-go counter for easy pick-up, counter seating with contemporary table-lamps - positioned appropriately, and a warm comfortable interior broken up with a modest ratio of booths to tables. Decorative pony walls and partitions infused with a few plants breaking up the space to create the right environment without causing you to feel you were eating in a banquet hall.

"So far so good," I thought to myself, as I reached for the menu to scan the offerings. The menu was, from a corporate standpoint, perfectly engineered. All the items were well placed, descriptors were well written, layout was crisp, and for a café, the offerings sounded appealing. My choice was easy... steak and eggs to feed my craving, and flapjacks – there's nothing like a pancake supper with a good steak and a side of eggs to fill that void. Well, so much for fantasy.

My food arrived and it was awful... I mean BAD, and I haven't said that in a long time. Sitting on my plate was the most puny, overcooked, soggy (figure that one out), piece of what they referred to as a steak. Next to that boil-in-the-bag piece of meat, was a small pile of little pale, un-seasoned, cubed potatoes, called home fries, and two pale looking eggs, at least they were over easy.

Now, as I get older, I have grown to focus more on the company than the meal, but this time I couldn't. I felt like Howard Beale, the acclaimed news anchorman for UBS TV in that 1976 movie "Network." I wanted to stand up and look at rest of the patrons in the restaurant and say, "look at your food – look at it will you and … get up now. I want all of you to get up out of your chairs. I want you to get up right now and go to the window, open it, and stick your head out and yell, I'm as mad as hell, and I'm not going to take this anymore!" Ah but alas, I contained myself. With a loss of appetite, I returned my food, and sat there with a cup of old warm coffee. I continued a nice dialog with my wife while waiting to depart.

You see this place with all the components to make a modern day restaurant a success, lacked one serious ingredient. They could not deliver what they had promised – good food. It takes passion to make good food. Someone in the kitchen has to be on his or her knees before a hot stove and find out how and what to cook. Passion is the key that separates real food from a cheap imitation. Passion is the door, the driving force, which brings all the right elements together. Passion will pull you to the consumer's table to check the pulse of their experience. Passion will drive you into the kitchen causing you to work endlessly on a dish until it is just right, its taste, texture, aroma, layers of flavor, presentation, all of it, are perfect. You will tear it apart and build it back up again – as many times as needed until it's right.

**Passion is contagious.** It's contagious with the staff and the patron. People are drawn to your passion. People want to be around people that believe… people that are truly excited about what they do. They want to brush up against you and get close to you. They want to catch a glimpse of something... they want to glean a new understanding, a new depth of what you're doing. They want an imparting of something. They want your mantel, so to speak. They want a double dose of the fire that is burning inside of you. They want to draw from the wellspring of your experience. They desire to taste of something grand. They want their cups to overflow.

**Now listen.... This is very important.** I am NOT talking about restaurants and the consumer.... I am talking about the answer to the greatest mystery of the 21st century. **I am talking about the Church.** I am talking about the great commission. I am talking about Jesus Christ and His desire to set a table in the community where you live and serve up a meal that is fit for Priests and Kings. **I am talking about Passion and the Pulpit.** I am talking about the ingredients needed to reach a dying world. I am talking about the difference between a lukewarm or a dead church and one that is alive on the inside with the presence and heartbeat of Jesus Christ.

The restaurant, in a real way, is parallel to our church buildings today. We build them on every street corner. We offer up verbal menus from the word of God for all to come and feast. We desire to restore man back into fellowship with their loving Father and introduce them to the "bread of life." Even the word "Restaurant" has its root meaning "to restore; a food that restores." Haven't we been given the great commission to restore mankind and bring them back into fellowship with their creator, to feed them real bread, living bread, the bread of life?

How often have we, the church, bought in to this corporate model. Instead of spending time on our knees before the hot stove of God's presence, we are in search for the right hook, a good program, and a new way to increase the tithe and raise the membership. Our real model is closer to Jesus in the garden of Gethsemane, than the hanging gardens of Babylon. We don't need spin. We need to be spent. Like change in the pocket of an Almighty God, we need to be sold out to Him. We need to seek Him until we sweat, as it were, great drops of blood. Only then will we have a message that is birthed in travail. Only then will we communicate the "Passion of Christ."

We get caught up in our various programs and events, how well we say the same old message, while forgetting what the fundamental mission was that brought us here to begin with. At times such as this, we have to go back to our first love and receive from Him the passion and simplicity that we knew when we first believed – where the mission was fresh and simplistic – the goals were souls and not much more.

That is not always a simple task. People have a tendency, no matter where they are or in what state they are in, to get comfortable. They settle into complacency and loose the desire for a deep love relationship. It becomes a forked-road marriage where each partner is headed in opposite directions. Neither a marriage nor the church will be able to survive in such a state. We, the bride of Christ, must be in submissive obedience to His master plan. Our churches need more of Him and less of us.

It's just like that; cookie-cutter, restaurant Jan and I ate at. It looked good, had all the spin but in the end – there was nothing solid to eat. It had become a "house-of-stale-bread" or a "house-of-bread" serving no bread at all, just old dried crumbs ground into the carpets from patrons long forgotten. When a restaurant runs out of its ability to serve food – people stop coming. The sad thing is that these people are hungry – they are thirsty – they are looking for someone somewhere to open their doors and invite them to come in and feast at the table of abundance.

Tragically, many churches have ended up in the same condition. A house-of-bread where the only mandate is to reminisce about the bread of the past – speculating how good it must have tasted. Yet, there are no ovens to bake what people want or need. It becomes a history lesson about bread. People come in hungry for the bread of life. They want to sink their teeth into savory hot loaves of freshly baked bread. They hunger and desire manna from heaven but all they get is a menu they can never order off.

Oh, there's talk about how wonderful the bread once was – they even sing about bread – but serve it fresh and hot – no way. All of this brings about a spiritual famine in the land. People go about their day hungry and thirsty for a living vibrant relationship with the bread of life – but are left unfilled and hopeless. The sad thing is that Jesus is now, more than ever before, ready to send fresh hot loves of His presence into their midst – if they would only seek His face and give Him back His church.

So what happens to the communities where we live, our neighborhoods, and our cities? What happens to our children? What happens to all the starving people around us desiring to sink their teeth into spiritual food that has substance and life giving power? They go hungry and the famine becomes more rigorous. Our churches become fast food outlets – scattered about on every street corner – but nothing of substance is really served there. What do people do when their spiritual hunger becomes spiritual malnutrition? They flock to anything or anyone that offers something resembling a loaf of bread. They window-shop on the streets of our cities and taste the offerings of the new age movement, Eastern mysticism, or the occult, in search for hot bread. They seek out astrologers and tarot card readers hoping to find living water to quench their dying souls.

People are a lot smarter than we think. If one of our churches lit the ovens of the Holy Spirit and started cooking hot loaves from heaven... word would travel... it would get around... people would do anything to get real bread... hot freshly baked bread... especially in times of great famine.

Consider the story of Ruth, found in the book of Ruth in the Old Testament.

> *"Now it came to pass, in the days when the judges ruled, that there was a famine in the land. And a certain man of Bethlehem, Judah, went to dwell in the country of Moab, he and his wife and his two sons. ...*
>
> *... Then she arose with her daughters-in-law that she might return from the country of Moab, for she had*

*heard in the country of Moab that the Lord had visited*
*His people by giving them bread."*

- Ruth 1:1,6

Naomi and her family left home and moved to Moab because there was a famine in Bethlehem. Bethlehem was the city of David; Bethlehem was the birthplace of the Messiah; Bethlehem was the birthplace of the bread of life. Bethlehem was the last place on earth you would think of as a place of famine. Even the literal translation of the word "Bethlehem" in the Hebrew means "the House of Bread." It should not have been a place of famine, but famine came, and Naomi left because they were hungry. They left because the House of Bread had no bread at all.

Why do people leave or never come into our churches – because there is no bread. Bread is the substance for life. The Jews knew the power of bread – they used its symbol during the Passover (feast of unleavened bread), the showbread was an integral part of the tabernacle and proof of the presence of God in the temple. In the book of Numbers, chapter four, it was called the bread of the Presence. The showbread literally means – show-up bread – the evidence that God has shown up in this place.

Naomi and her family are symbolic of the people that never enter, or leave, many of our churches today. They left Bethlehem and went to Moab trying to find bread. Oh, what lengths people will go through in search of some hot bread in times of famine. We see it all around us – people flock to nightclubs, casinos, and bars, in search for bread that will fill the void in their souls. They become slaves to sin, drugs, mental or physical abuse, and they accept it – believing it is their cup in life. Why do they believe this? The answer is simple – we have let them down, we have failed them and not offered them the reality of the living truth and the power of a gospel that will change their lives forever. We have become a franchise of the fast food gospel.

The good news is we do not have to except this state of spiritual melancholy. Jesus is more than ready to rain manna from heaven upon us. He wants His church back and is more than ready to hang a sign outside the "House of Bread" stating – "Welcome… Under New Management!" The turnaround is simple:

> "If My people who are called by My name will humble themselves, and pray and seek My face, and turn from their wicked ways, then I will hear from heaven, and will forgive their sin and heal their land."

> - 2 Chronicles 7:14

There is no other way. God wants to bake loaves of hot bread and serve them up to a people hungry for His presence. This really hit home for me one Sunday morning at church while taking communion. I walked up to the communion table to take communion. I stood there, held the bread in my hand, and began to thank the Lord for what He did for me. My heart was set on really digging into the moment. Suddenly, the Lord gave me an incredible vision.

## The Vision of the Bread of Life

I fell into a trance and saw myself standing in a café. The café was full of life, action, and buzzing with excitement. To my right was a large hearth stone oven. Right next to me was a chef with a wooden peel in his hand. He was pulling out of the oven large loaves of hot bread and tossing them into baskets. Waiters were moving about the café handing out loaves of this hot fragrant bread. Everyone was filled with incredible joy. The place was alive with enthusiasm and energy – and they were all smiling.

The counter in front of the oven was an "L" shape that wrapped around to the front of the café. In the corner next to floor-to-ceiling windows were two very large wine barrels – Napa Valley style. The wait staff was pouring wine from the spigots into large beer pitchers. They were running around pouring glasses of wine – smiling all the way. The front to the café was all windows, and the door was open.

The street in front of the café was alive with people rushing over to enter the café.... A paperboy was riding his bike had stopped in front of the café with a paper in his hand. He had an incredible smile on his face, almost animated. The paper was the *"Good News Journal"* and the headline across the front-page read, "This Is That," echoing Peter's famous words from Acts chapter two, in explanation of the out-pouring of the Holy Spirit on the day of Pentecost.

I asked the Lord what was going on, and He said,

> *"Religion has taken My communion and placed it in a box of lethargy. It lies dormant at the foot of the cross,*

*never moving to the place of resurrection and life. Yet, My kingdom is full of Life, where Mercy flows continuously from the vats of heaven and is waiting to be poured out and served up in Kingdom Café.*

*Heaven is so full of My grace that it comes out of the oven of My presence like loaves of warm bread, eagerly desiring to be served up, and full of life and abundance. When My people embrace the abundance of grace and mercy that I desire to pour out – people will flock in groves to get into My Kingdom and Joy will be the hallmark of My waitstaff.*

*The fire has been lit, the ovens are hot, the dough has been prepared for this hour, and the vats are already overflowing with My mercy. The bread and the wine point to the glory of what I have done, what I am doing, and what I will be doing in the days and months ahead. The gift of My atonement did not stop at the cross – it is perpetual – it moves to create a Kingdom here on earth... as it is in Heaven - full of royalty – a royal priesthood – sons and daughters of God reflecting the Glory of who I AM and what I AM doing... ageless, ceaseless, full of life and abundance.*

*The Kingdom Café is open – tell them to come – come to My banqueting table... the table has been set, destiny is today, see what I see – behold the beauty and the glory of the Kingdom Café. Oh how I love the life in this place."*

The next time you drive down the restaurant district of your neighborhood pay attention to all the types of restaurants you find there. Look at the ones that have a two-hour wait, in contrast to the restaurants whose parking lots are empty. Count the number of fast food outlets and cookie-cutter chains and see how many cars are lined up in the drive-thru.

Look at the churches in your neighborhood and use the same kind of guidelines you would to find true, hot, passionate food, try to find the one with a two-hour wait – to get in. I tell you, if a great restaurant opened its doors and served hot-out-of-the-oven bread, you would have to fight them off with a stick to stop them from coming in.

I challenge you – if people are willing to stand in line for two-hours to have a burger – how long will they stand in front of a church that is overflowing with the presence and power of the Holy Spirit. **The bread-of-life will draw them.** The new wine will keep them. No coupon, groupon, BOGO, or two-for-ones will bring them in. No early bird specials will cause them to beat down your doors. However, bread, life-giving bread, just out of the oven bread, served hot and fresh for this generation – will.

Humanity has a bread-shaped hole in its heart and the only thing that will fill it is Jesus. Let's get back to the culinary basics and bring forth hot bread to the nations. I look forward to the day when the lines outside our churches go on for blocks. I can't wait for the sweet aroma of the freshly baked bread of His presence to float through our streets filling the air like incense, drawing all those who are tired and needy. I look forward to the time when restaurant owners have to close down their restaurants because the ovens are turned up at the church down the street – fresh bread is being served and the

entire town is eating it up. Let's get on with the task at hand.
**Light the fire – kindle the stove – turn up the heat – let Jesus
show up and bring to the world the bread of His presence.**

> *"When the hour had come, He sat down, and the twelve
> apostles with Him. Then He said to them, "With
> fervent desire I have desired to eat this Passover with
> you before I suffer; for I say to you, I will no longer eat
> of it until it is fulfilled in the kingdom of God."*
>
> *Then He took the cup, and gave thanks, and said,
> "Take this and divide it among yourselves; for I say to
> you, I will not drink of the fruit of the vine until the
> kingdom of God comes."*
>
> *And He took bread, gave thanks and broke it, and gave
> it to them, saying, "This is My body which is given for
> you; do this in remembrance of Me."*
>
> *Likewise He also took the cup after supper, saying,
> "This cup is the new covenant in My blood, which is
> shed for you."*

- Luke 22:14-20

# CHAPTER 19

# Coffeehouse of Hope

*"Give ear, O my people, to my law; Incline your
ears to the words of my mouth. I will open my
mouth in a parable; I will utter dark sayings of
old, which we have heard and known, and our
fathers have told us.
We will not hide them from their children,
telling to the generation to come the praises of
the Lord, and His strength and His wonderful
works that He has done."*

- Psalm 78:1-4

*"And He said to them, "To you it has been given
to know the mystery of the kingdom of God; but
to those who are outside, all things come in
parables, so that 'Seeing they may see and not
perceive, And hearing they may hear and not
understand; Lest they should turn, And their
sins be forgiven them.'"*

*And He said to them, "Do you not understand this parable? How then will you understand all the parables?"*

- Mark 4:11-13

## The Parable… Given in a Dream

*The following parable was given to me in a dream.*

Once there was a Barista that loved his profession and took great care and pride in the coffee he brewed, so much so, that he said to himself, *"I am going to build me a café that serves up the finest coffee in all the world. In fact, my café is going to be so warm and welcoming that all who come in will taste of my cup and their lives will be filled with comfort and joy. It will be a place where people will gather and find rest for their souls."*

Well, as any good businessman would do, he surveyed the competition and assessed the needs of the marketplace. He was struck by the indifference of the people, how they would run into any coffeehouse and drink no matter the quality or how watered down it was. Some were running after instant coffee. Others wanted the sweeter varieties… like a caramel macchiato or vanilla latte that was so diluted all flavor was lost. And the beans… well no one knew the quality of a good beans… or the care it takes to produce the perfect cup, so he said to himself, *"I am going to change things. My coffee house will not be like this, for in my house – I will serve only the finest of beans… and I will pour only the finest cup,"* this desire to serve burned deep within his soul.

So he bought some land and built himself a coffeehouse. And when it was done the Barista stood back and marveled at the beauty, warmth, and simplicity of his new café... it was wonderful. He was now ready to open the doors to his new café.... There was one problem he had no coffee. Now this troubled the café owner, *"How can I sell the finest cup and not have the finest bean?"* So he looked to the bean traders to see what they offered, but did not care for the quality, their beans were either picked too early, or the wrong variety. For this Barista only the high mountain Arabica beans would do. Other beans were either low-mountain beans and often over roasted or burnt and lost all the essential oils, flavor, and aroma. So, he said to himself, *"I will head out myself and gather the beans I need."* So he closed the doors to his café and went on a journey in search for the finest of beans.

The Barista traveled to a faraway land. Its landscape was mountainous and terrain dangerous. In fact, this land was made up with some of the highest mountain ranges in the world and many were volcanic and active. The Barista knew that the best beans grew in regions such as this, so he picked the tallest volcanic mountain he could find and set out on his journey in search for the finest beans. After several days of hiking through the thickest of forests, he finely reached the summit. He searched and searched but found no beans, only ash and hardened lava, remnant for its last eruption. Then, as he circled the peak of the mountain, he came across a path that led him to a small luscious valley. On the edge of the valley was a single Arabica bush, but the bush had no life for it had been scorched in the heat of the eruption. He stood disheartened. Then, as if by fate, he glanced down at the base of the tree and saw nestled in the ashes, five little beans. *"I know what I will*

do," he said, *"I will plant the beans and wait for them to grow."*
So he gathered the beans in the palm of his hand, and took
some soil mingled with ash and journeyed to the center of the
valley where he found a cluster of tall shade trees. There he
planted his beans under the shade and safety of the trees.

For seven years, he waited for his trees to grow. Through rain,
and wind, and cold, and heat he camped at the side of his
bushes looking for the fruit he so longed to see. Then one day,
as the sun was breaking through the mist that had covered the
mountain top he saw it... his trees began to blossom. They were
covered with the most incredible white flowers he had ever
seen. And the aroma, like jasmine, filled the mountainside. But
after four days the flowers were gone, leaving behind them
perfect dark green berries.

"*Alas,*" the barista said, "*the berries I so long to see,*" and he
knelt down and thanked the God of Heaven for yielding a
harvest. But he knew that if he wanted to create the perfect cup
he must not pick them to soon or they will produce a bitter
cup, not fit for drinking. So he waited until they began to
ripen, at first to yellow, then light red and finally darkening to
a glossy deep red. Now it was time. He laid gunnysack at the
base of the bush and vigorously he shook the tree until all the
ripe berries had fallen onto his gunnysack. Likewise, he did to
all five trees. After gathering his berries, he knelt down and
sorted the good from the bad. Then placing the good berries
into massive bags he tied them off and threw them over his
shoulder and carried them down the mountain heading home
with a wonderful harvest.

When our Barista arrived at his café his eagerness to open his doors and serve his first cup was overwhelming, but he had to slow down, the time was not ready. He had to prepare the berries for roasting. First, he had to remove the flesh of the berry revealing the seeds or beans as we call them. Then he fermented them to remove the slimy film still present on the bean. When the fermentation was finished, he washed them with fresh water and laid them out to dry. But the work of the Barista was not done for the cup he desired to pour had to have a rich dark and aromatic flavor. To get to this level of excellence the beans needed to be roasted.

The roasting process was crucial as it developed caramelization, color, nuttiness, and most of all; it brings out the essential aromatic oils, which give the coffee its true flavor and aroma. Our Barista knew for the perfect cup, he did not want to over-roast it but still wanted a deep smooth cup with a subtle sugary flavor. Alas, the coffee was ready for cooling. Once cooled, he packed his beans in an airtight container until it was time for brewing.

Now, it was time. Now he could open the doors to his café and begin serving that perfect cup. So he went over to his espresso machine and placed his beans in the grinder. After grinding the beans he placed ground beans into the hopper and with a tamping device, he pressed the ground very tightly forming a puck, locked it into place on the espresso machine, and hit the brew button causing very hot water, under extreme pressure, to press its way through the grounds. The result produced a rich, almost syrupy beverage by extracting and emulsifying the oils in the ground coffee. He looked down at his little demitasse cup and said, "Perfect! This is just what I was looking for: a well-balanced cup with a reddish-brown crema. Now I can open my doors."

---

## The story and its interpretation...

*"My dear children listen to this story and understand. Do you not know that I would climb the highest mountain for you? Do you not know that I would search for you and bring you unto Myself?*

*Yes, I have called you unto Myself. I found you and pulled you out of the ashes and placed you in the palm of My hands. I held on to you as My own, and planted you under the shadow of My wings... and have protected you. I nourished you and watched as you grew.*

*I was there on the day you blossomed. Your faith in Me has been a sweet aroma in My temple. Your love for one another has been as jasmine, an aroma of adornment. I know the shaking you have endured, but I have gathered you up as a fine treasure and carried you upon My back, and brought you to this place inside of Me.*

*Do not fear or be dismayed. I have come that you might have life – and that more abundantly. But I want you to know that My presence and work in your life did not stop on the day you bloomed. Nor, did it stop when I saw the fruit of your love. No, it is because of your love and desire to draw closer to Me that I have pressed into your lives.*

*The work that I do calls for deep preparation. The value of the cup that I desire to pour is far richer than instant espresso. My gift for you is built upon perseverance. My desire for you is beyond anything you can imagine. Do you not know that everyone is seasoned with fire, and the fire you have experienced is the fire of purity?*

*I, Myself, have brought you to the roaster. I am the one that called you to that place. For though you walk through the flames of trial, the stench of the smoke shall not harm you. For what I am doing is for your benefit. For it is through this fire that the flesh is dried out, so that the oil of My presence within you would be drawn to the surface.*

*Yes, it is that oil that brings the flavor and fragrance of My Kingdom to others. I am preparing you. My desire is to pour you out upon the nations... so press in, and press on, know that in the end you shall be called blessed of My Father.*

*I know that many of do not understand this grinding process. Yet it is by this process that you, become We... for it is the rock of My presence that has brought you to this place. I have called you to cast all your cares upon Me – yes even your very lives.... And when you fall upon this rock you will be broken, but out of your brokenness will arise a heart set apart for Me, so press in, and press on, to that place that I have called you.*

*The pressure is on. You have been pressed on many sides, this I know, and this I understand. But please understand Me when I tell you, it is by this pressure and by this tamping, that My cup is created.*

*Do not fear and do not worry, cast your cares upon Me and let patience do its perfect work. Trust Me My child, you shall come through this time and you shall be a cup of blessing, for I have brought you unto Myself, and the cup I desire to pour – is a cup of blessing. This, My beloved, is the heart of the matter... press-in my love, press-on my beloved... for soon you will see the doors of My café open. My cup is full, and your cup shall surly overflow. Its' espresso time My children. Press-in, and press-on."*

# CHAPTER 20

# The Shaking

*"The poor and needy seek water, but there is none, their tongues fail for thirst. I, the Lord, will hear them; I, the God of Israel, will not forsake them. I will open rivers in desolate heights, and fountains in the midst of the valleys; I will make the wilderness a pool of water, and the dry land springs of water. I will plant in the wilderness the cedar and the acacia tree, the myrtle and the oil tree; I will set in the desert the cypress tree and the pine and the box tree together, That they may see and know, and consider and understand together, that the hand of the Lord has done this, and the Holy One of Israel has created it."*

- Isaiah 41:17-20

*"Along the bank of the river, on this side and that, will grow all kinds of trees used for food; their leaves will not wither, and their fruit will not fail. They will bear fruit every month, because their water flows from the sanctuary.*

*Their fruit will be for food, and their leaves for medicine."*

- Ezekiel 47:12

In the seasons ahead there is going to be a gracious shaking in the kingdom of God. The shaking is a shaking of release into greater levels of love, mercy, and tenderness. This season is a season of harvest. This harvest is the harvest of the fruit trees of heaven. From across spectrum of the kingdom, trees that have been fertilized, growing, and soaking in the sun of His presence are moving into realms of release and fruit-fullness. Let me explain.

During prayer a short while back, the Lord brought me to a quiet place. All around me, I saw ripples of water, as if I was submerged in an ocean and my eyes were just above the waterline. I was looking at the water and the water was vibrating all around me with the presence of Jesus.

As I watched the ripples, suddenly, I saw the face of Jesus. It looked as if he was sleeping with his face against a golden silken pillow. However, as I watched, I realized he wasn't sleeping at all. He was tenderly embracing the surface of the water. I understood the water as being the water of your life as a child of His.

Your life was infused with the water of His life. His life was fluid and it covered you. He was so enveloped in tender love and passion, for His desire over you, that, as He laid down, in tenderness, and He began to breathe upon the surface of the water. As He breathed His breath moved upon the water it causing ripples - and the ripples became waves – and the waves rolled out until they became a tsunami that flooded the whole earth.

Then I heard a song, a tender lullaby...

*The breath of the Lord is upon the waters*

*The breath of the Lord is upon the waters*

*His tender love is upon me*

*His tender love is embracing me*

*He is caressing me with the depth of His embrace*

*His love for me is stirring, stirring, ...stirring the deep places of my heart.*

As I listed to that melody I was overcome by the heart of the song...

> *His love is fluid.... His fluidity will overcome you in this season. His flowing love will bring rapture to your souls and a release of revelation and knowledge of Him - His heartbeat, passion, and love. His peace and presence will move upon you like waters upon the surface of the deep. His breath will be upon you like the dance of the wind, shaking, shaking, and shaking the very pillars of your soul.*
>
> *He is wooing you to a deeper place - a place of saturation, yes, marination... Marination that will bring transformation.*

*The ripples He is sending from you will be a proclamation to the nations.*

*What is produced in this season of tenderness and love will yield incredible fruit. During this season of marination and transformation, lives are going to change and fruit that has been ripening upon the vine in the last season is about to be released upon the face of the earth.*

**Let me explain...**

As I was watching the water, it all became quiet and dark like the night sky.... Then I heard the Lord say,

*"I am shaking and shifting the structures of the earth and calling for fruit in this season. I am bringing in the harvest and causing My voice to sound out in the highways and byways. Like a mighty whisper I am penetrating the hearts of many... and many, many, many shall hear and come unto to me. Byways shall become highways - crooked places shall be made straight. Plow horses are being sent out and the breaches are being repaired."*

Then he gave me a glimpse of the garden of His delight.

**Almond Trees:** Then I looked and saw Almond trees shaking in the wind and as the almonds fell to the ground branches sprung up and the almond branches began to bloom. The Lord said, "I am calling forth My almond branches, my royal priesthood, and they shall begin to bloom in the land and cause a fragrance to fill the air and begin to change the atmosphere."

**Apple Trees:** Then I looked and saw Apple trees shaken by the wind of His presence. Apples started to fall to the ground. As they fell, I saw workers of the harvest - the gathers collecting baskets of apples. The apples were collected and brought into the kitchen of the Most High God. There they were prepared, and the aroma of simmering apples began to fill the atmosphere of heaven - apples laced with cinnamon and raisins. Apples laced with sugar and spice. He took these fragrant apples, wrapped in the bread of His presence and baked them as pies - and then cut into wedges - and He said,

> *"With these wedges, I will pry open the dark places and transform doors that were once closed, windows of heaven; this is the process of My presence."*

And the Lord said,

> *"You are the apple of my eye and the desire of My heart and I am preparing you and enfolding you with My presence and for My purpose. I am about to serve you up to this planet and invade those that are, so-called, hard to reach - and to those hard to reach places.... And they shall open their doors to you because you bear my fragrance. You are sweet because I have simmered you in My love."*

**Date Palms:** And then I looked and saw the mighty Date palms of the desert, and they began to shake. I saw dates falling from the mighty palms. Then I heard the Lord Say,

> *"I have planted some of you at the gate of the desert and you have flourished in the dry places and have grown in the desert places and now I am beginning to*

*release your fruit." And the Lord said, "In this desert*
*place, I have courted you, yes, I have dated you and*
*showered you with My adoration and My love. Because*
*you have grown in the desert place, I will cause you to*
*become a river of life - and this desert will be*
*transformed into fertile fields. And gardens will grow*
*and harvest will come, and your branches will be as*
*shade to the broken."*

God is shaking the desert places, bringing sweetness to the barren lands - making you as date-nut bread to a hungry people.

Fig Trees: Then I looked and saw figs falling in the orchard and the figs were transformed into Fig-Newton, flakey and rich in flavor and aroma. And I heard the Lord say,

*"I am releasing my figs upon the land and opening*
*realms of creativity and invention. My people will be a*
*catalyst of creation - speaking creative life into this*
*season."*

Pine Trees: Then I saw tall pine trees lining the Mountain of the Lord and the Pine trees started to shake, and pine-cones started to fall and when they fell they revealed pine nuts, and the pine-cones became cones of protection, and the pine nuts began producing trees - that became ladders for others to climb the high mountain places of God.

Then I saw pesto blended with the basil of praise. I saw shrimp marinating in the pesto and God was calling those who were small in their own eyes to change their identity. And He said,

*"The small are about to become great in might. No
longer consider yourself as shrimp in my Kingdom... for
you are monster prawns, yes giants in the land - and
you are flavorful prawns - prawns in the hands of a
master chef who is about to serve you up as a new
course for this generation. You are mighty pine trees
planted upon the mountain of the Lord."*

**Tomatoes:** Then I saw the Lord walking in the tomato fields.
As He walked, ripe tomatoes began to fall to the ground, and
the Lord said,

*"This is a new fruit in the land, a new crop that will
penetrate the public places. They are a savory fruit, and
the meat of their calling will stretch across boundaries
and touch the high places - yes even the pinnacles of
power. And they shall release the flavors of Heaven to
those that many say, cannot be reached - But I say,
these have been created, to reach into that place and to
transform that dominion into the dominion of
Heaven."*

**Ancient Seeds:** The tide is turning and the geographical plates
of the planet are shifting and realigning - glory, glory, glory. I
looked and saw the mighty plates of the earth beginning to
move and shift. As they shifted I saw mighty seeds being
exposed, sprout, and grow. They were "Ancient seeds" planted
from the hand of the Ancient of Days, and these seeds are
about to be released into the earth, and the Lord said,

*"My people are about to bring forth a mighty root
system in the earth that will shake the very foundation
of the land. Trees, trees, trees are being shaken - and*

316 • FRED RAYNAUD

*fruit is coming forth. Heritage and inheritance is being released. Fruit from the past is being grafted into the fruit of the present. I am creating super fruit that will produce super food loaded with the nutrients and DNA of Heaven."*

This is a new season. This is a season of change and transformation. Press into his tenderness towards you. Press into the waters of life. Drink from the ocean of his love until your branches are so plump with his heartbeat – that your fruit falls into arms of the nations – ripe and ready for a hungry people.

This is your season. This is the year of fruitfulness... Press on Church and let His love overcome you....

# CHAPTER 21

# The Anointing

*"You shall put the turban on his head, and put
the holy crown on the turban. And you shall
take the anointing oil, pour it on his head, and
anoint him"*

- Exodus 29:6-7

*"Then you shall take the garments, put the
tunic on Aaron, and the robe of the ephod, the
ephod, and the breastplate, and gird him with
the intricately woven band of the ephod. 6 You
shall put the turban on his head, and put the
holy crown on the turban. 7 And you shall take
the anointing oil, pour it on his head, and
anoint him."*

- Exodus 29:5-7

A butterfly landed on my armchair. I was in Florida, and
it was gorgeous outside, so I wasn't surprised, except
that butterflies speak so deeply to my heart. They
speak of destiny and transformation. I had been sitting there
wondering about life and destiny, and there it was, this little

winged angel gazing up at me. I was immediately reminded about a word the Lord shared with me one summer.

For weeks that summer, the Lord had been sending me butterflies. When I asked Him what it meant He said,

> *"Transformation – pollination – impregnation - impartation. I am transforming My children to be a people called out by My name, to be a changed people – people that pulsate with the glory and beauty of My Kingdom. No longer will My children crawl around like caterpillars with their identity rooted in this world. They – have been transformed – renewed in their minds – a people that reflect My very nature – a people that have been transformed from this realm to the Heavenly. They have become butterflies of My reflective glory – they have taken flight, and in their flight they will pollinate the world around them with My kingdom, with My glory, with My love."*

A short while later, while I was at work, preoccupied with something, the Holy Spirit began to sing into my spirit. The volume of the singing was loud and getting louder. As I was walking towards the elevator His presence was increasing and the sound kept coming – then I stepped into the elevator and it became heavier – so much so, it took my breath away. Then the Lord said,

> *"I am taking you higher – Step into My presence – I am accelerating the timetable – I am taking you up higher – enter in – choose the penthouse – the pinnacle of My palace – step in and rest in my Glory."*

When I got home that night, I was sitting on my patio looking at the sun set between some tall pine trees by my house. Suddenly, I saw the Lion of the tribe of Judah – golden and powerful – filling the sky between the trees. He was moving towards me – big, fast, and powerful. As He moved closer, I could feel His presence increase – so much that I was startled and jumped back. I thought I was going to be overwhelmed and fall to the ground. This happened several times... and then it stopped – and my heart cried out – more Lord – I need more of You.

All that the Lord said was,

*"Suddenly, Suddenly, Suddenly,"*

But my heart wanted suddenly right now – and for days and days this hunger lingered – crying out - More of you....

Then that Friday night, a few days later, as I sought the Lord – praying for more, suddenly I saw the throne of God. Brilliant white light was shining from the throne. In front of the throne I saw Angels standing before a massive vat filled with golden oil. They were stirring this vat with very large paddles. Then Jesus stepped off His throne and stood before the vat. He peered into the vat until His reflection permeated the oil and His face covered the surface of the oil like a mirror. Then He bent over and dipped His face into the oil. When He stood back up His entire body was enveloped with golden oil. Then it was as if He was the oil – as if He was golden liquid. He began to shake His hands and massive drops of oil began to fall from the heavens.

I was lying down and saw this massive drop falling towards me – almost in slow motion. Then I heard the Lord say,

> "I AM the anointing – I AM the Christos – I Am all that you need – I have poured out Myself to release My anointing upon you – I AM all you need." Then the drops kept falling and as I look at these incredible golden drops – first the drops looked as if they were falling from an inverted golden crown – from the tips – then they appeared in the shape of keys – golden keys of oil."

And the Lord said,

> "My anointing is the key to unlock My presence with-in you – to unlock your destiny..."

And suddenly, it was as if I was looking into outer space and the heavens were filled with golden keys of oil – everywhere – like stars and planets move through the heavens.

Then the Lord said,

> "Behold the endless possibilities of My presence. Behold the endless possibilities of My presence in you. Today is the day of destiny. Today is the day that I unlock your tomorrows – your tomorrows are today – enter into My glory and know that I am He who holds the keys of David – who holds the keys of life and of death. Unlock the treasure chest within your spirit and release upon this land My Love, My power, My glory – for I AM glorified in you."

Isaiah 61 we read:

*"The Spirit of the Lord GOD is upon Me, because the Lord has anointed Me to preach good tidings to the poor; He has sent Me to heal the brokenhearted, To proclaim liberty to the captives, and the opening of the prison to those who are bound; To proclaim the acceptable year of the Lord, And the day of vengeance of our God; To comfort all who mourn, to console those who mourn in Zion, to give them beauty for ashes, the oil of joy for mourning, the garment of praise for the spirit of heaviness; That they may be called trees of righteousness, The planting of the Lord, that He may be glorified."*

*And they shall rebuild the old ruins, they shall raise up the former desolations, and they shall repair the ruined cities, the desolations of many generations. Strangers shall stand and feed your flocks, and the sons of the foreigner shall be your plowmen and your vinedressers. But you shall be named the priests of the Lord, they shall call you the servants of our God. You shall eat the riches of the Gentiles, and in their glory you shall boast. Instead of your shame you shall have double honor, and instead of confusion they shall rejoice in their portion.*

*Therefore in their land they shall possess double; Everlasting joy shall be theirs. "For I, the Lord, love justice; I hate robbery for burnt offering; I will direct their work in truth, and will make with them an everlasting covenant. Their*

> *descendants shall be known among the Gentiles,*
> *and their offspring among the people. All who see*
> *them shall acknowledge them, that they are the*
> *posterity whom the Lord has blessed." I will*
> *greatly rejoice in the Lord, My soul shall be joyful*
> *in my God; For He has clothed me with the*
> *garments of salvation,*
>
> *He has covered me with the robe of righteousness,*
> *as a bridegroom decks himself with ornaments,*
> *and as a bride adorns herself with her jewels. For*
> *as the earth brings forth its bud, as the garden*
> *causes the things that are sown in it to spring*
> *forth, so the Lord GOD will cause righteousness*
> *and praise to spring forth before all the nations."*

Rise up dear friends and be transformed... mount up on the wings of a butterfly - and slide into your destiny!

CHAPTER 22

# Thick Oil for a Chosen Generation

*"'The glory of this present house will be greater
than the glory of the former house,' says the
Lord Almighty. 'And in this place I will grant
peace,' declares the Lord Almighty."*

- Haggai 2:9

Something inside me is burning. I can't let it go. I yearn for that touch of the Master's hand that will shake the very foundation of my life and the lives of those around me. My heart is pounding in anticipation for Jesus to encounter His church like never before. I long for revival, true revival that is sustained for the long haul, a revival that grows from glory to glory, and does not dissipate through the years. I long for a touch of God on the land that will be greater than anything before it. I burn inside to see this generation leak with the presence of God. I long to see the reflection of Jesus on the face of His bride. I long to hear his heart beat and feel his embrace.

I grew up in the church in the midst of revival. The year was 1979. The Jesus movement was in transition from a beach salvation movement to a power encounter movement. John

Wimber of Vineyard Christian Fellowship had sparked something inside my heart that would forever change me. John had taught me that I could get as close to God as I wanted to, that I could serve Him with a level of intimacy that would overflow with prophecy, healings, signs, and wonders, to a starving broken planet. He taught me that "doing the stuff" was my birthright as a child of God, and that pursuit of His presence was the Kingdom.

Vineyard was birthed from a handful of burnt out pastors to become a major force in equipping the church worldwide to passionately seek the face of Jesus and reach out to the world through power encounters. We truly believed that when we pray, **"thy kingdom come, thy will be done, on Earth as it is in Heaven,"** we meant it, and so did Heaven! We were a church in the midst of revival.

Since the days of Pentecost, great revivals and awakenings have occurred throughout the centuries. But they have always faded away between the generations. Sure they have left their residue and incredible benefit to the body of Christ, but the burning heart nature of what we call revival – that heart pounding desire to seek his face – fades, and so often, in the wake we are left with another denominational spin off, but the heart of what birthed the revival disappears.

People have always asked, **"Why in the space of a couple generations do revivals dissipate?"** They go from a blazing fire of Glory to barely a flicker... then nothing – a puff of smoke – and it's gone. We haven't changed much since the times of Joshua. In Judges 2:7-11 when Joshua became leader, the bible says:

> *"So the people served the Lord all the days of Joshua, and all the days of the elders who outlived Joshua, who had seen all the great works of the Lord which He had done for Israel. Now Joshua the son of Nun, the servant of the Lord, died when he was one hundred and ten years old.*
>
> *And they buried him within the border of his inheritance at Timnath Heres, in the mountains of Ephraim, on the north side of Mount Gaash. When all that generation had been gathered to their fathers, another generation arose after them who did not know the Lord nor the work which He had done for Israel. Then the children of Israel did evil in the sight of the Lord, and served the Baals;"*

To be honest, that is my fear for this generation. The truth is, faith, anointing, ministries, mantles, gifts, and mighty moves of God cannot be transferred from generation to generation without personal power encounters and the desire of a people to burn for and seek after, with all their hearts, the face and presence of Jesus.

The good news, for this generation, is that God is on the move. There is a sense in the air that something big is about to happen. The gap between revivals is getting shorter and shorter. God is agitating our hearts. He is stirring the pot of our souls. He is shaking our very foundations. He so longs for a sustained move of his presence that he is not letting go; He is relentless in His pursuit. Really, He has taken hold of the hem of our garment, and will not let go, until the healing has begun. He is causing a desperation inside many that is truly making us miserable and it will not yield until we see and receive the fullness of what He longs for in this new era.

In my lifetime alone, since that incredible day in January 1979, when Jesus yanked me from the fires of hell and brought me into his presence as a child of the King, we have seen revival hit in pockets around the world. We saw the birth of revival in the Vineyard movement; we saw the flames of fire hit Toronto, Pensacola, Redding, Kansas City, Charlotte, and Mobile. This isn't just a western move. Today, God is beginning to take nations. He is establishing his Army around the world for a global harvest. However, what we are seeing today is just a trickle.

What Jesus desires to do for this generation is far beyond all of the moves of God in history. Jesus is waking the bride of Christ. We are so overdue. The coming move of God will be the sustained move of God. It will be unlike any before it. He is going to do a new thing. He is about to put his imprint on cities, states, regions, and countries, and, he is going to do it through everyday people. There is a personal outpouring that is going to take place that will reach the ends of the earth, and it will come through and be upon "average Joes", as we say in the states, people like you and me.

Repeatedly the Lord keeps showing me this very thing. He has not conceded, and I cannot shake it. Just yesterday, while driving to work, the Lord gave me a vision of the Shekinah Glory of God coming as a cloud. As I looked at the cloud it became a funnel cloud, and I heard the Lord say,

*"I am about to pour out my Shekinah glory on the individual. Like a funnel in the spout of a bottle, I shall pour My presence upon them and in them and they shall see and know My glory like no other generation."*

This personal outpouring will be rich with power and authority, but it will be wrapped up in a people, who, like Moses, have been to the mountain top, and have seen the lover of their souls... face-to-face. The anointing that is about to fall on the bride is thick with His presence, and will come upon all who seek after him and the beauty of His being.

The power and personal nature of this next move of God was reinforced in a dream the Lord had given me recently. In this dream, I saw a faucet in a bathroom like one would see in a typical home. The faucet was turned on, full force, and out poured thick black oil, like petroleum. When I saw it, I knew in my spirit that it was the oil of anointing. When I woke, instantly I saw visions of the earth, and inside the earth, I saw caverns of the deep filled with hot molten oil. They were just under the surface and scattered throughout the earth. As I looked, I saw oil wells sprouting up across the land. I saw layers of black shale just under the surface of the earth and the children of God holding clumps of shale in their hands. As they held the shale, it liquefied and flowed from the palms of their hands.

When I asked the Lord why the oil was black, he said,

*"Just as the blood of Able cried out from the ground for justice, so the residual anointing, life missions, ministries, destinies, and dreams from all of history are, even now, crying out to me. I have reserved, for this*

*generation, an anointing that is so thick it reeks with the history and legacy of My saints. Every lost dream, every shortened life call, every unfulfilled destiny, every mantle from every martyr, every mandate from every missionary, from every child in My house who has gone before you is stored up in me and is ready to be released upon the land.*

*That is why it is thick and black like oil, like petroleum. It is full of energy and power and this generation, more than any before it, knows what it means to be without it and the high cost it takes to obtain it. This anointing is redemption oil, redeeming all the lost anointings of history."*

Then he said,

*"Do you understand?"*

"Yes Lord," I responded. And in that moment I understood the thick blessing and rich heritage of the saints. I understood that this anointing was an answer to the heart cry of the saints in Revelation chapter 6:9-11.

*"When He opened the fifth seal, I saw under the altar the souls of those who had been slain for the Word of God and for the testimony which they held. And they cried with a loud voice, saying, "How long, O Lord, holy and true, until You judge and avenge our blood on those who dwell on the earth?" Then a white robe was given to each of them; and it was said to them that they should rest a little while longer, until both the*

> *number of their fellow servants and their
> brethren, who would be killed as they were, was
> completed."*

I understood that the judgment of God in these last days would begin with the love feast of the bride. It would begin with the fresh release of all the anointings throughout history, reduced and condensed into a mega-blast of his presence. I understood that Jesus would take the surplus from all who came before us and smear us with it, like smearing butter on hot toast.

He is about to give payback to the enemy. He is throwing down the trump card and the power and presence of the past will be more than our floor; they have become seeds - commingled and germinated for a new generation. You are God's secret weapon.

I also understood that we have to press in and remember and honor all that God has done before us. That we have to declare and decree with hearts of fire, that greater is He that is in us, than he that is in the world. God is about to flood the marketplace with saints smeared with his anointing. However, we have to remember how great and awesome our God is and believe His testimony. The bible says that the testimony of Jesus is the spirit of prophecy. All his wonders are available for release in our lives, today!

The word says:

> *"Remember the days of old, consider the years of many
> generations. Ask your father, and he will show you;
> Your elders, and they will tell you:"*

- Deuteronomy 32:7

And again in Joel 2:25…

> *"So I will restore to you the years that the*
> *swarming locust has eaten, the crawling locust,*
> *the consuming locust, and the chewing locust, My*
> *great army which I sent among you."*

Paul understood the heritage of the saints when he counseled
Timothy in 2 Timothy, chapter 1:5-7:

> *"When I call to remembrance the genuine faith*
> *that is in you, which dwelt first in your*
> *grandmother Lois and your mother Eunice, and I*
> *am persuaded is in you also. Therefore I remind*
> *you to stir up the gift of God which is in you*
> *through the laying on of my hands. For God has*
> *not given us a spirit of fear, but of power and of*
> *love and of a sound mind."*

And in Colossians he says:

> *"For this reason, since the day we heard about you, we*
> *have not stopped praying for you. We continually ask*
> *God to fill you with the knowledge of His will through*
> *all the wisdom and understanding that the Spirit gives,*
> *so that you may live a life worthy of the Lord and*
> *please Him in every way: bearing fruit in every good*
> *work, growing in the knowledge of God, being*
> *strengthened with all power according to his glorious*
> *might so that you may have great endurance and*
> *patience, and giving joyful thanks to the Father, who*
> *has qualified you to share in the inheritance of His holy*
> *people in the kingdom of light. For He has rescued us*

*from the dominion of darkness and brought us into the kingdom of the Son He loves, in whom we have redemption, the forgiveness of sins."*

- Colossians 1:9-14

Even the writer of Hebrews in chapter 11, understood the power of this rich thick anointing when he points us to the great cloud of witnesses.

*"All these people were still living by faith when they died. They did not receive the things promised; they only saw them and welcomed them from a distance, admitting that they were foreigners and strangers on earth."*

- Hebrews 11:13

He continues in verse 32:

*"And what more shall I say? I do not have time to tell about Gideon, Barak, Samson and Jephthah, about David and Samuel and the prophets, who through faith conquered kingdoms, administered justice, and gained what was promised; who shut the mouths of lions, quenched the fury of the flames, and escaped the edge of the sword; whose weakness was turned to strength; and who became powerful in battle and routed foreign armies. Women received back their dead, raised to life again. There were others who were tortured, refusing to be released so that they might gain an even better resurrection. Some*

> *faced jeers and flogging, and even chains and imprisonment. They were put to death by stoning; they were sawed in two; they were killed by the sword. They went about in sheepskins and goatskins, destitute, persecuted and mistreated— the world was not worthy of them. They wandered in deserts and mountains, living in caves and in holes in the ground. These were all commended for their faith, yet none of them received what had been promised,"*

And get this…

> *"...since God had planned something better for us so that only together with us would they be made perfect."*

- Hebrews 11:32-40

So His heart cry to us is this… in Chapter 12:1…

> *"Therefore, since we are surrounded by such a great cloud of witnesses, let us throw off everything that hinders and the sin that so easily entangles. And let us run with perseverance the race marked out for us,"*

You see…

> *"By faith Abel brought God a better offering than Cain did. By faith he was commended as righteous, when God spoke well of his offerings. And by faith Abel still speaks, even though he is dead."*

- Hebrews 11:4

But in Hebrews 12:22-24 he says…

> *"But you have come to Mount Zion, to the city of the*
> *living God, the heavenly Jerusalem. You have come to*
> *thousands upon thousands of angels in joyful assembly,*
> *to the church of the firstborn, whose names are written*
> *in heaven. You have come to God, the Judge of all, to*
> *the spirits of the righteous made perfect, to Jesus the*
> *mediator of a new covenant, and to the sprinkled blood*
> *that speaks a better word than the blood of Abel."*

- Hebrews 12:22-24

The blood of Jesus is speaking today. The blood of all the saints is speaking today. It is Christ's joy to anoint each of you, and your household with his payback plan.

When I was worshiping at church after the Lord had given me the dream of the faucet being turned on, I saw Jesus, in a bedroom with a pillow in his hand. He was having a pillow fight. The room was filled with joy as he swung the pillows around. The pillows were so stuffed full that as he swung they burst open and feathers were flying around everywhere. The room was so full of feathers that all you could see was a cloud of soft white feathers.

When I was praying about this I understood that trapped inside the pillow were dreams, dreams that that the Lord had placed in the hearts of his children, dreams of destiny and purpose, and the Lord's desire to bring breakthrough and release to long forgotten dreams.

As I was praying for a release of destiny in the lives of people in the church I saw the Holy Spirit fly in like a dove. His wings were dipped in the dark oil. As he flew over, a single oil dipped feather began to float down. As it approached, it became a quill pen. I then saw the pen begin to write. It was writing a signature – like a John Hancock, if you will.

I understood that the Holy Spirit was writing the dreams of promise, identity, and purpose on the hearts of his people. That He was engraving His purpose in their lives and signing His very name to it - like a decree. Like the signature on a check, you can take this check and deposit it, for it is decreed in heaven and engraved upon your hearts.

> *"Whoever has ears, let them hear what the Spirit says*
> *to the churches. To the one who is victorious, I will give*
> *some of the hidden manna. I will also give that person*
> *a white stone with a new name written on it, known*
> *only to the one who receives it."*

- Revelations 2:17

The Lord wants to tar-and-feather us, and send us out of the church building and into the streets. He is so concerned with our destiny, and the impact that this generation will have on the world, that He has not, and will not relent until his bride looks like Him. He is redeeming the time. You are a chosen generation. Do not underestimate the impact that you, as an individual, will have on this planet.

The last picture the Lord showed me regarding this anointing I saw an ocean size pool of this oil cover the whole earth. Then one drop fell from Heaven into the ocean of anointing causing ripples to flood the planet. Don't underestimate the impact of one drop upon your life can make. In the physics of God, drops become oceans.

Let us cry out and be smeared, tarred, and feathered!

> "The Redeemer will come to Zion, to those in Jacob who repent of their sins," declares the Lord.' As for me, this is My covenant with them," says the Lord. 'My Spirit, who is on you, will not depart from you, and My words that I have put in your mouth will always be on your lips, on the lips of your children and on the lips of their descendants—from this time on and forever,' says the Lord."

> - Isaiah 59:20-21

Reread Joel Chapter 2 for a snapshot of your destiny!

# CHAPTER 23

# Drink, My Bride

*"You, God, are my God, earnestly I seek you; I thirst for You, my whole being longs for You, in a dry and parched land where there is no water. I have seen You in the sanctuary and beheld Your power and your glory. Because Your love is better than life, my lips will glorify You. I will praise You as long as I live, and in Your name I will lift up my hands."*

- Psalms 63:1-4

*"I'm simply done with life. 57, not terminal or depressed. I was going to use the plastic bag, but too many failed attempt stories. I live in an apartment bldg, in California USA & if someone hears me moaning inside the bag & calls the police, it's BAD news for me. I've tried dehydration 4 times & have always failed & had water. ... I'm on another attempt at dehydration. Something always came up to deter my plan. It's going much better this time.*

*After 3 days of no food, I have no more hunger. Having no liquids is a lot tougher, but I've built up my courage & determination. I'm more willing to suffer dry-mouth, & I won't "cheat" by eating frozen grapes (they contain enough liquid to delay death). I've lost 50 pounds so there's not much for my body to live on itself. Some people might find this an agonizing way to die. It suits me. ... I'm very much at peace. I've made amends to all my friends & family. I've been an Atheist, but talked w/ several religious people about death. I believe I'll go to a nice place, & I'll recognize those I knew in some way. The dry-mouth is the hardest part of this method. At times it's really hard to swallow. So I go to sleep for a while. ..."*

*– From the Suicide Project -*
*http://suicideproject.org*

When I first read those words, it broke my heart. I found myself praying for her, asking God to give her living water, to show up and pour out his Spirit and open her eyes to the beauty of life in Christ. I'm sorry; I don't know the outcome of the writer. I pray she is still alive. She posted her journey on the Suicide Project website. That is all she wrote, two paragraphs of death, despair, and defeat. I pray someone at Suicide Project found a way to reach her - so very sad.

I found this story by accident. I was searching for stories about dehydration. When I was first diagnosed with diabetes I was in a state of dehydration. The sugar level in my body was killing me. I was constantly thirsty due to frequent urination. My mouth was dry. I experienced nausea, cramping, fatigue, confusion, sleepiness, and blurred vision. However, unlike the person above, I wasn't trying to kill myself. When my wife finely took me to the doctor's office, my blood sugar was 530. Thank God we caught it before I went into a coma. It's been five years, and I have had to make many life style changes – but all is good.

What really troubles me about the story above is that it does not have to be that way. We, the body of Christ, have the answer that this lady is searching for. We carry in us Kingdom life. Why did she want to die? Why wasn't someone there to give her hope? Where were the anointed ones? Sometimes I feel that we, the church, are a bit dehydrated and its hard to offer someone else water when you, yourself, are running on empty. I think we have gotten so used to running on empty that we don't realize we're drying out. Are we truly equipped to make a difference? Have we reached our full potential in Christ?

Unlike dehydration in the natural, spiritual dehydration may be harder to detect. In the natural, our bodies tell us we need water and instantly we move to fulfill that need. In the spirit realm, it's not as easy.

Signs like sexual immorality, impurity, and witchcraft, are obvious. It's the subtle signs of spiritual dehydration like complacency, jealously, fear, anger, selfish ambition, dissension, and discord that we often miss. Worse, we blame it on "quirks" in our personality or cultural upbringing. I think the number one sign so often missed is the lack of true thirst, that heart aching hunger for intimacy with Jesus. This one is so easily brushed off. If we aren't in "blatant sin" and are living a pretty good and decent life, then all is good, right? Not quite.

Many unsaved folks live good and decent lives. I believe the real test is our love meter with Jesus. A love meter measures your intimacy, hunger, and relationship with Christ. How hungry are we for him? Without an intimate relationship with Jesus, one that is constantly thirsting for more, we become like the old story of the frog in the water. If you throw a frog into boiling water, he will instinctively jump out to save its life. If, on the other hand, you drop him in ambient water (consider the lukewarm nature of the church of Laodicea in Revelation 3:14-22), then slowly turn up the heat; the frog will swim around until it boils to death.

You see a life that isn't constantly being filled with the love of God through relationship and intimacy will loose their ability to discern the true state of their condition, and find themselves floating in a sea of loneliness and spiritual isolation. And like that frog, in the end, if not caught in time, they will boil to death. For the Christian, a love relationship with Jesus is the life-line. In the book of Revelation, to the church at Ephesus, one of the greatest churches of the New Testament era, Jesus said this:

> *"I know your works, your labor, your patience, and*
> *that you cannot bear those who are evil. And you have*
> *tested those who say they are apostles and are not, and*

*have found them liars; and you have persevered and
have patience, and have labored for My name's sake
and have not become weary. Nevertheless I have this
against you, that you have left your first love.
Remember therefore from where you have fallen; repent
and do the first works, or else I will come to you quickly
and remove your lampstand from its place—unless you
repent."*

- Revelation 2:2-5

We know the truth of this in the natural. Ask anyone who is married, what their relationship would be like if their spouse was not madly in love with them, if they were complacent and took their mate for granted, if they never showed affection, or never showered them with love and attention. They would tell you the marriage is doomed, it's on the rocks. Sadly, it will end either in divorce or in the prison of unloving routine, two people trapped and separated by the invisible wall of hurt, hate, pride, and self-will.

Let me ask you a question: *Are you personally, at this time in your life, at a deep and agonizing level, hungry for more of the Lord? Are you so thirsty for him that, like the heartbeat of the of the bride in the Song of Solomon, if you can't find him, you're incomplete? Does your thirst cause you to and groan for Him? Do you dig and search for him, like a thirsty soul digging for water in a desert, not stopping until he finds water?*

You see Jesus is looking for a bride that truly craves him, one that is so in love with him she will do anything, just to be in his presence. The good news is we don't have to stay in that dry

place. We don't have to live that way. But we do have to repent.
We do have to change the way we think about Jesus. We have
to change the way we approach Him. Jesus is so eager to
embrace us and fill us with his presence. He is in fact,
chomping at the bit to do so. He is standing at the door, ready
to fill us again, and again, and again. And that filling is pure
bliss. So much so, that Peter, in the book of Acts responded to
the crowed like this....

> *"When the day of Pentecost came, they were all
> together in one place. Suddenly a sound like the
> blowing of a violent wind came from heaven and filled
> the whole house where they were sitting. They saw what
> seemed to be tongues of fire that separated and came to
> rest on each of them. All of them were filled with the
> Holy Spirit and began to speak in other tongues as the
> Spirit enabled them. Amazed and perplexed, they asked
> one another, what does this mean? Some, however,
> made fun of them and said, they have had too much
> wine. Then Peter stood up with the Eleven, raised his
> voice and addressed the crowd: Fellow Jews and all of
> you who live in Jerusalem, let me explain this to you;
> listen carefully to what I say. These people are not
> drunk, as you suppose. It's only nine in the morning!"*

- Acts 2:1-4, 12-14

These folks were so filled with new heavenly wine they
appeared to be drunk! Living water changes us. Being filled
with the presence of Jesus rocks our world. We become
undone. The good news is, when we drink and are full, we
thirst even more.... The Kingdom works that way. No, wonder

the first miracle recorded in the book of John was the wedding feast at Cana, where he turned water into wine to reveal his glory.

In the summer of 2010, I saw a vision of Jesus. He was leaning against an ancient well, like Jacob's well, with a cup in his hand. He looked at me, with a smile on his face, and said:

> *"Drink! – Come!*
>
> *All who are thirsty come to the living waters and drink... drink until your cup is overflowing.*
>
> *Drink until you are so full it flows into the streets. Drink until the land is saturated with my presence. Drink, My bride.*
>
> *Drink that I might shower you with My love.*
>
> *Drink that I might fill you with My presence, and endow you with My power and My passion.*
>
> *Drink My bride to overflowing and My glory shall rest upon you."*

I looked around and saw some folks really craving for more of Jesus, but others were not. It could have been fear or just uneasiness, but at the end of the day, the presence of Jesus was there to fill His children. I think that is the key, "being children, being childlike." Jesus wants us to come to him like a child. When we abandon all, and just want to seek his face like a child – the windows of heaven open up and the rain begins to fall – the floodwaters start to raise and the wonder and beauty of the lover of our souls, rushes in. You see children know how to dream. They aren't shackled by duty. They aren't preoccupied to fill a series of repetitive tasks and projects. They just want to play with their Poppa. They just want to soak in the waters of life. They just want to be held by Daddy.

Sometimes folks feel the Lord's presence or listen to a word from the Lord and it really resonates in their hearts, but that resonation soon dissipates, and is replaced with another activity. That encounter moment is taken away, they have robbed themselves of the true purpose of resonation: to draw them in and closer to Jesus; to be filled with the healing work of His hand; to be immersed into the living water – and be changed. Instead of allowing time to baste in the moment through worship, or quietness, or meditation, or simply waiting, they rush off to the next task and that Holy Spirit moment of filling, passes them by. They miss the rich blessing that only comes through marination and patiently waiting on the gentile grace-fullness of Holy Spirit. The modern demands of our cultural and the rigidness of tight schedules can kill off the move of God as much as anything else.

Yet, Jesus still needs to go to Samaria. He still stands at Jacob's well looking for someone to take the drink from His hand. Jesus told the woman at the well in the fourth chapter of John:

> *"If you knew the gift of God and who it is that asks you for a drink, you would have asked him and he would have given you living water."* ... *"Everyone who drinks this water will be thirsty again, but whoever drinks the water I give them will never thirst. Indeed, the water I give them will become in them a spring of water welling up to eternal life."*

- John 4:10, 13-14

And in John chapter 7 in desperation, he cried out...

*"On the last and greatest day of the festival, Jesus stood
and said in a loud voice, "Let anyone who is thirsty
come to me and drink."*

- John 7:37

This burning desire to drink and be filled with the presence
Jesus is unstoppable. Everywhere I turn the Lord keeps saying
the same thing. I can't shake it. Then (summer of 2012), I saw
the following:

In the vision, I saw myself standing backstage, as it were. I was
peering at the side of the stage looking at a soft cream-white
curtain. I approached the curtain and reached out to touch it.
As I touched it, I was struck by its softness. I looked up to see
how high the curtain went and saw the curtain shoot straight
up into the heavens. As I was peering into the heavens, I
realized it wasn't a curtain at all... it was the robe of Jesus. I was
holding the hem of his garment. I was overcome with the Holy
Spirit, and I heard the voice of Isaiah:

*"In the year that King Uzziah died, I saw the Lord, high
and exalted, seated on a throne; and the train of his
robe filled the temple..."*

- Isaiah 6:1

And like Isaiah, I was undone. Then I heard the Lord say,

*"The stage has been set. The time has arrived. My Spirit yearns to fill My temple, and I shall fill My temple, until the whole earth is filled with My Glory. Don't you know that you are the temple of the Holy Spirit? Open up your hearts and let me in..., open up your hearts and let me in. Open the doors of your hearts and let ME IN."*

And I cried out in my spirit – **have your way God, have your way!!!!** Fill us God fill us to overflowing. And I looked around again and knew the Spirit of the living God was there to fill his bride to overflowing.... I wanted to shout it out – wake up oh bride – be filled with His glory, be filled with His fullness, be filled and see the glory of the Lord! But the time wasn't right, so I sat there, filled, yet sad inside. The heart cry of Jesus hovered over that place like the Shekinah glory, but the bride was still sleeping.

Moments later the Lord showed me the oceans of the world and farmers were plowing on the surface of the ocean. They were in rows, all plowing in unison. As I watched the farmers were transformed into people riding wave-runners riding the wake of His presence.

Instantly I understood the riders were His Last Days messengers, preparing the way for His coming, preparing for the next great wave of His presence. They were the sent-out-ones. They were the voices of those shouting in the wilderness, "prepare ye the way of the Lord." They were the forerunners on wave-runners, riding the wave of his Glory, a wave so big, like a tsunami, it will flood the land.

You see the Lord's cry is no different than what He spoke to the prophet Malachi…

> *"I will send my messenger, who will prepare the way before me. Then suddenly the Lord you are seeking will come to his temple; the messenger of the covenant, whom you desire, will come," says the Lord Almighty. But who can endure the day of his coming? Who can stand when He appears? For He will be like a refiner's fire or a launderer's soap."*

> - Malachi 3:1-2

The Lord is getting us ready, but this season requires a bride whose lamps are full and lit and whose cups are overflowing. While I was praying about this I saw the Lord standing in Heaven. His head was bent down towards the earth. His mouth opened and water came gushing out like a waterfall. I looked at the waterfall and saw salmon swimming upstream, towards Jesus. I heard the Holy Spirit say, "Swim to me my children, swim and spawn a new generation, spawn life." And I knew that Jesus was birthing something that has generational impact, and this move will reach generations to come (Psalms 36:9).

> *"For with you is the fountain of life; in your light we see light."*

Jesus is calling us into a new level of oneness that will have everlasting impact.…

> *"My prayer is not for them alone. I pray also for those who will believe in me through their message, that all of*

*them may be one, Father, just as you are in me and I
am in you. May they also be in us so that the world
may believe that you have sent me. I have given them
the glory that you gave me, that they may be one as we
are one — I in them and you in me—so that they may
be brought to complete unity."*

- John 17:20-23

*"For I will pour water on the thirsty land, and streams
on the dry ground; I will pour out my Spirit on your
offspring, and my blessing on your descendants. They
will spring up like grass in a meadow, like poplar trees
by flowing streams."*

- Isaiah 44:3-4

After this the Lord showed me trees weeping golden sap, and I
knew that all,

*"...Creation waits in eager expectation for the children
of God to be revealed. ... We know that the whole
creation has been groaning as in the pains of childbirth
right up to the present time."*

- Romans 8:19, 22

Then I saw the wooden floors of an old shack. I looked at the
floor with all its grain exposed, and saw that even the floors
were weeping. Then I saw the walls of the shack, and I saw the
grain in the wood, and I knew that the grain was revealing
years of brokenness. It was revealing a people bound by a
structure of pain and fear.

Then I saw Jesus peering through a knothole in the wall. Outside was the wondrous beauty of his presence. It lit up the sky. I knew that the Lord had come to bring healing and restoration. I knew that the Lord was releasing healing and restoration to His church. I knew that he was breaking the walls that bound and shaking the wooden foundation that is stopping His children from obtaining their potential. I understood that He was peering inside our hearts and asking us to open up to Him and trade the shack of shackles for a mansion on a hill.

Then I saw Jesus walking quietly on a green hill, dressed in a simple cream-white robe, like a monk would wear, only cream-white, no gold, it was common, and simple. He removed His hood revealing His crown; it too was soft and simple, almost understated like a whisper. It had the words faithful and true inscribed on it. Large red rubies were studded between the words and around the crown.

As I was looking, I felt that the Lord was coming in quietness, almost like He was coming in secret. And the Lord brought this scripture to my mind:

> *"You go to the festival. I am not going up to this festival, because my time has not yet fully come." After he had said this, he stayed in Galilee. However, after his brothers had left for the festival, he went also, not publicly, but in secret."*
>
> - John 7:8-10

I knew that this season was also a season of the quietness of Christ. Jesus is coming to us quietly and in secret. He will whisper in our ears, and He will share with us His secret things. This is the place of being still before Him. He will show up when we least expect it. He will enter situations that we think He has no interest in. He, himself will spy out the land. He, himself, will ride the wind like a whisper and invade our hearts in a new intimate way. He will show us a side of His nature that we have never seen before. We will look upon Him, and see a completely new revelation of His presence. Know this:

> *"The secret things belong to the Lord our God, but the things revealed belong to us and to our children forever, that we may follow all the words of this law."*

- Deuteronomy 29:29

And

> *"I will give you hidden treasures, riches stored in secret places, so that you may know that I am the Lord, the God of Israel, who summons you by name."*

- Isaiah 45:3

This experience will be like that of John in the book of Revelation. John was the beloved. John was the youngest of the disciples; he had walked with Jesus for three years. He was there when Jesus was transfigured. He had his head on the breast of Jesus at the last supper. He stayed by him at the foot of the cross, and raced Peter to the tomb on that Easter morning. He was there at Pentecost, and served Him for nearly 70 years, as a church father, until his exile on the isle of Patmos.

Yet, as a man who knew Jesus so well, who walked with him so long, he was about to encounter Jesus like he never did before. Check it out…

> *"I, John, your brother and companion in the suffering and kingdom and patient endurance that are ours in Jesus, was on the island of Patmos because of the word of God and the testimony of Jesus. On the Lord's Day I was in the Spirit, and I heard behind me a loud voice like a trumpet, which said: "Write on a scroll what you see and send it to the seven churches: to Ephesus, Smyrna, Pergamum, Thyatira, Sardis, Philadelphia and Laodicea."*
>
> *I turned around to see the voice that was speaking to me. And when I turned I saw seven golden lampstands, and among the lampstands was someone like a son of man, dressed in a robe reaching down to his feet and with a golden sash around his chest. The hair on his head was white like wool, as white as snow, and his eyes were like blazing fire. His feet were like bronze glowing in a furnace, and his voice was like the sound of rushing waters. In his right hand he held seven stars, and coming out of his mouth was a sharp, double-edged sword. His face was like the sun shining in all its brilliance.*
>
> *When I saw him, I fell at his feet as though dead. Then He placed his right hand on me and said: "Do not be afraid. I am the First and the Last. I am the Living One; I was dead, and now look, I am alive forever and ever! And I hold the keys of death and Hades. "Write,*

*therefore, what you have seen, what is now and what will take place later."*

- Revelation 1:9-19

We are moving towards a new encounter with Christ. We shall see Him like we've never seen him before, Get ready church.

After this I saw cream-white sheets hanging on a clothesline and the wind was blowing them dry.... Spring aroma filled the air... and then I saw the face of a bride behind a cream-white veil... She was getting ready to step out from behind the veil.

I understood the Lord was drying out our garments, getting them ready to wear – His bride is at the door and in His heart, He is crying out…

*"Gather the people, consecrate the assembly; bring together the elders, gather the children, those nursing at the breast. Let the bridegroom leave His room and the bride her chamber."*

- Joel 2:16

*"Let us rejoice and be glad and give him glory! For the wedding of the Lamb has come, and his bride has made herself ready."*

- Revelation 19:7

And we shall join Him in His cry…

*"The Spirit and the bride say, "Come!" And let the one who hears say, "Come!" Let the one who is thirsty come;*

*and let the one who wishes take the free gift of the water of life."*

- Revelation 22:17

And He will rejoice over us…

*"For Zion's sake I will not keep silent, for Jerusalem's sake I will not remain quiet, till her vindication shines out like the dawn, her salvation like a blazing torch. The nations will see your vindication, and all kings your glory; you will be called by a new name that the mouth of the Lord will bestow.*

*You will be a crown of splendor in the Lord 's hand, a royal diadem in the hand of your God. No longer will they call you Deserted, or name your land Desolate. But you will be called Hephzibah, and your land Beulah; for the Lord will take delight in you, and your land will be married. As a young man marries a young woman, so will your Builder marry you; as a bridegroom rejoices over his bride, so will your God rejoice over you."*

- Isaiah 62:1-5

Be filled dear children. Drink until you're full and overflowing. Let him whisper in your ear. Let him heal the brokenness in your heart. Let him rebuild the foundations of your life. Let him drape you with clean cream-white garments and give you the season of the bride. So you can fulfill "who" you are in Christ. It's your destiny.

# Chapter 24

# Verily, Verily

*"And he saith unto him, Verily, verily, I say
unto you, Hereafter ye shall see heaven open,
and the angels of God ascending and descending
upon the Son of man."*

- John 1:51, KJV

I find it fascinating, every time I read these two little words from Jesus, "verily, verily." This duet appears 25 times in the New Testament and only in the book of John, and only spoken by Jesus. You lose the impact of this combination in the newer translations such as the NIV, where they use the words "Very truly," or "Most assuredly" in the NKJV. The Greek here is actually the word "amēn." Its origin is Hebrew. It is often translated trustworthy, surely, so be it, amen, truly, and verily. According to Strong's, it has been called the best-known word in human speech. The word is directly related - in fact, almost identical - to the Hebrew word for "believe" (amam), or faithful, and it carries the notion of being "firm." Thus, it came to mean "sure" or "truly," an expression of absolute trust and confidence.

What strikes me is when the word is spoken twice, as a lead-in to a statement or proclamation. In scripture, Jesus is the only one to use that pairing. Listen to some of the statements Jesus proclaimed with this pairing:

*"Jesus answered and said unto him, Verily, verily, I say unto thee, Except a man be born again, he cannot see the kingdom of God."*

- John 3:3, KJV

*"Then answered Jesus and said unto them, Verily, verily, I say unto you, The Son can do nothing of himself, but what he seeth the Father do: for what things so ever he doeth, these also doeth the Son likewise."*

- John 5:19, KJV

*"Verily, verily, I say unto you, He that heareth my word, and believeth on him that sent me, hath everlasting life, and shall not come into condemnation; but is passed from death unto life."*

- John 5:24, KJV

*"Verily, verily, I say unto you, The hour is coming, and now is, when the dead shall hear the voice of the Son of God: and they that hear shall live."*

- John 5:25, KJV

*"Jesus answered them and said, Verily, verily, I say unto you, Ye seek me, not because ye saw the miracles, but because ye did eat of the loaves, and were filled."*

*"Jesus said unto them, Verily, verily, I say unto you,
Before Abraham was, I am."*

- John 8:58, KJV

*"Verily, verily, I say unto you, He that believeth on me,
the works that I do shall he do also; and greater works
than these shall he do; because I go unto my Father."*

- John 14:12, KJV

Each of those statements, are powerful, foundational,
statements of our faith. They breathe of the eternal manifest
presence of Jesus and His kingdom! In ancient Hebrew, if I was
going to describe to you, say, a "hole" in the road, if its size was
average, I would say, "hole," however, if it was a large hole, I
would say, "hole, hole". If it was a massive crater, I would say,
"hole, hole, hole." The importance of this is the weight Jesus
puts in what he is about say, "Verily, verily, I say unto you...."
In other words, He is saying,

> *"listen up, what I am about to tell you is extremely
> important and it is critical that you believe it."*

This truth is magnified even more when we read in the book of
Revelation the following:

> *"And the four beasts had each of them six wings about
> him; and they were full of eyes within: and they rest not
> day and night, saying, Holy, holy, holy, Lord God
> Almighty, which was, and is, and is to come."*

- Revelation 4:8

You cannot help but notice the repetition of the word "Holy." Here the bigness of God's Holiness is magnified by the unending proclamation of the living creatures surrounding His throne. The very thought of that makes you want to lie prostrate and simply worship and soak in His presence.

This thought hit home with me recently when I was reflecting on all that God had been speaking into my spirit recently. There has almost been a speed, a sense of urgency to what He has been saying. Generally, God has always driven me to the same three core messages when He speaks – pointing believers to their destiny - pointing believers to Heaven and driving them into His presence – and pointing out the hour in which we live and the call to the Bride of Christ.

These three themes have been a general message of my life. I think they are hard-wired into my system, who I am as a Christian and a prophet. However, in this current season there is a real sense of urgency. In the fall of 2011 the Lord gave me a word to the church, the Lord emphasized the powerful anointing that has been set aside for this generation in this place and time. He has also emphasized the place of the Bride in this hour, and the need for her to press in, and be filled with His presence. It has been a call to get equipped, if you will, for the task that is in front of her. Both messages are consistent with my life theme. What was different is the speed and repetition that the messages were coming; I mean daily, several times during the day.

Let me illustrate this with just a few of the words the Lord has spoken to my heart.

A short time after the above incident, while driving to church I saw a vision of intense rain. The rain was so forceful it was horizontal. I was soaking wet, running into the rain. I had an incredible sense of joy as I forced myself forward into the rain. I knew in my spirit that this was the latter rain of God that He was coming like a storm upon us. I also knew that this rain was a driving rain pushing us forward into our destiny, but more so, into His presence. The words of Hosea and Joel filled my mind.

> "Then shall we know, if we follow on to know the Lord: his going forth is prepared as the morning; and he shall come unto us as the rain, as the latter and former rain unto the earth."

> - Hosea 6:3

> "Be glad then, ye children of Zion, and rejoice in the Lord your God: for he hath given you the former rain moderately, and he will cause to come down for you the rain, the former rain, and the latter rain in the first month. And the floors shall be full of wheat, and the vats shall overflow with wine and oil. And I will restore to you the years that the locust hath eaten, the cankerworm, and the caterpiller, and the palmerworm, my great army which I sent among you."

> - Joel 2:23-25

Joel actually summed up what the Lord had been speaking to my heart. Not only was His presence coming in intensity but the outflow of that move would be a global harvest (the wheat) bringing about the filling of His children (vats of wine) and the anointing (vats of oil) from His presence. I saw the tables turned on the enemy and a restoration of all things to King Jesus, brought about by His great and mighty army. When I was reflecting on this, I heard the Lord say,

> *"Proclaim this to My children. Blow a trumpet in Zion, sound an alarm on My Holy Mountain. I am coming like the rain, and every eye shall see Me, and the wetness of My presence shall saturate everything in My path."*

A short time later, I looked up and saw, what looked like the sky dissolving. It was like those old movie film clips, where, at the end of the movie, the heat from the projector bulb burns the filmstrip and you watch as the film dissolves in front of your eyes. I instantly understood that what I was seeing was the kingdoms of this world dissolving and making way for the Kingdom of Heaven to fill all. Then I remembered the words of Peter:

> *"But the day of the Lord will come as a thief in the night; in the which the heavens shall pass away with a great noise, and the elements shall melt with fervent heat, the earth also and the works that are therein shall be burned up. Seeing then that all these things shall be dissolved, what manner of persons ought ye to be in all holy conversation and godliness, Looking for and hasting unto the coming of the day of God, wherein the heavens being on fire shall be dissolved, and the elements shall melt with fervent heat? Nevertheless we, according to his promise, look for new heavens and a new earth, wherein dwelleth righteousness.*

*Wherefore, beloved, seeing that ye look for such things,*
*be diligent that ye may be found of him in peace,*
*without spot, and blameless."*

- 2 Peter 3:10-14

This was a message of seriousness. A wake-up call, if you will, to be mindful and diligent during the hour in which we live. It was reminiscent of the words of Isaiah and John:

*"All the stars in the sky will be dissolved and the*
*heavens rolled up like a scroll; all the starry host will*
*fall like withered leaves from the vine, like shriveled figs*
*from the fig tree."*

- Isaiah 34:4

*"I watched as he opened the sixth seal. There was a*
*great earthquake. The sun turned black like sackcloth*
*made of goat hair, the whole moon turned blood red,*
*and the stars in the sky fell to earth, as figs drop from a*
*fig tree when shaken by a strong wind. The heavens*
*receded like a scroll being rolled up, and every*
*mountain and island was removed from its place."*

- Revelation 6:12-14

Then a short time later, I saw Jesus. I could only see His feet up to His calves. He was wearing old worn-out work jeans like overalls. He had on construction-style work boots that were worn and dusty. He was walking between the rows of crops on a farm, examining the harvest. Then the words of Jesus filled my mind:

*"The harvest truly is plentiful, but the laborers are few. Therefore pray the Lord of the harvest to send out laborers into His harvest....' Let both grow together until the harvest, and at the time of harvest I will say to the reapers, 'First gather together the tares and bind them in bundles to burn them, but gather the wheat into my barn'"*

- Matthew 9:37-38, 13:30

Then I heard the Lord say,

*"See how fat the kernels of wheat are? See, even now they are bursting at the seams. I have walked the fields of harvest. I have seen the seeds of My labor. Look, the time is ready, even at hand, for the Son of Man to reap the wages of His sacrifice. The Harvest is ready; the kernels are ripe for the threshing floor. Come my children; let us gather together the harvest of My labor."*

Can you sense the urgency of the message? It is a call to press in and co-labor with our Lord and Savior, for the harvest is ripe and ready to reap.

Then, a short time later, I saw a revolutionary patriot digging in the dirt. I thought he was digging for water, so I asked the Lord what he was doing. He said,

*"He is not digging for water, he is barring treasure for a future generation. You are that generation. It is the inheritance of this generation sowed into the soil of this land. Release the treasure, that this country may seek*

*me again, and I will pour out a blessing on them that*
*will flood the whole earth."*

And I knew that the revival that birthed the founding of this nation would come again, like the rain, and renew the land for a great and mighty harvest.

Then, as I was reflecting on all that the Lord had spoken He showed me the following:

I saw the horizon just after dusk. On the horizon were twelve massive candles burning. I asked the Lord what they were. He said,

> *"These are the guardians of transition. The governments of this world shall be relinquished and the Government of My Kingdom shall fill the earth even as the oceans of this world cover the surface of the deep. For the heavens shall roll up like a scroll and every mountain shall flee, and everything that exalts itself against Me shall be humbled. Nothing shall stand against the tsunami of my presence. I am coming, and My watchmen and guardians are standing by, ready, and brightly lit."*

The power of this vision was breathtaking. The bigness of the word echoed deep in my soul. I could hear the thunder of His footsteps. I could feel the atmosphere of the planet changing. I knew that we were entering into a new season, a season unlike any other. I understood that the candles were the church. I was reminded of the words of John in Revelation 1:12-15,

> *"Then I turned to see the voice that spoke with me. And having turned I saw seven golden lampstands, and in the midst of the seven lampstands One like the Son of Man, clothed with a garment down to the feet and girded about the chest with a golden band. His head and hair were white like wool, as white as snow, and His eyes like a flame of fire; His feet were like fine brass, as if refined in a furnace, and His voice as the sound of many waters"*

But, then it hit me, yes it was the church, but in the context of this vision it was the church dressed in Bridal attire and she was fully engaged in what the Groom was about to do. Listen to the words of John in Revelation 21:9-27.

> *"Then one of the seven angels who had the seven bowls filled with the seven last plagues came to me and talked with me, saying, "Come, I will show you the bride, the Lamb's wife." And he carried me away in the Spirit to a great and high mountain, and showed me the great city, the holy Jerusalem, descending out of heaven from God, having the glory of God. Her light was like a most precious stone, like a jasper stone, clear as crystal. Also she had a great and high wall with twelve gates, and twelve angels at the gates, and names written on them, which are the names of the twelve tribes of the children of Israel: three gates on the east, three gates on the north, three gates on the south, and three gates on the west.*

Now the wall of the city had twelve foundations, and on them were the names of the twelve apostles of the Lamb. And he who talked with me had a gold reed to measure the city, its gates, and its wall. The city is laid out as a square; its length is as great as its breadth. And he measured the city with the reed: twelve thousand furlongs. Its length, breadth, and height are equal. Then he measured its wall: one hundred and forty-four cubits, according to the measure of a man, that is, of an angel.

The construction of its wall was of jasper; and the city was pure gold, like clear glass. The foundations of the wall of the city were adorned with all kinds of precious stones: the first foundation was jasper, the second sapphire, the third chalcedony, the fourth emerald, the fifth sardonyx, the sixth sardius, the seventh chrysolite, the eighth beryl, the ninth topaz, the tenth chrysoprase, the eleventh jacinth, and the twelfth amethyst. The twelve gates were twelve pearls: each individual gate was of one pearl. And the street of the city was pure gold, like transparent glass.

But I saw no temple in it, for the Lord God Almighty and the Lamb are its temple. The city had no need of the sun or of the moon to shine in it, for the glory of God illuminated it. The Lamb is its light. And the nations of those who are saved shall walk in its light, and the kings of the

> earth bring their glory and honor into it. Its gates shall not be shut at all by day (there shall be no night there). And they shall bring the glory and the honor of the nations into it. But there shall by no means enter it anything that defiles, or causes an abomination or a lie, but only those who are written in the Lamb's Book of Life."

Isaiah captures the same type of urgency:

> "Awake, awake, O Zion, clothe yourself with strength. Put on your garments of splendor, O Jerusalem, the holy city. The uncircumcised and de-filed will not enter you again. Shake off your dust; rise up, sit enthroned, O Jerusalem. Free yourself from the chains on your neck, O captive Daughter of Zion. For this is what the Lord says: You were sold for nothing, and without money you will be redeemed…Listen! Your watchmen lift up their voices; together they shout for joy. When the Lord returns to Zion, they will see it with their own eyes. Burst into songs of joy together, you ruins of Jerusalem, for the Lord has comforted his people, he has redeemed Jerusalem…Depart, depart, go out from there! Touch no unclean thing! Come out from it and be pure, you who carry the vessels of the Lord. But you will not leave in haste or go in flight; for the Lord will go before you, the God if Israel will be your rear guard.

> - Isaiah 52:1-3, 8-9, 11-12

So the beauty of the Bride, as Heaven sees her, is breath taking, is unshakable, untouchable, full of God's glory, covered with fine jewels, and pearls, and her gates are open to all. Angels stand guard at her gates. She is simply glorious, without spot or blemish.

So I ask you, how serious does the Lord get? I mean, seriously folks, how serious is He when He keeps saying the same thing over, and over? Do you sense that we are in new a season of transition? Do you hear the sound of Heaven calling you to a higher place? Do you feel the sound of drum beat? Do you hear footsteps of the King? I do and I want to call you to a place of listening, and pressing in to the throne room.

Sometimes, when we hear words that seem so big and so broad, we don't really know what to do. We say to ourselves things like, "that was cool," or "awesome God," and we continue to go about our day. Alternatively, we find ourselves feeling inadequate, unable to respond. I have good news for you.

The Lord never speaks to us about great promises, only to dangle them in front of like carrots on a stick, with no real desire to bring about what He has promised. Sure, He responds to our hunger and thirst for him, and He does call us to seek him, to knock, and to dig. He responds to our worship, yes, in a very powerful way, but it is His joy to bring us the Kingdom.

It is His joy to set our hearts ablaze. It is His heart's desire that we would be transformed into that beautiful Bride and He longs to make that happen. However, this pursuit is not something we have to struggle with or muster up in the flesh. More than anything, He wants us to come to Him like little children, free from the fear of performance, free to leap in to Poppa's lap and enjoy His companionship.

The last vision I had this week before writing this sums up the "How" of moving into the place of intimacy. I saw Jesus sitting on the throne. He was full of joy, to the point of laughter. He was sitting like a grandpa calling his grand kids to jump into his lap. There was such eagerness in His expression. He was so proud of the growth of His kids. He was so pleased with them how they were learning and how they responded to the simple things. He just wanted to hug on them and cuddle with them. He wanted to play with them and give them all the joy that was in His heart.

> *"But Jesus called them unto him, and said, Suffer little children to come unto me, and forbid them not: for of such is the kingdom of God. Verily I say unto you, Whosoever shall not receive the kingdom of God as a little child shall in no wise enter therein."*
>
> - Luke 18:16-17

The key to moving in this next move of God will be the intimate manifestation of the Church being like Children, in their love towards Jesus, for such is the Kingdom of God!

One last thing, on the way to Church this morning, the Lord gave me a vision of storm clouds. I saw the sky and it was dark with a massive thick black cloud. As I was watching the cloud suddenly, from the center of the cloud, it burst open, exploding the cloud into hundreds of smaller clouds. The smaller clouds looked like men's hands with lightning bolts in each fist. The clouds were heading in all directions, north, south, east, and west. I knew that clouds represented the church. I understood that the rain of His presence that was about to come was going to transform us, we were going to move from rain seekers to rain delivers. We were not only going to bring the rain of His presence to the world, but like the lightning bolts, we were bringing the power of God with signs and wonders, thunder, and lightning.

A couple of hours later, I was standing in the doorway that leads outside to my porch. I was watching the rain literally hammer the backyard. The wind was blowing, leaves were flying, and now, the Holy Spirit came upon me and said,

> *"As you see in the natural, so shall you see in My Spirit. Prepare for rain." I started to praise God, crying out, "Send your rain God, and rain down on us!"*

Then I recalled the words of Elijah:

> *"Then Elijah said to Ahab, 'Go up, eat and drink; for there is the sound of abundance of rain.' So Ahab went up to eat and drink. And Elijah went up to the top of Carmel; then he bowed down on the ground, and put his face between his knees, and said to his servant, 'Go up now, look toward the sea.'*

> *So he went up and looked, and said, 'There is nothing.' And seven times he said, 'Go again.'*

> *Then it came to pass the seventh time, that he said, 'There is a cloud, as small as a man's hand, rising out of the sea!' So he said, "Go up, say to Ahab, 'Prepare your chariot, and go down before the rain stops you.'"*

*Now it happened in the meantime that the sky became*
*black with clouds and wind, and there was a heavy*
*rain. So Ahab rode away and went to Jezreel."*

- 1 Kings 18:41-45

I propose to you that Elijah was not only seeing the natural rain for Ahab, and the nation, but was seeing the rain of God in these last days, and the church transformed. Get ready church... prepare for rain, and we, like Elijah's servant, will look faithfully, until we see the first cloud.

# CHAPTER 25

# A word of Grace

*"My heart is overflowing with a good theme; I recite my composition concerning the King; my tongue is the pen of a ready writer.*

*You are fairer than the sons of men; Grace is poured upon your lips; Therefore God has blessed You forever. Gird Your sword upon Your thigh, O Mighty One, with Your glory and Your majesty. And in Your majesty ride prosperously because of truth, humility, and righteousness; And Your right hand shall teach You awesome things. Your arrows are sharp in the heart of the King's enemies; the peoples fall under You.*

*Your throne, O God, is forever and ever; A scepter of righteousness is the scepter of Your kingdom. You love righteousness and hate wickedness; Therefore God, Your God, has anointed You with the oil of gladness more than your companions. All Your garments are scented with myrrh and aloes and cassia, out of the ivory palaces, by which they have made you glad. Kings' daughters are among Your honorable women; at Your right hand stands the queen in gold from Ophir.*

*Listen, O daughter, Consider and incline your ear;*
*Forget your own people also, and your father's house;*
*so the King will greatly desire your beauty; because He*
*is your Lord, worship Him. And the daughter of Tyre*
*will come with a gift; the rich among the people will*
*seek your favor. The royal daughter is all glorious*
*within the palace; her clothing is woven with gold. She*
*shall be brought to the King in robes of many colors; the*
*virgins, her companions who follow her, shall be*
*brought to you. With gladness and rejoicing they shall*
*be brought; they shall enter the King's palace.*

*Instead of Your fathers shall be Your sons, whom You*
*shall make princes in all the earth. I will make Your*
*name to be remembered in all generations; therefore*
*the people shall praise You forever and ever."*

- Psalms 45

They call this Psalm "The Glories of the Messiah and His Bride." A poetic prophet of the sons of Korah wrote it. It was set to the tune of the "Lilies," pointing us to love writings of the Song of Solomon, and speaks of the passion of the King for His bride. In fact, the writer calls this psalm, "A song of love." It was a royal wedding song and was more than likely sung at the wedding of King David or Solomon and one of his princesses. Charles Wesley was so moved by this psalm he paraphrased it in his hymn, "My heart is full of Christ, and longs its glorious matter to declare." Prophetically, it speaks of Christ and His love for the church.

The first nine verses speak to the glorious nature and splendor of the King and His might against all falsehood, pride, and injustice. The next five verses speak directly to the bride. The writer is calling her to the high place; he is exhorting her to forsake her old life and accept her new position as queen, with all its sacrifices, duties, rewards, and pleasures, but above all to yield herself fully to the King.

It is fitting to end this book on the Bride of Christ. In fact, I thought I was done with this book after completing the previous chapter. However the Lord had another idea. You see He woke me up out of an incredible dream the other day, and for the last two days I haven't been able to shake it.

In the dream I was taken to the throne room of God. I saw myself walking up to the throne to embrace my King. Above the throne was a banner with the word "commission" written across it. I saw myself walk between two pillars that lead to the throne. Then I saw myself exit the throne through two other pillars on the right. I was dressed in a white bridal gown with boots on. The time between entering the first two pillars and exiting the second set of pillars my mind was filled with incredible revelations regarding the Bride of Christ and her commission and destiny. I understood that the foundation of her commission was found in the loving embrace of her King, and in that embrace, in her love fellowship with her husband, she would be endued with power and glory to fulfill her call.

Then, as I walked away, in my new bridal attire, instantly I was standing in the workplace, holding the elbow of a young lad. I looked down at his elbow and saw the residue of scar tissue from surgery, where they pieced together his elbow with metal pins. I began to pray and commanded the metal to leave his body.

As I was praying this young man jumped back with a startled look and said, "What are you doing to my arm?"

I watched as the Lord began to miraculously recreate his elbow and remove all the metal from his body. They boy was smiling ear-to-ear, blown away at what was happening. Then I looked out to the crowd and said,

> *"Join with me loved ones, say the name of Jesus, and watch the Glory of the Lord."*

Instantly, everybody began to say "Jesus" in perfect harmony. Their voices filled the atmosphere like a Holy choir from heaven. As they spoke I saw the metal plate in the boy's head dissolve and eject from his body. Then I woke.

Taken-back by the dream, I began to pray, and my prayers continued throughout the day. At the time I didn't know what the dream meant… whether it was literal, in the sense that I would see this boy and bring the King's healing gift to him, or whether it was something more.

By noon, as I was standing outside reflecting on the dream's meaning, the Lord spoke to me very load and clear. *"Tell them…"* He said,

> *"Tell them how much I love them, how much My heart burns for My bride. Tell them that My love for them is unshakeable, it is so deep that My heart beats with passion at the very thought of her. Tell My bride that I am head-over-heals for her, and in this hour, I shall take her into the wedding chamber and there she will know the tenderness of My touch. I shall wrap My arms*

*around her and caress her with Holy love and with fire. In my embrace I will shower her with My desires. I shall cover her with My presence and trade her earthly garments with the wardrobe of heaven. I will put rings on her fingers and bells on her toes. I shall engrave her heart with My image and she shall see what I see. She shall feel as I feel. She shall touch others even as I have touched her. She shall be a queen in My kingdom, and her garments will radiate her beauty because she has looked upon the face of her lover.*

*In this hour, this hour of the Bridal Shower, I shall wrap myself around her in My embrace, she shall see My heart for her and for humanity and in so doing, she will rise with a burning conviction, yes with a Holy commission, and return to the land that I send her, and there she shall reach out and bring the love touch to all she encounters.*

*Yes, My love touch is amazing, for in that touch is wrapped up all the mysteries of creation. She shall speak and limbs will be created. She shall whisper and the ears of the deaf shall be restored. Where ears do not exist, they shall be created at the breath of My bride. For this is the hour of the Bridal Shower, and the rain she has so longed to see will come even as the wind blows upon the garment of my bride, as she walks amongst the hosts of heaven. Her aroma is like sweet raspberries. The very taste of her brings healing to the land, for she has been to the wedding chamber and felt My embrace. She has kissed the lips of her lover and has left changed into the beauty I saw the day I created her.*

*This is how I feel about My bride, she is the lover of My soul. Prepare for the bridal shower My bride and come to me. Let me embrace you and give you My heart."*

As He spoke those words to me I could feel His love flow over me like warm oil. Liquid love covered my heart and I, like the psalmist, took up the pen of a ready writer. As I began writing I was suddenly caught up in the Spirit to the worship song "Dying to Return," by Vineyard. As the sounds of this song flooded my heart, I saw Jesus in this incredible montage. As I heard these words His love filled my heart.

"He walked with a smile"

I saw Him as the Son of Man, strong and eloquent, walking along dusty roads, smiling and touching all along the side of the road. His features radiated with mission and purpose. With every touch His face beamed with the most incredible smile. Then He turned, looked into my eyes... and smiled. The song continued.

"He walked with peace"

And I was overcome by His peaceful nature. Peace flowed out from Him like waves of light flooding the atmosphere. Then, it was as if he was looking around, but no one really understood the true meaning of His life mission. He was listening to the hearts of those around Him. The road was lined with people, some wanted food, others healing, others just desiring to see miracles, and there were others there, mocking Him in unbelief. Yet, in all, it seemed that no one understood. Then, like before, He turned and looked at... and smiled. It was a smile that said,

*"I know... and they will soon know... when its finished."*

And the song continued.

**"But His heart cried out"**

And when I heard those words I could see His heart pour out to the Father, the only one that knew the road He was one, the only one that truly understood. Then He bowed His head as if He heard the words from His Poppa respond back to Him,

*"All is well My Son ... it is almost finished, your almost there."*

Then He lifted His head in perfect peace and strength, and with Holy confidence He looked over at me again, and smiled, and His smile carried so much weight in it. It was like a smile of assurance in the outcome of His destiny. And the song continued.

**"He was alone"**

And instantly I saw Him in His loneliness on this planet. His heart was in perfect unity with His Father and the Holy Spirit, but He walked as a man alone. I could feel the ach in His heart, desiring the lover of His soul, to be united with her so that she would see and understand fully His love for her. The song continued.

**"He broke the world - Made all things new"**

And I saw Him on the road to the cross, as venomous words spewed out of the mouths of all around Him. His heart was torn at the blindness of the crowed. Yet, again, at that moment

He turned and looked in My eyes, and smiled. My heart tore with His love and I was overtaken and undone. The lover of my soul was hurting, and in His hurt was the soul desire to embrace me. As the onlookers mocked Him, and tried to crush His spirit, He stood silent, and then turned again to me… and smiled.

"And He tore my heart as He stood silent…"

And I was overwhelmed by His beauty and His tenderness, His love and desire for me was killing me and I saw Him, in His sacrificial journey, to redeem me and bring me to Himself, and I was undone.

"So beautiful, So beautiful"

And I saw Him as His heart cried out in the garden, and I saw Him as they spit on Him, and the cat-of-nine-tails came ripping down, tearing open His flesh. And with every scourge, I could see His eyes, His incredibly tender and loving eyes. I saw the strength of His perseverance, as the whip ripped across His back… Then as before, He turned and looked again, and the whip came lashing down, and as His eyes met mine… He smiled. I was undone.

Then I saw them as they mocked Him and put that scarlet robe upon His back and pressed that crown of thorns into His skull. I saw blood began to run down the sides of His face, and onto the ground, onto the earth that He created.

And I saw Him as they nailed nine-inch spikes into His hands and feet and hung Him on the cross. And I saw Him, as He cried out:

"Where are You?"

"Where are You?"

"My God why have You forsaken me?"

And I was so moved, my body began to shake, and tears filled my heart at the sight of this perfect man hung between heaven and earth... alone.

"Up there alone this perfect man"

And my heart was overcome at the sight of His sacrifice and I watched, as He turned, and once again, looked at me in my eyes... and smiled. Then He turned and said, "It is finished... I'll be back," and He smiled again. And I saw Him as He gave up His Spirit to the Father.

"Dying to return the Son was killed"

And I understood like never before, the words of the writer of Hebrews when he wrote:

> "Therefore we also, since we are surrounded by so great a cloud of witnesses, let us lay aside every weight, and the sin which so easily ensnares us, and let us run with endurance the race that is set before us, looking unto Jesus, the author and finisher of our faith, who for the joy that was set before Him endured the cross, despising the shame, and has sat down at the right hand of the throne of God."
>
> - Hebrews 12:1-2

The same passion and love for you that drove Him to the cross is the same passion and love that drives His desire for you today. It is that same unshakeable passion that desire to embrace His bride, the lover of His soul. He will not stop until He can embrace you and wrap you in the wedding garments of His good pleasure. Consider the words of John.

> *"And I heard, as it were, the voice of a great multitude, as the sound of many waters and as the sound of mighty thunderings, saying, "Alleluia! For the Lord God Omnipotent reigns! Let us be glad and rejoice and give Him glory, for the marriage of the Lamb has come, and His wife has made herself ready." And to her it was granted to be arrayed in fine linen, clean and bright, for the fine linen is the righteous acts of the saints.*
>
> *Then he said to me, "Write: 'Blessed are those who are called to the marriage supper of the Lamb!'"*

- Revelation 19:6-9

Readiness happens in His presence. Readiness takes place in intimacy. Transformation takes place when we snuggle up to Him and open our hearts to receive the fullness of His love for us.

The commission of this next season will be the commission of the bride, it will usher in the power of God like never seen before, and it will be birthed from a Lover, to the beloved, and will change humanity forever.

> *"Then I, John, saw the holy city, New Jerusalem, coming down out of heaven from God, prepared as a*

*bride adorned for her husband. And I heard a loud*
*voice from heaven saying, "Behold, the tabernacle of*
*God is with men, and He will dwell with them, and they*
*shall be His people. God Himself will be with them and*
*be their God. And God will wipe away every tear from*
*their eyes; there shall be no more death, nor sorrow, nor*
*crying. There shall be no more pain, for the former*
*things have passed away."*

- Revelation 21:2-4

**Your destiny is calling you…**

*"And the Spirit and the bride say, "Come!" And let him*
*who hears say, "Come!" And let him who thirsts come.*
*Whoever desires, let him take the water of life freely."*

- Revelation 22:18

I looking for the day the rain comes down in sheets of liquid
love. I am looking for the season of the saints where the bridal
shower of the Bride shakes the very foundations of the earth.
Where limbs are created where there were no limbs. Where eye
sockets are filled with the creative love touch of Jesus. Where
the deaf hear, for the first time, the voice of Jesus as He
whispers in their newly created ears how much He loves them.
I am looking for the day when average Joes step out in
thunderous power and change the face of nations. I am looking
for the day that the lover of our souls embraces us with His
passion and pushes us into our destiny. I'm waiting for the rain
of God! Let's move the heart of God and worship Him on His
throne. It's time church. Get ready, get ready, get ready!

My prayer is that this book series has helped to light a fire in your soul and push you to that higher calling of our Lord – so shake the dust off your feet and don't look back. This is the season of the bride…. Rise up dear ones and embrace your King, for He is madly in love with you.

# CHAPTER 26

# Final Thoughts

*""My heart is overflowing with a good theme; I recite my composition concerning the King; my tongue is the pen of a ready writer.*

*You are fairer than the sons of men; Grace is poured upon your lips; Therefore God has blessed You forever. Gird Your sword upon Your thigh, O Mighty One, with Your glory and Your majesty. And in Your majesty ride prosperously because of truth, humility, and righteousness; And Your right hand shall teach You awesome things. Your arrows are sharp in the heart of the King's enemies; the peoples fall under You.*

*Your throne, O God, is forever and ever; A scepter of righteousness is the scepter of Your kingdom. You love righteousness and hate wickedness; Therefore God, Your God, has anointed You with the oil of gladness more than your companions. All Your garments are scented with myrrh and aloes and cassia, out of the ivory palaces, by which they have made you glad. Kings' daughters are among Your honorable women; at Your right hand stands the queen in gold from Ophir.*

*Listen, O daughter, Consider and incline your ear;*
*Forget your own people also, and your father's house;*
*so the King will greatly desire your beauty; because He*
*is your Lord, worship Him. And the daughter of Tyre*
*will come with a gift; the rich among the people will*
*seek your favor. The royal daughter is all glorious*
*within the palace; her clothing is woven with gold. She*
*shall be brought to the King in robes of many colors; the*
*virgins, her companions who follow her, shall be*
*brought to you. With gladness and rejoicing they shall*
*be brought; they shall enter the King's palace.*

*Instead of Your fathers shall be Your sons, whom You*
*shall make princes in all the earth. I will make Your*
*name to be remembered in all generations; therefore*
*the people shall praise You forever and ever."*

- Psalm 45

They call this Psalm *"The Glories of the Messiah and His Bride."* A poetic prophet of the sons of Korah wrote it. It was set to the tune of the *"Lilies,"* pointing us to love writings of the Song of Solomon, and speaks of the passion of the King for His bride. In fact, the writer calls this psalm, "A song of love." It was a royal wedding song and was more than likely sung at the wedding of King David or Solomon and one of his princesses. Charles Wesley was so moved by this psalm he paraphrased it in his hymn, *"My heart is full of Christ, and longs its glorious matter to declare."* Prophetically, it speaks of Christ and His love for the church.

The first nine verses speak to the glorious nature and splendor of the King and His might against all falsehood, pride, and injustice. The next five verses speak directly to the bride. The writer is calling her to the high place; he is exhorting her to forsake her old life and accept her new position as queen, with all its sacrifices, duties, rewards, and pleasures, but above all to yield herself fully to the King.

It is fitting to end this book on the Bride of Christ. In fact, I thought I was done with this section after completing the previous chapter. However the Lord had another idea. You see He woke me up out of an incredible dream the other day, and for the last two days I haven't been able to shake it.

In the dream I was taken to the throne room of God. I saw myself walking up to the throne to embrace my King. Above the throne was a banner with the word "*commission*" written across it. I saw myself walk between two pillars that lead to the throne. Then I saw myself exit the throne through two other pillars on the right. I was dressed in a white bridal gown with boots on. The time between entering the first two pillars and exiting the second set of pillars my mind was filled with incredible revelations regarding the Bride of Christ and her commission and destiny.

I understood that the foundation of her commission was found in the loving embrace of her King, and in that embrace, in her love fellowship with her husband, she would be endued with power and glory to fulfill her call.

Then, as I walked away, in my new bridal attire, instantly I was standing in the workplace, holding the elbow of a young lad. I looked down at his elbow and saw the residue of scar tissue from surgery, where they pieced together his elbow with metal pins. I began to pray and commanded the metal to leave his body.

As I was praying this young man jumped back with a startled look and said, "*What are you doing to my arm?*"

I watched as the Lord began to miraculously recreate his elbow and remove all the metal from his body. The boy was smiling era-to-ear, blown away at what was happening. Then I looked out to the crowd and said, "*Join with me loved ones, say the name of Jesus, and watch the Glory of the Lord.*" Instantly, everybody began to say, "*Jesus*" in perfect harmony. Their voices filled the atmosphere like a Holy choir from heaven. As they spoke I saw the metal plate in the boy's head dissolve and eject from his body. Then I woke.

Taken back by the dream I began to pray, and my prayers continued throughout the day. At the time I didn't know what the dream meant … whether it was literal, in the sense that I would see this boy and bring the King's healing gift to him, or whether it was something more.

By noon, as I was standing outside reflecting on the dreams meaning, the Lord spoke to me very loud and clear. "Tell them…" He said,

> "*Tell them how much I love them, how much My heart burns for My bride. Tell them that My love for them is unshakeable, it is so deep that My heart beats with passion at the very thought of her. Tell My bride that I am head-over-heals for her, and in this hour, I shall take her into the wedding chamber and there she will know the*

*tenderness of My touch. I shall wrap My arms around her and caress her with Holy love and with fire. In my embrace I will shower her with My desires. I shall cover her with My presence and trade her earthly garments with the wardrobe of heaven. I will put rings on her fingers and bells on her toes. I shall engrave her heart with My image and she shall see what I see. She shall feel as I feel. She shall touch others even as I have touched her. She shall be a queen in My kingdom, and her garments will radiate her beauty because she has looked upon the face of her lover. In this hour, this hour of the Bridal Shower, I shall wrap myself around her in My embrace, she shall see My heart for her and for humanity and in so doing, she will rise with a burning conviction, yes with a Holy commission, and return to the land that I send her, and there she shall reach out and bring the love touch to all she encounters.*

*Yes, My love touch is amazing, for in that touch is wrapped up all the mysteries of creation. She shall speak and limbs will be created. She shall whisper and the ears of the deaf shall be restored. Where ears do not exist, they shall be created at the breath of My bride. For this is the hour of the Bridal Shower, and the rain she has so longed to see will come even as the wind blows upon the garment of my bride, as she walks amongst the hosts of heaven. Her aroma is like sweet*

388 • FRED RAYNAUD

> *raspberries. The very taste of her brings healing to the land, for she has been to the wedding chamber and felt My embrace. She has kissed the lips of her lover and has left changed into the beauty I saw the day I created her. This is how I feel about My bride, she is the lover of My soul. Prepare for the bridal shower, My bride, and come to me. Let me embrace you and give you My heart."*

As He spoke those words to me I could feel His love flow over my like warm oil. Liquid love covered my heart and I, like the psalmist, took up the pen of a ready writer. As I began writing I was suddenly caught up in the Spirit to the worship song *"Dying to Return,"* by Vineyard. As the sounds of this song flooded my heart, I saw Jesus in this incredible montage. As I heard these words His love filled my heart.

"He walked with a smile…."

I saw Him as the Son of Man, strong and eloquent, walking along dusty roads, smiling and touching all along the side of the road. His features radiated with mission and purpose. With every touch His face beamed with the most incredible smile. Then He turned, looked into my eyes … and smiled. The song continued.

"He walked with peace…."

I was overcome by His peaceful nature. Peace flowed out from Him like waves of light flooding the atmosphere. Then, it was as if he was looking around, but no one really understood the true meaning of His life mission. He was listening to the hearts of those around Him. The road was lined with people, some wanted food, others healing, others just desiring to see miracles, and there were others there, mocking Him in unbelief. Yet, in all, it seemed that no one understood. Then, like before, He turned and looked at me ... and smiled. It was a smile that said, "I know ... and they will soon know ... when its finished." The song continued.

**"But His heart cried out...."**

When I heard those words I could see His heart pour out to the Father, the only one that knew the road He was on, the only one that truly understood. Then He bowed His head as if He heard the words from His Poppa respond back to Him, *"All is well My Son ... it is almost finished, you're almost there."* Then He lifted His head in perfect peace and strength, and with Holy confidence He looked over at me again, and smiled, and His smile carried so much weight in it. It was like a smile of assurance in the outcome of His destiny. The song continued.

**"He was alone...."**

Instantly I saw Him in His loneliness on this planet. His heart was in perfect unity with His Father and the Holy Spirit, but He walked as a man alone. I could feel the ache in His heart, desiring the lover of His soul, to be united with her so that she would see and understand fully His love for her. The song continued.

**"He broke the world - Made all things new...."**

I saw Him on the road to the cross, as venomous words spewed out of the mouths of all around Him. His heart was torn at the blindness of the crowed.  Yet, again, at that moment He turned and looked in My eyes, and smiled. My heart tore with His love and I was overtaken and undone. The lover of my soul was hurting, and in His hurt was the soul desire to embrace me. As the onlookers mocked Him, and tried to crush His spirit, He stood silent, and then turned again to me … and smiled.

"And He tore my heart as He stood silent…."

I was overwhelmed by His beauty and His tenderness, His love and desire for me was killing me and I saw Him, in His sacrificial journey, to redeem me and bring me to Himself, and I was undone.

"So beautiful, So beautiful…."

I saw Him as His heart cried out in the garden, and I saw Him as they spit on Him, and the cat-of-nine-tails came ripping down, tearing open His flesh. With every scourge, I could see His eyes, His incredibly tender and loving eyes. I saw His the strength of His perseverance, as the whip ripped across His back… Then as before, He turned and looked again, and the whip came lashing down, and as His eyes met mine… He smiled. I was undone.

Then I saw them as they mocked Him and put that scarlet robe upon His back and pressed that crown of thorns into His skull. I saw blood begin to run down the sides of His face, and onto the ground, onto the earth that He created.

I saw Him as they nailed nine-inch spikes into His hands and feet and hung Him on the cross. I saw Him, as He cried out:

"Where are You?"

"Where are You?"

"My God why have You forsaken me?"

I was so moved, my body began to shake, and tears filled my heart at the sight of this perfect man hung between heaven and earth ... alone.

"Up there alone this perfect man...."

My heart was overcome at the sight of His sacrifice and I watched, as He turned, and again, looked at me in my eyes ... and smiled. Then He turned and said, "It is finished ... I'll be back," and He smiled again. I saw Him as He gave up His Spirit to the Father.

"Dying to return the Son was killed...."

I understood like never before, the words of the writer of Hebrews 12:1-2 when he wrote:

> *"Therefore we also, since we are surrounded by so great a cloud of witnesses, let us lay aside every weight, and the sin which so easily ensnares us, and let us run with endurance the race that is set before us, looking unto Jesus, the author and finisher of our faith, who for the joy that was set before Him endured the cross, despising the shame, and has sat down at the right hand of the throne of God."*

The same passion and love for you that drove Him to the cross is the same passion and love that drives His desire for you today. It is that same unshakeable passions, that desires to embrace His bride, the lover of His soul. He will not stop until He can embrace you and wrap you in the wedding garments of His good pleasure. Consider the words of John.

> *"And I heard, as it were, the voice of a great multitude, as the sound of many waters and as the sound of mighty thunderings, saying, "Alleluia! For the Lord God Omnipotent reigns! Let us be glad and rejoice and give Him glory, for the marriage of the Lamb has come, and His wife has made herself ready." And to her it was granted to be arrayed in fine linen, clean and bright, for the fine linen is the righteous acts of the saints.*
>
> *Then he said to me, "Write: 'Blessed are those who are called to the marriage supper of the Lamb! '"*
>
> - Revelation 19:6-9

Readiness happens in His presence. Readiness takes place in intimacy. Transformation takes place when we snuggle up to Him and open our hearts to receive the fullness of His love for us. The commission of this next season will be the commission of the bride, it will usher in the power of God like never seen before, and it will be birthed from a Lover, to the beloved, and will change humanity forever.

> *"Then I, John, saw the holy city, New Jerusalem, coming down out of heaven from God, prepared as a bride adorned for her husband. And I heard a loud*

THE SEER'S GIFT • 393

*voice from heaven saying, "Behold, the tabernacle of God is with men, and He will dwell with them, and they shall be His people. God Himself will be with them and be their God. And God will wipe away every tear from their eyes; there shall be no more death, nor sorrow, nor crying. There shall be no more pain, for the former things have passed away."*

- Revelation 21:2-4

**Your destiny is calling you...**

*"And the Spirit and the bride say, "Come!" And let him who hears say, "Come!" And let him who thirsts come. Whoever desires, let him take the water of life freely."*

- Revelation 22:18

I look for the day the rains come down in sheets of liquid love. I am looking for the season of the saints where the bridal shower of the Bride shakes the very foundations of the earth. Where limbs are created where there were no limbs. Where eye sockets are filled with the creative love touch of Jesus. Where the deaf hear, for the first time, the voice of Jesus as He whispers in their newly created ears how much He loves them. I am looking for the day when average Joes step out in thunderous power and change the face of nations. I am looking for the day that the lover of our souls embraces us with His passion and pushes us into our destiny. I'm waiting for the rain of God! Let's move the heart of God and worship Him on His throne. It's time church. Get ready, get ready, get ready!

My prayer is that this book has helped to light a fire in your soul and push you to that higher calling of our Lord – so shake the dust off your feet and don't look back. This is the season of the bride…. Rise up dear ones and embrace your King, for He is madly in love with you.

This series includes the following books:

- **The Seer's Gift** - a look at the Language of Visions and Dreams (this volume).
- **The Seer and Healing** - How visions and dreams operate in the ministry of healing.
- **Pictorial Language of a Seer** - a reference work on similes, metaphors, and symbolism commonly seen in the life of the believer.

# Aurora

*"Oh, that You would rend the heavens! That
You would come down! That the mountains
might shake at Your presence — As fire burns
brushwood, as fire causes water to boil — To
make Your name known to Your adversaries,
that the nations may tremble at Your presence!
When You did awesome things for which we did
not look, You came down, the mountains shook
at Your presence. For since the beginning of the
world men have not heard nor perceived by the
ear, nor has the eye seen any God besides You,
who acts for the one who waits for Him.*

- Isaiah 64:1-4

I can think of no better topic to end this book then with the
topic of being embraced and filled with the Holy Spirit of
promise. You see, deep in the heart of every person there
is a yearning for God. For those that know Him, it is a heart cry
for more of Him and it increases with every passing touch of
His presence. Like estranged lovers, we ache to see His face, to
hear His whisper, and to feel His breathe upon our lives. For

those that don't, it is the hollow sound of searching, trying to fill a craving they don't understand. Like an ancient dry well scarred by the desert heat, their voice echoes in the wind, crying out for the source of living water.

This desire is not new; it is built into our DNA. We were created to know Him and seek after more of His presence in our lives. Expressions of that desire are seen in our passions, hunger, creative nature, need for love, and our ability to dream. Those traits are but a reflection of the One we are groaning for. We are after all, created in His image. When these innate abilities go unchecked by heaven's purpose they spin off into worldly desires, lusts, and the pursuit of false fulfillment. However, when they are ignited by Holy passion they become the catalyst in bringing the Kingdom of Heaven to earth, and the fulfillment of who we were created to be, and our identity blossoms.

Consider the words of Isaiah, *"Oh, that You would rend the heavens! That You would come down!"* In this verse Isaiah sums up the cry and desire of all creation. It is not only a cry for presence, but also a cry for influence, a call for God to invade earth and explode in the hearts of humanity. Yet, from the moment Adam and Eve sinned, the answer to that cry was put in motion, and from the seed of the women would come forth a redeemer, Jesus, who conclusively, would unite humanity back to his Creator.

Isaiah heard the whisper of this promise. You can hear it in many of his prophecies, Isaiah 9:6; 11:1; and 61, to name a few. Those that know Him hear that same whisper. For those that don't, Isaiah leaves them with the reality of their condition, and this promise (Isaiah 32:13-16):

*"On the land of my people will come up thorns and briers, yes, on all the happy homes in the joyous city; Because the palaces will be forsaken, the bustling city will be deserted. The forts and towers will become lairs forever, a joy of wild donkeys, a pasture of flocks—*

*Until the Spirit is poured upon us from on high, and the wilderness becomes a fruitful field, and the fruitful field is counted as a forest. Then justice will dwell in the wilderness, and righteousness remain in the fruitful field...."*

In this passage Isaiah acknowledges God's awareness of the pain and travail caused by sins invasion upon the planet. However, he also leaves all of us this promise, *"Until the Spirit is poured upon us from on high, and the wilderness becomes a fruitful field."* That is what we all want. For those that have experienced God's touch through the kiss of the Holy Spirit, our yearning is for more of Him. For those that don't, their true craving is to be filled with the giver of life, the Holy Spirit of comfort.

John the Baptist echoed the same promise, not knowing that the answer to that promise was headed in his direction.

*"I indeed baptize you with water unto repentance, but He who is coming after me is mightier than I, whose sandals I am not worthy to carry. He will baptize you with the Holy Spirit and fire. His winnowing fan is in His hand, and He will thoroughly clean out His*

*threshing floor, and gather His wheat into the barn; but He will burn up the chaff with unquenchable fire."*

*Then Jesus came from Galilee to John at the Jordan to be baptized by him. And John tried to prevent Him, saying, "I need to be baptized by You, and are You coming to me?"*

*But Jesus answered and said to him, 'Permit it to be so now, for thus it is fitting for us to fulfill all righteousness.'"*

- Matthew 3:11-15

Suddenly, he saw the Lamb of God approaching. Struck by his own need, he pleads, "*I need to be baptized by You, and you are coming to me?*" In other words, I am not worthy to do such a thing, to be in your presence. Please baptize me with Holy fire!

Then Jesus responded, "**Permit it to be so....**" The answer to all the cries of history, past and present, was looking him in the eyes. A proclamation was made, Jesus was declaring to the entire universe, now is the time, and today is the day of your visitation.

At that, John baptized Him, and in doing so, a rift was torn in the universe and the Heavens opened, the Spirit of the living God had come.

*"And immediately, coming up from the water, He saw the heavens parting and the Spirit descending upon Him like a dove. Then a voice came from heaven, "You are My beloved Son, in whom I am well pleased."*

- Mark 1:10-11

That was not just a quaint prophetic act; it was a violent act. One in which the Spirit of God tore through the heavens and forever changed the atmosphere and creation. The rending that Isaiah cried out for just took place and the Spirit of God filled the Son of God, in His humanity. It was the same power and rending that we saw at the cross when the veil of the temple was torn from top to bottom, and the earth quaked, and the rocks split (Matthew 27:51).

> *"Then, behold, the veil of the temple was torn in two from top to bottom; and the earth quaked, and the rocks were split,"*

At the Jordan we saw Heaven open and the Spirit descend upon the promised one. At the cross we saw Heaven open and the veil of the temple tore, giving all believers access to the throne room of God. Today, every believer is living under that same open Heaven. Without that access and your ability to abide in Christ and be filled with the Holy Spirit, you can do nothing (John 15:4). However, if you live desiring to want more, and you seek His face, you will be filled, for you are the temple of the Holy Spirit. You were created to house the thunderous presence of Almighty God. When you die to your old man, and seek the giver of life, you will see as Isaiah did (Isaiah 6:1):

> *"In the year that King Uzziah died, I saw the Lord sitting on a throne, high and lifted up, and the train of His robe filled the temple."*

That word for *"filled"* in Hebrew has the essence of continual motion. In other words, His robe filled, and kept on filling, the temple. What a wondrous thing it is to know that God's desire to fill us is not a one-time event. He is looking to fill us to overflowing, and continue that process until we see Him face-to-face. However, filling is for the thirsty. God wants you so thirsty for Him that nothing else will satisfy. To be filled you not only have to thirst, but you have to go after Him and drink. No one can force you to thirst, seek, or drink. Those acts are yours alone. By them you will be filled or not, its really all up to you. You see faith mingled with thirst and seeking produces drinking. When you stir your hearts desire to press in, no matter the cost, a cup of blessing will await you.

> *"On the last day, that great day of the feast, Jesus stood and cried out, saying, "If anyone thirsts, let him come to Me and drink. He who believes in Me, as the Scripture has said, out of his heart will flow rivers of living water." But this He spoke concerning the Spirit, whom those believing in Him would receive; for the Holy Spirit was not yet given, because Jesus was not yet glorified."*

> *- John 7:37-39*

Jesus desires to fill you with the Spirit. Other than the kingdom of Heaven and doing the works of the Kingdom, it was the promise He talked about the most. He called it the promise of the Father. Consider the following Scriptures:

> *"And I will pray the Father, and He will give you another Helper, that He may abide with you forever—the Spirit of truth, whom the world cannot receive, because it neither sees Him nor knows Him; but you know Him, for He dwells with you and will be in you....*

*But the Helper, the Holy Spirit, whom the Father will send in My name, He will teach you all things, and bring to your remembrance all things that I said to you."*

*- John 14:16-18, 26*

*"But when the Helper comes, whom I shall send to you from the Father, the Spirit of truth who proceeds from the Father, He will testify of Me."*

*- John 15:26*

*"I still have many things to say to you, but you cannot bear them now. However, when He, the Spirit of truth, has come, He will guide you into all truth; for He will not speak on His own authority, but whatever He hears He will speak; and He will tell you things to come. He will glorify Me, for He will take of what is Mine and declare it to you. All things that the Father has are Mine. Therefore I said that He will take of Mine and declare it to you."*

*- John 16:12-15*

One of the first acts of Jesus after He was resurrected was to commission and empower His disciples. His desire was that they would do just as He had done. Their mission was to follow the model of Jesus and heal the sick, cast out demons, and raise the dead. They were to be totally dependent upon the Father and to walk filled with the Holy Spirit. After He spoke to them about their mission, He breathed on them, and declared, "Receive the Holy Spirit."

*"So Jesus said to them again, "Peace to you! As the Father has sent Me, I also send you." And when He had said this, He breathed on them, and said to them, "Receive the Holy Spirit."*

- John 20:21-22

Then a little while later He lit the fire again, only this time the filling of the Spirit was coming in power, and it was not just for them, but for all who tarry for His promise.

*"Behold, I send the Promise of My Father upon you; but tarry in the city of Jerusalem until you are endued with power from on high."*

- Luke 24:49

His desire for them to be filled was unstoppable. He met with them again and proclaimed:

*"And being assembled together with them, He commanded them not to depart from Jerusalem, but to wait for the Promise of the Father, "which," He said, "you have heard from Me; for John truly baptized with water, but you shall be baptized with the Holy Spirit not many days from now."*

- Acts 1:4-5

**Suddenly it happened!**

*"When the Day of Pentecost had fully come, they were all with one accord in one place. And suddenly there came a sound from heaven, as of a rushing mighty*

*wind, and it filled the whole house where they were*
*sitting. Then there appeared to them divided tongues,*
*as of fire, and one sat upon each of them. And they*
*were all filled with the Holy Spirit and began to speak*
*with other tongues, as the Spirit gave them utterance."*

- Acts 2:1-4

This filling was not a one-time event:

*"For the promise is to you and to your children, and to*
*all who are afar off, as many as the Lord our God will*
*call."*

- Acts 2:39

We are to seek Him with all our hearts and be filled with His
glory and presence. This is our heart's pursuit, and when the
Glory comes it will shake the very foundations of our lives. My
desire for you, as you read this book, is to be filled to
overflowing. My heart's cry is that you would be so ignited by
the flame of His presence that you would set the world ablaze
with the love of our Master. When we come together as
believers we should expect no less than what the priests of the
old covenant experienced.

*"And it came to pass, when the priests came out of the*
*holy place, that the cloud filled the house of the Lord, so*
*that the priests could not continue ministering because*
*of the cloud; for the glory of the Lord filled the house of*
*the Lord."*

- 1 Kings 8:10-11

That is church my friends. That is the heart cry of Him who sits upon the throne. He so desires to fill you that He will not relent until He has a bride so full of Him, that she glows with the glory of the lover of her soul.

---

## Let me illustrate

To illustrate the Lord's desire to fill His house with His presence and purpose, let me share with you a vision the Lord gave me a while back at church on Father's Day.

I was caught up in worship and as I was worshiping I saw in space what looked like the lights of Aurora. They were brilliant, tall and streaming down in colors, shades of blue, green, red and white. They filled the heavens with such incredible brilliance I was awestruck.

I asked the Lord what it was and He said, "*It is the rain of Heaven.*" In an instant, I was watching the rain of Heaven come down in sheets of light. Then, all of a sudden, Jesus stepped through the light like He was opening a shower curtain. He was beaming with the same brilliant light, only more glorious, majestic, sparkly, incredible. His hands were cupped, and beaming out from the sides, and between His fingers were beams of more incredible, colorful, light. It was like He was holding a ball of brilliance. Suddenly, He opened His hands, and out shot the dove of promise, with His wings extended as if ready to fly. It too, was draped in incredible light. The colors were amazing.

Then Jesus said, "*This is the promise of the Father. It is the Father's gift on this Father's day.*"

I was blown away. How awesome it is that the Father would send His only begotten Son, to give us not only His precious Son, but also the Gift of promise, the Holy Spirit, to all that are thirsty and desire to be wrapped in the glorious light of His presence.

Dear ones, before you do anything. Before you read any further, stop what you are doing and praise the name of Jesus. Worship Him in His splendor. Don't settle for anything less than His sweet presence. Lay on the floor if you have to, but don't stop until the lover of your soul kisses you and fills you with the Spirit of promise. Praise Him, and seek to be filled, even at this moment. Call on the Holy Spirit, and cry out ...

> *"Send me the Father's promise, Lord. Fill me Lord. Make me an instrument of your peace and alter my life course with your love and beauty. Come Holy Spirit, Come!"*

# Bibliography

Doug Addison, Prophecy, Dreams, and Evangelism, 2005, Streams Books, 1st Ed.

James W. and Michal Goll,

Dream Language, 2006, Destiny Image Publishing, 1st Ed.

Angelic Encounters, 2007, Strang Communications/Chrisma House, 1st Ed.

John Crowder, The New Mystics, 2006, Destiny Image, 1st Ed.

Jim Driscoll, The Modern Seer, 2010, Orbital Book Group, 1st Ed.

Gary Oates, Open My eyes Lord, 2008, Open Heaven Publications, 1st Ed.

Kris Vallotton, Developing a Supernatural Lifestyle, 2007, Destiny Image, 1st Ed.

Jonathan Welton, The School of the Seer, 2009, Destiny Image, 1st Ed.

Dr. Bill Hamon, Apostles, Prophets, and the Coming Moves of God, 1997, Destiny Image, 1st Ed.

Graham Cooke, Approaching the Heart of Prophecy, 2009, Brilliant Books, 1st Ed.; Developing Your Prophetic Gifting, 1994, Chosen Books, 1st Ed.

Randy Clark, Ministry Training Manual, 2004, Global Awakening, 1st Ed.

# About the Author

Fred Raynaud, WCMC – is an author, speaker, and retired Master Chef by trade. He serves the body of Christ as a prophetic revivalist and is president of Kingdom Wind Ministries. He lives with his wife in Florida.

For more information, please visit our website at http://kingdomwind.org

Made in the USA
Middletown, DE
24 September 2022

11152717R00228